Federal taxation in America

Authoritative and readable, this brief survey is a comprehensive historical overview of the U.S. federal tax system. Its coverage extends from the ratification of the Constitution to the present day. Brownlee describes the five principal stages of federal taxation in relation to the crises that led to their adoption—the formation of the republic, the Civil War, World War I, the Great Depression, and World War II—and discusses the significant modifications during the Reagan presidency. While focusing on federal policy, Brownlee also attends to the related history of state and local taxation.

This historical account recognizes the power of democratic forces outside the government, the influence of institutions and expertise inside the government, and the potency of ideas as an independent creative force that may lend intention to democratic forces, governmental deliberations, and resulting policies. This "democratic-institutionalist" interpretation is a novel and major contribution to the history of taxation and public finance.

Now in a new edition, Brownlee adds a new chapter focusing on the current tax policies of the George W. Bush administration. This discussion is set in a larger analysis of contemporary tax and fiscal issues, including war finance, Social Security, and Medicare.

W. Elliot Brownlee is Professor of History at the University of California, Santa Barbara. He is author and editor of numerous books, including *Funding the Modern American State, 1941–1995: The Rise and Fall of the Era of Easy Finance* (Cambridge, 1996).

WOODROW WILSON CENTER SERIES

Continued on page following index

Federal taxation in America

A short history
Second edition

W. Elliot Brownlee
University of California, Santa Barbara

WOODROW WILSON CENTER PRESS

AND

CAMBRIDGE
UNIVERSITY PRESS

CAMBRIDGE UNIVERSITY PRESS
Cambridge, New York, Melbourne, Madrid, Cape Town, Singapore, São Paulo, Delhi

Cambridge University Press
The Edinburgh Building, Cambridge CB2 8RU, UK

Published in the United States of America by Cambridge University Press, New York

www.cambridge.org
Information on this title: www.cambridge.org/9780521545204

WOODROW WILSON CENTER PRESS
One Woodrow Wilson Plaza
1300 Pennsylvania Avenue, NW, Washington, DC 20004-3027

http://www.wilsoncenter.org

First edition published 1996
Second edition published 2004

A catalogue record for this publication is available from the British Library

ISBN 978-0-521-83665-4 hardback
ISBN 978-0-521-54520-4 paperback

Transferred to digital printing 2009

For Mary Margaret

Contents

Acknowledgments

The first edition of this book developed from a 1993–96 project of the Woodrow Wilson International Center for Scholars that studied the financing of the federal government since World War II. I am grateful to Michael J. Lacey, then director of the Division of United States Studies at the Woodrow Wilson Center, for conceiving and organizing the project, and for pressing me to set the history of taxation and public finance in the broader history of American government and society. Edward Berkowitz, Hugh Heclo, Carolyn Jones, Cathie Martin, Stanford Ross, Herbert Stein, Eugene Steuerle, and Julian Zelizer were the other participants in the Woodrow Wilson Center project. They brought a wealth of experience and scholarly insight to bear on the history of taxation and public finance, and I found their advice invaluable.

Frank Smith, executive editor of Social Sciences at Cambridge University Press, and Joseph Brinley, director of the Woodrow Wilson Center Press, proposed that I write this book and then revise it for a second edition. I am grateful for their encouragement, sage advice, and exceptionally efficient support. Carolee Belkin Walker, former senior editor at the Woodrow Wilson Center Press, provided excellent editorial guidance and support for the first edition. Yamile Kahn did the same for the second edition.

In writing the first edition, I benefited greatly from the suggestions of reviewers W. Andrew Achenbaum, Brian Balogh, and William J. Barber. I appreciated as well the comments of Michael Bernstein, Robert M. Collins, Peter Lindert, Richard Musgrave, Ed Perkins, Richard Sylla, and John Wallis on an overview of the first edition I presented at a 1994 conference on "Fiscal Crises in Historical Perspective" sponsored by the All-UC (University of California) Group in Economic History.

Since the first edition appeared, colleagues at various conferences and seminars on tax policy have helped me think about the long-term development of taxation in the United States. They include Bruce F. Davie (annual meeting of the National Tax Association, 1996); Joel Slemrod (conference, "Does Atlas Shrug? The Economic Consequences of Taxing the Rich," University of Michigan Business School, 1997); Robert Kenzer (seminar, University of Richmond, 1998); Ben Baack (Policy History Conference, 1999); Laura Kalman, Stanley N. Katz, and Dennis Ventry (conference, American Society for Legal History, 1999); Anthony J. Badger (seminar, Sidney Sussex College, Cambridge University, 2001); Gareth Davies, David A. Hollinger, and R. Laurence Moore (seminar, Rothermere American Institute, Oxford University, 2001); Steve Sheffrin (International Conference on the History of the Reagan Presidency, University of California, Santa Barbara, 2002); and Andrew DeWit, Naohiko Jinno, and Sven Steinmo (seminars, Center for International Research on the Japanese Economy, University of Tokyo, 2002). I have tried to make the most of their suggestions in revising the first edition, particularly with regard to the impact of the so-called Reagan Revolution and subsequent conservative initiatives. I am also grateful for the astute comments of C. Eugene Steuerle, who read a draft of the second edition.

The University of California, through both fiscal crises and periods of economic euphoria, has been superbly encouraging of scholarship. I am indebted to the Santa Barbara campus for sabbatical and various other important forms of support.

As my dedication suggests, my largest debt is to Mary Margaret Brownlee. She has read virtually every draft of the manuscript. Her sharp critical eye saved me from numerous errors, and her historical insight suggested many fruitful lines of inquiry.

Santa Barbara
October 2003

Introduction: Taxation and national emergencies

Since the late 1970s, radical reform of the federal tax system has been a matter of serious discussion. And that discussion has prompted important changes in the tax system. Of particular note were the reforms that President Ronald Reagan engineered. These amounted to the most significant changes in federal tax policy in peacetime since the New Deal of President Franklin Roosevelt. The so-called Reagan Revolution, however, did not abandon the income tax that had been crafted during World War II. Indeed, the Reagan administration actually increased the capacity of the income tax for raising revenue. But in the 1990s, other powerful conservatives, led by Newt Gingrich and the congressional architects of the "Contract with America," began calling for eradicating the income tax and replacing it with either a national tax on consumption or a "flat tax." In 2002, president George W. Bush joined those voices by proposing a broad tax on consumption that would take the place of the progressive income tax. In 2003, in response, Congress enacted tax cuts that may have initiated the shift of federal finance toward a system of consumption taxation.

As part I of this book suggests, there would be nothing extraordinary about the emergence of a new tax regime—that is to say, a system of taxation with its own characteristic tax base, rate structure, administrative apparatus, and social purpose. The United States has had five such regimes since the founding of the republic. There would be nothing new, either, about such a shift beginning gradually. For example, the adoption of a tax regime based on income taxation had its origins in a long period of political agitation and legislative experimentation. Even the 1913 ratification of the Sixteenth Amendment to the Constitution, which provided a constitutional basis for income taxation, and the adoption of income-tax legislation in that same year, did not produce a dramatic change. The income tax was a highly tentative experiment until 1916, when America prepared to enter World War I and settled on it as the primary means of raising taxes for the war.

What would be without precedent, however, is a decisive shift to a new tax regime in the absence of a national crisis or emergency. The moments of sweeping change in tax regimes have come invariably during the nation's great emergencies—the constitutional crisis of the 1780s, the three major wars, and the Great Depression. Thus, on the one hand, the history of American taxation is not encouraging for reformers who would seek a new regime in periods of political stability, peace, and prosperity. On the other hand, history suggests that American political leaders have been creative and resourceful, capable of embracing drastic changes in the federal tax system if the right political and economic circumstances converge. Further, the meaning of "crisis" is, to a large extent, in the eye of the beholder. Many conservatives, for example, believe that the nation is experiencing a long-term crisis of confidence in government that compels a reconstruction of public institutions, including instruments of taxation. Perhaps the tax cuts that the Bush administration engineered in 2001, 2002, and 2003 will turn out to be the first steps in the adoption of a new tax regime.

The need to understand the sources of this conservative reconstruction, its potential significance, and the likelihood of it succeeding were very much on my mind as I revised the first edition of this book. Consequently, in this second edition, I have significantly expanded the coverage of the past twenty-five years. To do this, I have added part II, in which I seek to connect contemporary tax issues, and especially the prospects for fundamental tax reform in the twenty-first century, with the earlier history of tax regimes in America.

The core of this book, however, remains part I. It seeks to explore the association between the growth of government since the early republic and the history of federal taxation. The association has been close, just as conservative critics of the federal tax system have perhaps suspected. Part I examines the political, economic, and intellectual underpinnings of American tax regimes to help explain the enormous growth of the federal government, which, like the development of taxation, has hinged on the nation's great crises.

The history discussed in part I turns on the government's need for vast new revenues to meet national emergencies. These crises invariably forced political leaders to reexamine thoroughly the nation's financial options. In so doing, those leaders faced issues that went far beyond the financial problem of meeting demands to increase government spending. The great crises—each of which involved the meaning or survival of the nation—stimulated debate over national values. At the same time, each of the great crises intensified ideological and distributional divisions within American society. Because wars required the sacrifice of lives as well as treasure, they were especially powerful stimulants of social division. The resulting political conflicts often centered on issues of taxation; tax politics was always an important vehicle for the expression of both national values and the underlying social and ideological conflicts that the emergencies only intensified.

Within the economic and social turbulence of each crisis, the political leaders in the executive and legislative branches of the federal government struggled to establish coherent tax policies. On the whole, the crisis conditions strengthened the power of these leaders, and the tax systems they implemented further enhanced their influence. Political leaders mobilized party government and administrative techniques, including professional expertise, to expand the capacity and productivity of the federal tax system. To be sure, there was always tension between executive and legislative leaders over tax policy, and both the president and Congress had to address the demands of local interests. But during the Civil War and World War I, the common partisan loyalties and shared social values of the nation's political leaders largely overcame the pressures that tended to fragment American government. Consequently, during those two emergencies, the nation's political leadership created tax regimes with a high degree of coherence and intention.

Tension between the executive and the legislative branches intensified during the 1920s and once again during the late 1930s. The demands of local interests on the federal government also increased during these same periods. Consequently, the administration of Franklin D. Roosevelt found it more difficult to shape the new tax regimes demanded by national emergencies than had the administrations of Abraham Lincoln during the Civil War and Woodrow Wilson during World War I. But appeals to party loyalty worked to Roosevelt's advantage, and he proved resilient in forging coalitions both inside and outside the federal government. As a result, the two tax regimes produced by the New Deal and World War II bore the imprint of his administration more than that of Congress, and the imprint of a national interest more than that of local interests.

Within the conflicted politics of each of the emergencies, the leaders of the federal government worked to persuade Americans to accept new taxes. During wartime, the architects of national mobilization made taxation part of larger strategies of persuading

Americans to accept sacrifice. In the Civil War and each of the two world wars, they crafted new tax programs designed both to implement sacrifice and to convince the mass of taxpayers that their sacrifices were fair. In the process, the new tax systems acquired the symbolic function of expressing the goals of the federal government. The high-tariff system of the Civil War, for example, came to represent the federal government's commitment to create a powerful national market and to protect capitalists and workers within that market.

To help make the case for fairness, the nation's political leaders experimented with progressive income taxes during the Civil War and then introduced them on a grand scale during the two world wars. The adoption of progressive taxes during those two wars took into account and exploited powerful impulses, stimulated by the forces of democracy and industrialization, for a restructuring of American society. As a consequence, both wars produced major advances in the cause of progressive taxation at the same time that they broadened the social and financial base for funding warfare and other purposes of the federal government.

During World War I, progressive impulses were so strong that the framers of tax policy launched major initiatives that were designed to tax capital and to democratize production and finance. The most radical initiatives—most notably, the rigorous taxation of corporate excess profits—did not survive the postwar reaction of the 1920s, but they continued to influence tax policy until World War II, when the requirements of unprecedented mobilization and the fear of postwar depression led the framers of progressive tax measures to focus on the taxation of the much larger base of salaries and wages, rather than that of rents, interest, and profits.

The tax regimes of the two world wars did not produce a social revolution. But they did establish tax policy that was far more progressively redistributional than it had been before World War I, and they did establish a responsibility for the federal government to redistribute income according to ideals of social justice. These regimes became a powerful expression of the democratic ideals of the nation.

The social tensions—tensions of class and section—created by industrialization might have led the nation eventually to adopt progressive income taxation even in the absence of war. But historical contingency played a powerful role. The wartime mobilizations and the fact that both mobilizations were managed by the leadership of the Democratic Party—which was more strongly committed to progressive income taxes and more opposed to regressive taxes on consumption than the Republican Party—accelerated the process. In addition, by contributing to the resolution of wartime social crises, the emergency-driven tax policies acquired a legitimacy and cultural force that sustained them well after the emergencies were over.

The opportunity to establish new taxes provided policy architects with openings to modernize the tax system, in the sense of adapting it to new economic and organizational conditions and thereby making it a more efficient producer of revenue. No process of "modernization" closely dictated the selection of options. But in each crisis, policymakers discovered that the organizational maturing of industrial society had created a new menu of feasible options. For example, because of the prior development of financial accounting for the management of large corporations and the collection of Social Security payroll taxes, during World War II the federal government was able to establish a broad-based income tax— one that reached wages and salaries as well as the income from capital. Exploiting the new tax options during each emergency provided a structure and an administrative apparatus that allowed the federal government to capitalize effectively on postcrisis economic expansion.

By creating instruments of taxation that had acquired an independent legitimacy and were administratively more robust, each crisis opened up new opportunities for proponents of expanded government programs to advance their interests after the emergency was over. Postwar leaders were able to forge new expenditure programs—both direct and indirect—without incurring the political costs associated with raising taxes or introducing new ones. The popularity of the expenditure programs, in turn, reinforced the popularity of the tax system behind the programs. Thus, the crisis-born enhancement of tax capability contributed to the much-discussed "upward ratchet" effect that emergencies had on government spending.

Each new tax regime drew political strength from the fact that it increased not only the federal government's size but also its centralization. The relative growth of federal taxation was most rapid during the five national emergencies. To some extent, the expansion of federal taxation undercut the tax base of state government. But the federal government offset this and won state and local support for its tax regimes by assuming part of the burden of financing public services from states and localities after the crisis, and by finding ways to expedite the levying and collecting of state and local taxes. In the process, the federal government often also contributed to the centralization of taxation *within* states.

Indirect expenditure programs were particularly important to the political survival of new tax regimes after national emergencies. These indirect programs, which are now known as "tax expenditures," were networks of privileges—deductions, exemptions, and credits—within the tax code. They resulted from the resurgence of local interests after the emergencies. These programs reduced tax bases and often made rate structures less progressive. But they left intact the fundamental intent of the emergency tax regimes. In fact, they provided significant political protection to the new regimes.

The survival of each emergency-born tax system in the post-crisis era lent the nation's tax system an increasingly layered, or diversified, quality. Each new regime preserved important elements of its predecessor—elements that had survived earlier postcrisis political tests. Thus the World War II system contained not only the features that lent it distinction but also those that it had inherited from the Civil War, World War I, and Great Depression regimes.

In the absence of a new national emergency, the systems of the early republic, the Civil War, World War I, and the New Deal might have survived much longer. Each of them produced adequate revenues to fund expansive postcrisis programs. Each of the systems faced substantial criticism, but in each instance political leaders developed successful strategies, including compromises on tax policy, for preserving the regime. Nonetheless, each tax system proved inadequate—both politically and economically—to meet the fiscal demands of a subsequent national emergency, and each gave way to a new system.

In the absence of a new national emergency, the World War II tax regime remains in place today. To be sure, during the 1980s, the federal government embarked on significant tax reform. But ironically enough, the reforms, which were part of the "Reagan Revolution," turned out to strengthen the World War II tax regime. Reagan's successors, George H. W. Bush and Bill Clinton, did not advance the reforms, but they also—largely through tax increases—enhanced the fiscal capacity of the World War II regime.

President George W. Bush, however, has launched a program that purports to have begun comprehensive reform of the nation's fiscal system, including taxation. His approach has been incremental, and his accomplishments are as yet limited, but his ambition is sizable and he may be able to carry his program further. For President Bush to have a chance of finishing this job, however, the nation may have first to pass through an episode of extreme fiscal stress. Such an episode could materialize if the Bush tax cuts turn out to have made the tax system inadequate to meet the economic challenges facing the nation during the twenty-first century. But the outcome of such a crisis may disappoint conservative forces. The new regime might turn out to be rather different from the kind of regime the Bush administration would favor. The history of federal taxation in America may provide some guidance regarding the likely nature of a new tax regime.

Part I

The historic regimes

1

The formative tax regimes, 1789–1916

Modern American tax regimes began with the ratification of the U.S. Constitution in 1788. The new Constitution established powers and requirements that have had an enduring influence on the nation's tax regimes. The Constitution gave the new federal government clear and broad powers to impose "indirect" taxes—taxes on commerce that consumers would pay only indirectly, through intermediaries— as well as the power to borrow and the exclusive power to create money. But the Constitution restricted the ability to levy "direct" taxes—taxes levied directly on individuals. This restriction had a major impact on the form of future federal tax regimes and on the division of tax effort between the federal government and the governments of states and localities.

The framers of the Constitution provided only the skeleton of a state. It was up to the leaders of the new republic to develop the central instruments of government, including government finance. These leaders experimented with many of the specific taxing instruments allowed by the Constitution, but they made extensive use only of the taxation of imports. They discovered that import taxes met most of their needs for tax revenues while minimizing political discord. Therefore, the tax regime that followed the creation of

13

the new constitutional order was based on customs duties; it lasted until the Civil War, making it the longest in American history.

Only during the Civil War did politicians begin to exercise in earnest the wide range of tax instruments possible under the Constitution. As republican leaders forged the modern American nation-state, they greatly enhanced the scale and scope of public finance. The core of their wartime system of finance became an expression of national strength in the postwar era. Taken together, the framing of the Constitution and the fighting of the Civil War set the foundations for the tax systems that financed American nationhood during the twentieth century.

THE REGIME OF THE EARLY REPUBLIC

Before the American Revolution, taxation was relatively light in the British colonies that would form the United States. Public services, such as education and roads, were limited in scale, and the British government heavily funded its military operations from across the Atlantic. In 1763, however, after the expensive Seven Years' War, the British initiated a program to increase taxes levied on Americans, especially through "internal" taxes such as the Stamp Act (1765) and the Townshend Acts (1767). But colonial resistance forced the British to repeal these taxes quickly (with the exception of the tax on tea), and the overall rate of taxation in America remained low until the outset of the Revolution, at least by contemporary British standards. Nonetheless, taxation became central to the revolutionary contests between Britain and America over rights.

Tax rates and types of taxation varied substantially from colony to colony, and even from community to community within particular colonies, depending on modes of political organization and the distribution of economic power. British taxing traditions were diverse, and the various colonies and local communities had a rich array of institutions from which to choose: taxes on imports and exports; property taxes (taxes on the value of real and personal assets); poll taxes (taxes levied on citizens without any regard for their property, income, or any economic characteristic); excise (sales) taxes; and faculty taxes, which were taxes on the implicit incomes of people in trades or businesses. The mix varied, but each colony made use of virtually all these different modes of taxation.

Fighting the Revolution forced a greater degree of fiscal effort on Americans. At the same time, the democratic forces that the Revolution unleashed energized reformers throughout America to restructure state taxation. These reformers focused on abandoning deeply unpopular poll taxes and shifting taxes to wealth as measured by the value of property holdings. The reformers embraced "ability to pay"—the notion that the rich ought to contribute disproportionately to government—as a criterion to determine the distribution of taxes. The reformers were aware that the rich of their day spent more of their income on housing than did the poor and that a flat, ad valorem property levy was therefore progressive. Some conservative leaders also supported the reforms as necessary both to raise revenue and to quell social discord. The accomplishments of the reform movements varied widely across the new states; the greatest successes were in New England and the Middle Atlantic states.[1]

During the Revolution, while state government increased taxes and relied more heavily on property taxes, the nascent federal government failed to develop effective taxing authority. The Continental Congress depended on funds requisitioned from the states, which usually ignored calls for funds or responded very slowly. There was little improvement under the Articles of Confederation. States resisted requisitions and vetoed efforts to establish national tariffs.

---

[1] The complicated story of tax reform during the American Revolution is ably told by Robert A. Becker, *Revolution, Reform, and the Politics of American Taxation, 1763–1783* (Baton Rouge: Louisiana State University Press, 1980).

The fundamental structure of the federal tax system, as well as that of modern tax regimes, emerged from the formative emergency for the American federal government—the revolutionary crisis that extended through the formation of the U.S. Constitution. At its heart, the crisis was a constitutional struggle to define the basic ideas underlying the federal government: ideas of representation and consent, constitutionality and rights, and sovereignty.

At the same time Americans were forging their ideas of government, they were struggling with an array of practical problems. Among the most pressing were how to finance the Revolutionary War debts, and how to establish the credit of the nation in a way that would win respect in international financial markets. In the process of resolving problems that were both profound and mundane, the framers of the Constitution gave shape to the fiscal institutions they believed the new federal government—and a new nation—would need to survive and prosper.[2]

The Constitution reflected the desire of James Madison, Alexander Hamilton, and its other leading supporters to provide the new central government with far greater capacity to tax than the old national government had enjoyed under the Articles of Confederation. The protracted fiscal crisis of the 1780s convinced Madison and Hamilton that the new representative government must have the fiscal power required to create a strong and meaningful nation. A central goal was to fund the foreign debts that the Confederation

---

[2] For a survey of taxation during these formative years, one that "places taxation at the center of the movement that produced the Constitution" (p. 8), see Roger H. Brown, *Redeeming the Republic: Federalists, Taxation, and the Origins of the Constitution* (Baltimore: Johns Hopkins University Press, 1993). The best survey of the concrete fiscal problems that were associated with financing the American Revolution, and that subsequently influenced the framers of the Constitution, is E. James Ferguson, *The Power of the Purse: A History of American Public Finance, 1776–1790* (Chapel Hill: University of North Carolina Press, 1961).

had inherited from the Revolutionary War, and to do so in a way that would win the confidence of the international financial markets to which the new nation would have to turn for capital. In the process of funding the debts, the new government would both nurture and demonstrate the fiscal virtue of the citizens of a republic.

Consequently, whereas the Confederation had only been able to exhort the states to contribute voluntarily to the federal treasury, the Constitution now gave the new government fiscal authority commensurate with its sovereignty. In the words of Article I, Section 8, of the Constitution, Congress had the general power "to lay and collect taxes, duties, imposts, and excises." In addition, Section 8 established the power "to borrow money on the credit of the United States" and "to coin money, regulate the value thereof, and of foreign coin."

The new fiscal powers, and especially the powers to tax and coin money, illustrated the trust in the new government held by the founders and the ratifiers of the Constitution. But another provision of the Constitution seemed to express worry about the taxing power—Article I, Section 9, which severely limited federal taxation of property. The clause specified: "No capitation, or other direct tax shall be laid, unless in proportion to the census."

Identifying the basis for this limitation lies at the heart of interpreting the fiscal intentions of the framers of the Constitution. On its surface, Article I, Section 9, might seem to express a Lockean liberalism—a line of thinking that emphasized individualism, celebrated the pursuit of private self-interest and financial gain, and regarded with suspicion any governmental initiatives that might impede the search for individual gain. Much evidence with regard to the general political culture of eighteenth-century America reinforces the interpretation that it was a society of profit-maximizing tax resisters. Then, as now, numerous Americans of all classes cheated, evaded taxes, exploited loopholes in the tax code, migrated to low-tax havens, sought political groups and representatives committed to reducing taxes, and welcomed constitutional restrictions on taxation. They became especially recalcitrant during periods of economic adversity, such as the deflationary 1780s.

The major obstacle to this interpretation of Article I, Section 9, is the fact that eighteenth-century Americans generally preferred direct taxation—especially of property—to any other form of tax. Property taxation was almost everywhere the instrument of choice for local governments. The limitation on the federal government's use of property taxation had far more to do with attitudes regarding the proper sphere of the federal government than it did with the scope of government in general or the proper forms of taxation.

Understanding both the enthusiasm for property taxation at state and local levels and the worries about federal use of the property tax requires recognition that the central language of the Revolution contained much more than Lockean liberalism's emphasis on private rights. That language embraced as well a classical republicanism, or a civic humanism, which stressed communal responsibilities. These ideas focused on the threat of corruption to public order, the dangers of commercialism, and the need to foster public virtue. The founders, and even Adam Smith, held these ideas of classical republicanism in tension with those of liberalism.[3]

Commitments to civic humanism could create pressure for higher taxes, rather than lower. For example, the ideal of a harmonious republic of citizens equal before the law created demands for taxes

---

[3] A useful introduction to the modern intellectual history of the Revolutionary era is found in the essays in *The American Revolution: Its Character and Limits*, ed. Jack P. Greene (New York: New York University Press, 1987). For important suggestions as to the long-run influence of civic humanism, see Dorothy Ross, "The Liberal Tradition Revisited and the Republican Tradition Addressed," in *New Directions in American Intellectual History*, ed. John Higham and Paul K. Conkin (Baltimore: Johns Hopkins University Press, 1979), 116–31. On Adam Smith as a civic humanist, see Donald Winch, *Adam Smith's Politics: An Essay in Historiographic Revision* (Cambridge: Cambridge University Press, 1978).

to destroy islands of privilege by taxing the rich more heavily. That ideal also embraced the notion that taxpaying was one of the normal obligations of a citizenry bound together in a republic by ties of affection and respect. This communal thinking went further, emphasizing the direct relationship between wealth and the responsibility to support government and public order. It embraced enlightened self-interest and included a citizen's ability to pay as a criterion in determining patterns of taxation. In the first canon of taxation proposed in *The Wealth of Nations*, Adam Smith declared: "The subjects of every state ought to contribute towards the support of the government, as nearly as possible, in proportion to their respective abilities." In an era when most wealth was in the form of real estate, the property tax—in particular, the taxation of property according to its value—became popular because it seemed to offer the greatest potential for taxing according to ability to pay.

American governments were aware, as was Adam Smith, that the rich of their day spent more of their income on housing than did the poor and that a flat, ad valorem property levy was therefore progressive. Smith was cautious in advancing the desirability of progressive taxation, but he wrote: "It is not very unreasonable that the rich should contribute to the public expense, not only in proportion to their revenue, but something more than in proportion." The development of new property taxes stalled during the hard deflation of the 1780s. But even conservative elites began to understand the potential of property taxation to raise revenue and quell social discord. Proponents of tax reform worried that the new national government might preempt the use of property taxation by state and local governments. Thus, restricting the national government's ability to levy property taxes represented an expression of civic humanism.[4]

---

[4] Adam Smith, *An Inquiry into the Nature and Causes of the Wealth of Nations* (New York: Modern Library, 1937), 777, 794.

The limitation on the federal use of direct taxation also reflected the fact that the framers of the Constitution thought about taxation in the context of the corruption of the British Parliament and the monarchy and sought to prevent similar abuse by the new federal government. They believed that local control was necessary for the equitable operation of the property tax. The federal government, they feared, might become too far removed from the people or captured by a powerful faction. The consequence might be abuse of the property tax. Moreover, framers who were associated with a particular industry or section of the country often worried that the federal government might single out their industry or section for discriminatory property taxation. Slaveowners, for example, worried about federal property taxation that would single out slave property. Representatives of rural districts worried about taxation that might favor town dwellers over farmers—for example, the taxation of property holdings on the basis of their acreage rather than their value. Urban commercial interests worried about the reverse—federal taxation of property holdings on the basis of their value.

Such fears, in turn, fueled the fear of factionalism that James Madison, a civic humanist, expressed in *Federalist* No. 10. He predicted that "the most common and durable source of factions" would be "the various and unequal distribution of property." He concluded that the issue of taxation, more than any other, created an opportunity and temptation for "a predominant party to trample on the rules of justice." He regarded the large scale of the republic as the fundamental protection against factionalism, but in his mind Article I, Section 9, provided additional security. Giving even further protection was the requirement of Article I, Section 8, that "all duties, imposts, and excises shall be uniform throughout the United States." This clause prevented Congress from singling out a particular state or group of states for higher rates of taxation on trade, and it reflected the hope of Madison and his *Federalist* coauthor

Hamilton that the new Constitution would foster the development of a national marketplace.

Madison and the other framers of the Constitution did not regard Article I, Section 9, as crippling the new federal government. Indeed, they were confident that Article I, Section 8, established the means for the new government to acquire the economic resources it needed to fulfill its promise. They believed that the Constitution, even with the limitation, left the way open for the new federal government to raise the tax revenues it needed through indirect taxes—for example, tariffs and excises, which the federal government collected indirectly through intermediaries such as merchants.

Tariffs, in fact, turned out to provide the core of federal finance. On July 4, 1789, even before Congress had created the Treasury, President George Washington signed into law a tariff act designed to raise revenues for the new government. The act established a complex set of duties on imports, rebates for reexported goods, and special favors for imports carried in American vessels. The act yielded more than $1 million a year.

Alexander Hamilton, the first secretary of the treasury, needed to expand federal tax revenues to accomplish the highest priority of his ambitious financial program: paying off, in full, the loans that foreign governments had made to the Continental Congress during the Revolution. In 1790, the principal and unpaid interest on these loans together amounted to roughly $11.6 million. Hamilton proposed that the federal government pay the interest out of tax revenues while, over a fifteen-year period, raising enough capital to repay the principal. The interest payments would require, he estimated, about $3 billion in tax revenues a year.

In January 1790, in his "Report on the Public Credit," the first of a series outlining his financial program, Hamilton recommended how Congress ought to raise these revenues. He urged increasing tariffs over a broad range of goods and introducing internal taxation in the form of an excise tax on distilled spirits. He stopped short of proposing direct taxes—by which he, and the Constitution, meant poll taxes and property taxes. He worried that these taxes would create a popular backlash, and he wanted to encourage the states to cooperate with his financial program by leaving direct taxation as the exclusive province of state and local governments. In August 1790 Congress adopted, with only minor changes, Hamilton's proposal for increasing tariffs. At the same time, Congress asked Hamilton to submit a formal proposal for establishing the tax on distilled spirits. In December 1790, Hamilton did so. And in March 1791, with little debate, Congress adopted it in the Excise Act of 1791.

In December 1791, Hamilton recommended modifications of the new tariff system as part of an ambitious program to promote the nation's industrial advancement. In the "Report on Manufactures," his last report to Congress, he declared that the development of modern manufacturing in America would be difficult because of "fear of want of success in untried enterprises" and competition from European manufacturers, who had reaped the benefits of their governments' mercantilist policies.[5] He proposed, among other policies, tariffs to protect new industries and exemptions from tariffs for raw materials needed for industrial development. Such policies would, he argued, encourage Americans to spend their money and energy to advance industrial technology. Although Congress rejected most of Hamilton's broad program for industrialization, in March 1792 it did pass most of the tariff program he had proposed: increases in tariffs on manufactured goods, including the iron and steel of Pennsylvania, and reductions in tariffs on raw materials.

---

[5] Alexander Hamilton, "Report on Manufactures," quoted in *The Reports of Alexander Hamilton*, ed. Jacob E. Cooke (New York: Harper & Row, 1964), 140.

Even after the increases in 1792, the tariff rates were relatively low and did not impede trade significantly. And between 1789 and 1815, the tariff revenues accounted for about 90 percent of total federal tax revenues.[6]

From 1789 through the War of 1812, the most heated controversies regarding taxation concerned excise taxes rather than tariffs. Excises turned out to arouse the very factionalism that Madison had feared because they seemed to single out unfairly particular classes of producers. President Washington and Secretary Hamilton discovered this after Congress, in 1791 and 1792, followed their recommendation and enacted the nation's first excise taxes—on distilled spirits. Despite the fact that Congress structured the tax to favor whiskey production at the expense of rum production, the tax touched off the Whiskey Rebellion of 1794. Washington had to raise 15,000 troops to discourage the Pennsylvania farmers who had protested, waving banners denouncing tyranny and proclaiming "Liberty, Equality, and Fraternity."[7]

The protest ended any substantial Federalist interest in excise taxation. But Hamilton and other leading Federalists wanted to wield all the taxing powers provided by the Constitution. In 1792, Hamilton explained to Washington that enactment of the whiskey excise was desirable so that "the authority of the National Government should be visible in some branch of internal Revenue; lest a total non-exercise of it should beget an impression that it was never to be exercised & next that it ought not to be exercised."[8]

---

[6] U.S. Bureau of the Census, *Historical Statistics of the United States: Colonial Times to 1970, Part 2* (Washington, D.C.: U.S. Government Printing Office, 1975), 1106.

[7] See Thomas P. Slaughter, *The Whiskey Rebellion: Frontier Epilogue to the American Revolution* (New York: Oxford University Press, 1986).

[8] Hamilton to Washington, August 18, 1792, *The Papers of Alexander Hamilton*, ed. Harold C. Syrett (New York: Columbia University Press, 1967), vol. 12, 236–37.

Hamilton and Washington had a dual purpose. For one thing, they were preparing, in particular, for wartime and international crises, during which trade might be inadequate for the federal government's revenue needs. For another, they were promoting taxpaying as an expression of republican citizenship, and even of loyalty to the new nation. But in the wake of the Whiskey Rebellion, Hamilton understood the popular hostility toward excises. The Federalists experimented further with excises but limited them almost exclusively to goods and services consumed by the affluent. These taxes included levies on carriages and snuff manufacturing (1794) and stamp duties on legal transactions, including a duty on probates for wills (1797)—a first step in the development of the federal estate tax.

The Federalists also wanted to exercise the power to levy direct taxes. In 1798, to help finance the naval buildup against France, they imposed a direct tax on property and assigned revenue goals to the states on the basis of population, just as the Constitution required. The property taxed included all dwelling houses, lands, and large slave-holdings. Once again, to blunt the reaction to the tax's distributional effects, they gave it a progressive twist—requiring each state, in raising its share of revenue, to tax houses at rates that increased along with their value.

None of the Federalist experiments with more progressive forms of excise or direct taxes worked well, except to establish precedents for future tax initiatives. The measures raised little revenue and, even in their progressive form, contributed to Federalist political defeats in 1798 and 1800. Subsequently, in 1802, Thomas Jefferson's administration led in abolishing all excise and direct taxes. Prospects were dismal for using internal taxes to demonstrate republican commitment to the new federal government.

Hamilton's economic policies may have undermined the future of the Federalist Party, but they established a fiscally strong federal government, just as he had planned. For example, the federal government collected enough revenue to pay interest on the public debt ($2.8 million in 1793), fund the army and navy (more than $1 million in 1792), and still balance the 1793 federal budget. Throughout the critical 1790s, tax revenues more than covered the federal government's interest payments on the national debt, despite the fact that these payments accounted for more than half of federal expenditures—a larger share than at any time since, including during the most dramatic national emergencies. By 1795, the regular payment of interest enabled the Treasury to float new loans in the Netherlands and pay off its debts to Spain and France. The new European loans contributed to a dramatic economic expansion that began in the early 1790s and continued for a decade. Thus, Hamilton's fiscal policies were an important part of a model of a central government that worked creatively, positively, and effectively to unleash the nation's economic energies.

The revenue system not only serviced the nation's debt but also proved adequate to meet almost all the other needs of the new federal government. It required virtually no tax revenues to carry out two of its most important economic functions—maintaining a customs union and distributing public land. (Public land sales roughly covered the costs of administering the land system.) But for other important activities, the new government did require tax revenues. It used indirect taxes to finance the undeclared naval war with France in the late 1790s and Jefferson's war against the Barbary pirates. Tariff revenues, in combination with the debt finance that the general taxing power made possible, funded the Louisiana Purchase. Moreover, these revenues, along with land subsidies, allowed presidents from Jefferson through John Quincy Adams to implement the ambitious program of internal improvements designed by Albert Gallatin, Jefferson's secretary of the treasury. The federal government paid off all its debt by 1836, and in 1837 customs duties also enabled President Martin Van Buren's Treasury to undertake a major distribution of surplus revenues to the states for internal improvements.[9]

As the federal government emphasized tariff revenues and removed itself from the realm of direct taxation, state and local governments forged ahead with the development of revenue systems that relied heavily on property taxes. Most dramatic was the use of property taxation by state governments. Two fundamental forces—the democratization of politics and the industrialization of the economy—accelerated the property-tax movement. As the Industrial Revolution gathered force during the 1820s and 1830s, Jacksonian reformers extended the scope of property taxation, trying to tax all forms of wealth. By the Civil War, they had created in most states the elements of a general property tax designed to reach not only real estate, tools, equipment, and furnishings but also intangible personal property such as cash, credits, notes, stocks, bonds, and mortgages. Some states simply expanded the statutory definitions of what constituted property for tax purposes. Other states added constitutional provisions for uniformity (requiring that properties of equal value be taxed at the same rate) and for universality (requiring that all property be taxed). For example, Ohio's 1851 constitution provided that "laws shall be passed taxing by a uniform rule all moneys, credits, investments in bonds, stocks, joint-stock companies or otherwise; and also all real and personal property, according to its true value in money" (Article 12, Section 2). Ohio had launched general property-tax reform as early as 1825

---

[9] For a survey of federal taxation in the early national period, see Henry Carter Adams, *Taxation in the United States, 1789–1816* (Baltimore: Johns Hopkins University Press, 1884). No twentieth-century historian has written a survey of taxation, let alone public finance, in the early national period, but a political scientist has made a useful effort for the federal government. See Dall W. Forsythe, *Taxation and Political Change in the Young Nation, 1781–1833* (New York: Columbia University Press, 1977).

and had garnered sustained increases in taxes on personal property. But empowered by its 1851 constitution, in only two years it doubled its assessment of personal property—to about two-thirds the value of real property. In the same two-year period, both state and local tax collections nearly doubled.

By the 1860s, in much of the nation, property taxation was the dominant source of state and local revenues. As a consequence of property taxation's apparent success in serving their fiscal purposes, state and local political leaders became increasingly vigilant in watching for possible federal incursions into their property-tax base. At the same time, state and local governments often resented the fact that the financial instruments of the federal government, including federal bonds, remained beyond their reach. In 1819, in *McCulloch v. Maryland*, the Supreme Court of Chief Justice John Marshall ruled unconstitutional a Maryland tax on the Baltimore branch of the Bank of the United States. In 1823, in *Weston v. Charleston*, the Marshall Court specifically ruled unconstitutional state or local taxes on federal bonds.[10]

---

[10] For overviews of the antebellum reform movement for general property taxation, see Sumner Benson, "A History of the General Property Tax," in *The American Property Tax: Its History, Administration, and Economic Impact,* ed. George C. S. Benson et al. (Claremont, Calif.: Claremont Men's College, 1965), 31–52. Also see Richard T. Ely, *Taxation in American States and Cities* (New York: Thomas Y. Crowell, 1888), 131–45; on Ohio's property-tax experience, see 146–59, 456. The major exceptions in the increasing reliance by state governments on property taxation were in the South, where the waxing movement to protect slavery increasingly shielded slaves from state taxation. In North Carolina, for example, during the 1840s and 1850s the state government relied on investment income from banks and railroads and on borrowing to reduce its reliance on property taxes. See Richard Sylla, "Long-Term Trends in State and Local Finance: Sources and Uses of Funds in North Carolina, 1800–1977," in *Long-Term Factors in American Economic Growth*, ed. Stanley L. Engerman and Robert E. Gallman, National Bureau of Economic Research, Studies in Income and Wealth, vol. 51 (Chicago: University of Chicago Press, 1986), 832–35. Another valuable

After the federal government withdrew from direct and excise taxation, it relied primarily on tariffs for its revenue needs. Low tariffs proved to be a great financial success, producing revenue during periods of expanding foreign trade, which began as early as the 1790s, when American merchants profited handsomely from the Napoleonic Wars. Economic growth, which began to increase in a significant and sustained way during the 1820s, meant continuing increases in the per capita demand for imported goods and, in turn, increases in tariff revenues per capita. The flow of most ocean commerce through a few major ports provided the setting for well-administered tariffs. Low tariffs proved inexpensive to collect, and their collection did not require force.

Low tariffs were also a political success. When tariff rates were low, they won popularity. Other advantages proved important as well. Low tariffs were widely diffused or more general in their scope; they did not seem to penalize particular groups the way excises did. Taxes on imported luxury goods seemed to tax extravagant living, and tariffs were useful in economic diplomacy. To almost all Americans, tariffs seemed a legitimate and reasonable exercise of power by the new government. In short, low and moderate tariffs allowed the leaders of the early republic to limit the political divisiveness of taxation. In their effort to create a republic that was both strong and just, the early leaders of the United States relied on relatively low tariffs to raise substantial revenues yet keep tax issues from arousing the disruptive forces of factionalism.

The nation's leaders broke from the reliance on low tariffs on only two occasions. One was during the War of 1812, when a sharp decline in foreign trade ruined customs revenues. Congress

state-level study is Peter Wallenstein, *From Slave South to New South: Public Policy in Nineteenth-Century Georgia* (Chapel Hill: University of North Carolina Press, 1987).

responded by reviving excise taxation and by imposing direct taxes on houses, land, and slaves in 1813, 1815, and 1816. The federal government, following Article I, Section 9, assigned these taxes to the states according to population, as measured by the 1810 census. Each state, in turn, generally met its revenue assessment with a state property tax allocated to counties according to the distribution of taxable property. Congress also enacted duties on liquor licenses, carriages, refined sugar, and even distilled spirits. At the very end of the war, President Madison's secretary of the treasury, Alexander J. Dallas, proposed adopting an inheritance tax and a tax on incomes. But the war ended before Congress acted.

In all, taxation financed more than 40 percent of expenditures during the War of 1812, and the war was so popular that there was no significant political backlash against the temporarily high tax levels. No permanent changes in either the level or kind of federal taxation emerged from the war.

The other break with low tariffs came during the period of experimentation with protectionism from the 1820s through the early 1830s. The rationale for this move was industrialization—protecting America's high-wage workers and high-cost industries as they learned how to meet their British competition. The major departure in this direction came in 1824, when Congress enacted a 35 percent tax on imported iron, woolen, and cotton goods. The act also increased tariffs on imported raw materials, including flax, hemp, iron, lead, molasses, and raw wool.

But protection had little beneficial effect on American industries, most of which had developed on their own the ability to compete with their British counterparts. Moreover, Southern planters and Western farmers generally resisted measures that seemed to increase the price of manufactured goods. Southern politicians, especially in South Carolina, denounced the 1828 tariff legislation as the "Tariff of Abominations" and vowed to overturn it in the future, one way or another. In addition, during the Nullification Crisis of 1832–33, high tariffs came to symbolize federal power for South Carolinians worried about the future of slavery.

Consequently, in 1833 Congress began to reduce tariffs, enacting a measure that provided for a gradual, biennial reduction of the tariff so that by 1842 rates would return to the modest levels set in 1816. In 1846, Congress passed the Walker Tariff, which reduced tariffs even further; only lip service to the principle of protection remained. The Walker Tariff paralleled Britain's repeal of the Corn Laws in the same year, and it seemed to herald the adoption of free trade throughout the Anglo-American world.

The Mexican War began in the same year that Congress adopted the Walker Tariff. The financing of the war demonstrated once again the enormous revenue potential of low customs duties in a period of economic expansion. The economic recovery that had begun in the early 1840s, coupled with the lower import duties, produced an upsurge in federal revenues that enabled the federal government to pay for the war without any increase in tax rates or introduction of new taxes. Tax revenues covered more than 60 percent of wartime expenditures, and the continued buoyancy of customs duties enabled the federal government to nearly pay off its Mexican War debts by the time of the Civil War. The nation could look forward to funding future wars of territorial or imperial expansion in a similar fashion—as long as those wars were not substantially larger in scope and did not disrupt the federal government's ability to raise revenue through international trade.

Had it not been for the Civil War, changes in the federal government's tax policies might well have been minimal during the rest of the nineteenth century. Low tariffs for revenue, the borrowing power that Secretary Hamilton's financial program had helped establish, and the federal government's enormous land resources would probably have been adequate to meet federal needs if a great national emergency had not intervened.

THE CIVIL WAR REGIME

The Civil War was the first great national emergency. In fact, it may well have been the crucible for modern American nationhood. It certainly transformed the federal government and its revenue systems. It was the nation's first modern war in the sense of requiring an enormous quantity of capital. The Union's war costs drove up government spending from less than 2 percent of the gross national product to an average of 15 percent, close to the 20 percent level reached in the early 1990s. These capital requirements evoked an emergency taxation program of unprecedented scale and scope. It employed all the taxes provided for by the framers of the Constitution.[11]

Broad electoral support within the North enabled the newly dominant Republican Party to meld its interests with those of the federal government and to achieve a great deal of latitude in setting national tax policy. Despite the dramatic break with the modest liberal state of the past, Republican leaders did not face significant resistance to the huge new taxes or need to rely on coercion for their collection. The Republicans were able to persuade the American public to accept the massive broadening of the fiscal foundation of the federal government. Taxpaying became a way for Americans to demonstrate their loyalty to the Union government and to the American nation.

The Republicans introduced a tax system composed primarily of high tariffs and excise taxes, which had been so unpopular during the early republic. These new taxes funded about 20 percent of wartime expenditures. Republican Congresses increased tariffs

---

[11] For suggestions of the significance of the Civil War to the meaning of the American nation, see Carl Degler, "One among Many: The United States and National Unification," in *Lincoln, the War President: The Gettysburg Lectures*, ed. Gabor S. Boritt (New York: Oxford University Press, 1992), 91–119.

every year during the war, and the Tariff Act of 1864 imposed duties that were almost half the total value of all dutiable imports.[12]
They also imposed excise taxes on virtually all consumer goods. To
administer these taxes, in 1862 Republicans created the office of the
commissioner of internal revenue. The first commissioner, George
S. Boutwell, described the office as "the largest Government department ever organized."[13] During and after the war, this system
of consumption taxation became the centerpiece, in turn, for both
the Republicans' ambitious new program of nation building and
national economic policy.[14]

The Republican consumption taxes were regressive, taxing people with lower incomes at higher rates than those with higher incomes. Republican leaders generally preferred such taxes, but they
also recognized that regressive taxes might undermine confidence in
the Republican Party and the war effort, particularly in Western and
border states. Consequently, they looked for a supplementary tax
that bore a closer relationship to a citizen's ability to pay than did
the tariffs and excises. The twin goals would be to raise additional
tax revenue, thus easing inflationary pressures, and to convince taxpayers that the wartime fiscal system was fair.

The leadership had few options. The rudimentary accounting
methods followed by homes, farms, and businesses meant that the

---

[12] The standard history of tariff legislation remains Frank W. Taussig, *The
Tariff History of the United States* (New York: G. P. Putnam's Sons, 1931).
[13] George S. Boutwell, *Reminiscences of Sixty Years in Public Affairs* (New
York: Greenwood Press, 1968 reprint), vol. 1, 313.
[14] On the ways in which the Republicans powerfully fused the interests of
party, the state, and the nation during the Civil War, see Richard F. Bensel,
*Yankee Leviathan: The Origins of Central State Authority in America,
1859–1877* (Cambridge: Cambridge University Press, 1990), 1–237. For
a similar treatment of economic policy, see Heather Cox Richardson, *The
Greatest Nation of the Earth: Republican Economic Policies during the Civil
War* (Cambridge, Mass.: Harvard University Press, 1977). Richardson's book
contains a useful chapter surveying Civil War tax legislation; see 103–38.

most practical method to raise huge amounts of revenue quickly was the one they had already chosen: taxing goods at the point of importation or sale. Even this approach required the swift development of a large administrative apparatus for the collection of excises.

Less practical, but perhaps feasible, was adapting the administrative systems that state and local governments had developed for property taxation. Secretary of the Treasury Salmon P. Chase and Thaddeus Stevens, chair of the Ways and Means Committee in the House of Representatives, favored this approach at first, and they proposed an emergency property tax modeled after one adopted during the War of 1812. But virtually everyone regarded a property tax as a direct levy, and Article I, Section 8, of the Constitution required the federal government to allocate a direct tax among the states on the basis of population rather than property values. Members of Congress from Western states (including the Great Lakes states), border states, and poorer Northeastern states protested that this would mean a higher rate of taxation on property in their states. They also complained that the tax as written would not reach the personal property held as real estate improvements and as "intangibles" such as stocks, bonds, mortgages, and cash. Congressman Schuyler Colfax of Indiana declared, "I cannot go home and tell my constituents that I voted for a bill that would allow a man, a millionaire, who has put his entire property into stock, to be exempt from taxation, while a farmer who lives by his side must pay a tax."[15]

In response to the complaints, the leadership took note of how the British Liberals had used income taxation in financing the Crimean War as a substitute for heavier taxation of property. Justin S. Morrill of Vermont, who chaired the Ways and Means Subcommittee on

[15] *Congressional Globe*, 37th Congress, First Session (Washington, D.C.: U.S. Government Printing Office, 1861), 248.

Taxation and was a staunch proponent of high tariffs, introduced a
proposal for a new and very different tax—the first federal income
tax. Congressional leaders viewed the tax as an indirect tax because
it did not directly tax property values.[16]

The first income tax was ungraduated, imposing a basic rate
of 3 percent on incomes above a personal exemption of $800.[17]
Amendments in subsequent war years reduced the exemption and
introduced graduation. In 1865, the tax imposed a 5 percent rate
on incomes between $600 and $5,000 and 10 percent on incomes over $5,000. The rates seem low by current standards, and
the Republicans considered imposing even higher rates on larger
incomes. Nonetheless, the wartime Republicans imposed higher
taxes—perhaps twice as high—than the wealthy were used to paying under the general property tax.[18] The tax reached well into

---

[16] The most informative scholarship detailing the development of income-tax
legislation between the Civil War and World War I remains Roy G. Blakey
and Gladys C. Blakey, *The Federal Income Tax* (London: Longmans, Green,
1940), 1–103; also see Sidney Ratner, *American Taxation: Its History as a
Social Force in Democracy* (New York: W. W. Norton, 1942), 13–340;
and Edwin R. A. Seligman, *The Income Tax: A Study of the History, Theory, and Practice of Income Taxation at Home and Abroad* (New York:
Macmillan, 1914). Robert Stanley has revised this scholarship, emphasizing the conservative forces behind the development of the federal income
tax through 1913. In explaining the adoption of the first federal income tax,
he emphasizes the Republican desire to provide political protection for the
consumption-based tax regime. See Robert Stanley, *Dimensions of Law in
the Service of Order: Origins of the Federal Income Tax, 1861–1913* (New
York: Oxford University Press, 1993).

[17] The federal government had no scientific way to measure personal income,
but Congress came surprisingly close to setting the exemption close to average annual family income, which was about $900 in 1870. See U.S. Bureau
of the Census, *Historical Statistics of the United States: Colonial Times to
1970*, 41, 240.

[18] For evidence that propertied New Yorkers paid substantially higher income taxes than property taxes, see Seligman, *Income Tax*, 473–75. On

the affluent upper middle classes of the nation's commercial and industrial centers.

The administrative machinery that the commissioner of internal revenue devised to collect the income tax relied heavily on taxpayer cooperation. Compliance was high, prompted by patriotic support for the war effort and by the partial enactment of British "stoppage at the source" (meaning collection at the source or the withholding of taxes by corporations and others who make payments of income). The commissioner lacked the administrative capacity to obtain earnings reports or collect taxes from farms and small businesses, where most Americans earned their income. But the law did require corporations—railroads, banks, and insurance companies, primarily—to collect taxes on dividends and interest, which constituted a large share of the income of the affluent citizens the law was designed to tax. Also, the law required agencies of the federal government to collect taxes on salaries, which grew substantially during the wartime mobilization.

By the end of the war, more than 10 percent of all Union households were paying an income tax, and the rate of taxpaying probably reached 15 percent in the Northeastern states, where the federal government collected three-fourths of its income-tax revenues. These households probably constituted roughly the slice of society that economic historians have estimated as owning 70 percent or more of the nation's wealth in 1860. The income base for taxation was so substantial that in 1865 the tax, even with its low rate, produced nearly $61 million—21 percent of federal tax revenues for that year. (Various excises accounted for 50 percent, and tariffs made up the remaining 29 percent.) With the end of hostilities and the resumption of full-scale foreign trade, customs revenues more than doubled in 1866, but income-tax revenues still accounted for

congressional opposition to even higher rates, see Richardson, *Greatest Nation of the Earth*, 129 ff.

15 percent of all tax revenues. (The share of customs duties rose to 37 percent, while that of excises fell slightly, to 48 percent.)[19]

The Republican wartime government built the kind of revenue system necessary to establish a powerful modern state. But the rudimentary administrative apparatus available for direct taxation essentially prevented Abraham Lincoln's administration from financing a much larger share of the war through tax revenues. Even so, taxes, almost all of them new, financed about a fifth of the Union's war costs.[20]

During the late 1860s and early 1870s, Republican Congresses phased out most of the excise taxes, which the general public resented in peacetime and blamed for postwar increases in the cost of living. Abolishing the excise taxes made it easier for the Republican leadership to phase out the income tax as well. Congressional Republicans generally wanted to respond to the demands of

---

[19] These estimates are based on the well-known data on taxpayers developed by the commissioner of internal revenue for 1866. By contrast with my emphasis, Robert Stanley, citing a figure of only 1.3 percent of the American people paying income taxes, claims that the tax did not reach the middle class. Stanley arrives at a lower number, and a serious underestimate of the social reach of the income tax, by including the Confederate population and by not estimating taxpaying households. See Stanley, *Dimensions of Law in the Service of Order*, 39–40, 263–64. On estimates regarding the distribution of income and wealth, 1790–1860, see W. Elliot Brownlee, *Dynamics of Ascent: A History of the American Economy* (New York: Alfred A. Knopf, 1979), 134–36.

[20] In addition to imposing broad-based taxes, the Union government borrowed from the middle class as well as from the wealthy and created a functional money supply. Critiques of the borrowing and monetary policies of Secretary of the Treasury Chase abound. See, e.g., Robert A. Love, *Federal Financing: A Study of the Methods Employed by the Treasury in Its Borrowing Operations* (New York: Columbia University Press, 1931), 74–117. For a more positive view of Chase, see John Niven, *Salmon P. Chase: A Biography* (New York: Oxford University Press, 1995).

extremely affluent citizens, who had accepted the income tax only as an emergency measure and now lobbied vigorously to ensure first its reduction and then its discontinuance at its sunset date of 1870. Little organized support emerged for permanent income taxation, and only a minority of the party's congressional leadership thought about the tax as a valuable rhetorical shield to protect regressive tariffs. Fewer still actually liked the distributional effects of the tax. Consequently, beginning in 1867, the Republican leadership increased the exemptions and lowered the rates. In 1870, Congress—mistakenly fearing a deficit—extended the tax, but then allowed it to expire in 1872.

Republicans, however, maintained the consumption basis of the federal tax system by keeping two elements of the Civil War tax system. First, they retained the high tariffs. Frequent revisions of the tariff schedules left intact the fundamental structure of the tariff system. Until the Underwood-Simmons Tariff Act of 1913 significantly reduced the Civil War rates, the ratio between duties and the value of dutiable goods rarely dropped below 40 percent and was frequently close to 50 percent. The highest rates were imposed on manufactured goods—particularly metals and metal products, including iron and steel, cotton textiles, and certain woolen goods. On many manufactured items, the rate of taxation reached 100 percent. By 1872, tariff duties dominated federal revenues; except in a few years of severe depression and during the financing of the Spanish-American War, they would do so until 1911.

Second, Republicans left in place the taxes on alcohol and tobacco products and a few taxes on luxury items such as perfumes and cosmetics. Buoyant, price-inelastic demand for alcohol and tobacco products meant that taxes on them yielded substantial revenues, even after the federal government reduced the tax rates. In the years before World War I, revenues from levies on alcohol and tobacco always produced at least a third of all federal tax revenues, and by the mid-1890s they averaged close to a half. During the period 1911–13, alcohol and tobacco taxes produced even more revenue than did tariffs.

The Republican taxes worked politically and survived into the postwar period, despite their regressiveness, partly because, like consumption taxes in general, they escaped the notice of many taxpayers. But at least as important was the fact that the taxes won public acceptance, for a variety of reasons. Most critically, the new tax regime had acquired political momentum by helping to finance a war that defined the meaning of the American nation. For most of Northern society, the Union victory had enhanced the legitimacy of Republican tax measures and, more generally, its program of nationalist state building and economic development.

Important as well to the acceptance of the taxes was the popularity of the programs they funded. After the Civil War, the consumption-tax regime financed popular military operations, including the early phases of Reconstruction in the South, the continuing warfare with Native American tribes, and the initiation of a modern navy. Most of the tax revenues that financed the Spanish-American War came from a doubling of the taxes on tobacco and alcohol products.

Broadly popular new programs of public works and transfer payments were also all visibly financed by consumption taxes. These federal programs rewarded loyalty to the Union cause and to the Republican Party. Community leaders throughout the North became accustomed to feeding from what became known as the "pork barrel"—the annual Rivers and Harbors Bill funded by consumption-tax revenues. Republican governments also used consumption taxes to fund the nation's first major system of social insurance: an ambitious program of pensions and disability benefits for Union veterans and their dependents.

As the pensions grew decidedly generous during the 1880s and 1890s, they became a central element in the strength of the

Republican Party and continued to be important politically and economically into the twentieth century. Disbursements for disability and old-age benefits, all funded from consumption taxes, soared after the 1879 Arrears Act and the 1890 Dependent Pension Act liberalized benefits. This benefit spending remained at a high level until World War I, and during the late 1890s pensions required about 45 percent of all federal receipts. The taxes that funded the transfer payments were regressive, but the distribution of benefits was progressive—at least within the states of the victorious Union. The portion of the American population who received Civil War pensions, especially in Northern states, compared well with the levels provided by the German and Danish old-age systems, although it fell short of the level provided by British old-age pensions before World War I. In addition, Americans participating in the Civil War benefit system enjoyed terms of coverage, such as eligibility for benefits, that were reasonably generous when compared with those offered by European social programs.[21]

State and local governments, particularly when under the control of Republicans, welcomed the government centralization that the new social programs created. State and local leaders appreciated the way in which the programs satisfied demands for public works and welfare that they would otherwise have had to meet. From the 1880s through the first decade of the twentieth century, urbanization accelerated significantly, requiring cities to invest more in parks, schools, hospitals, transit systems, waterworks, and sewers. State governments increased their investments in higher education and began to aid localities in financing schools and roads.

---

[21] See William H. Glasson, *Federal Military Pensions in the United States* (New York: Oxford University Press, 1918). Also see Theda Skocpol, *Protecting Soldiers and Mothers: The Political Origins of Social Policy in the United States* (Cambridge, Mass.: Harvard University Press, 1992), 102–51; see 130–35 for the international comparisons.

The federal programs were especially welcome because they indirectly relieved the beleaguered system of property taxation used by state and local governments. Industrialization and economic instability after the Civil War undermined the egalitarian promise of the general property tax to apply to all wealth at the same rate. The self-assessment procedures commonly used were inadequate to expose and determine the value of cash, credits, notes, stocks, bonds, and mortgages, especially in the nation's largest cities. The insensitivity of assessment procedures to changes in price level increased the inequities during the economic crises of the late nineteenth century. State and local governments began to develop the modern property tax, with its standardized assessment practices and its focus on real estate.[22]

The Republican consumption-tax system also remained popular because of its regulatory dimensions. The enactment of the system represented a stunning victory for economic protectionism and, more generally, for government regulation through taxation. In sum, the system established tax incentives, disincentives, and subsidies as important, popular, and permanent elements of the federal revenue structure.

The high excise taxes on alcohol and tobacco appealed to much of the middle-class population as discouragements to, and punishments for, the consumption of commodities thought to be sinful and threatening to a virtuous republican social order. At the same time, the distilling and brewing industries valued the taxes because they provided legitimacy and meant tacit support from the federal government in the struggle against prohibitionist forces.

---

[22] On the complex difficulties with the general property tax, see Clifton K. Yearley, *The Money Machines: The Breakdown and Reform of Governmental and Party Finance in the North, 1860–1920* (Albany: State University of New York Press, 1970), 3–95, 137–65.

American business leaders lauded the regulatory effects of the tariff system. Manufacturers welcomed the protection they believed the tariffs afforded them against foreign competitors, and they praised the tendency of a favorable trade balance with Europe to encourage capital formation in America. During the 1870s and 1880s, manufacturers became especially enthusiastic about the high-tariff system because it allowed them to build national marketing organizations, free of worries about disruptions caused by European competitors. The high tariffs provided benefits not so much to the infant industries favored by Adam Smith as to the giant American corporations that were integrating vertically and gaining a long-term advantage over European firms, which were restricted to smaller markets.

Bankers and members of the financial community generally favored less emphasis on protection, more attention to the stimulation of international trade, and reductions in spending on lighthouses and pensions, coupled with further tax reductions. Nonetheless, they liked the way in which substantial taxes on consumption forced increases in the nation's rate of saving and facilitated the repayment of the wartime debt. By using consumption taxes to finance the war debt and interest payments (the latter rendered in the gold collected by customs duties), the Republican leadership transferred significant amounts of capital from consumers to holders of federal debt (Europeans as well as Americans), who tended to be wealthier than the average consumer and more likely to invest. And creditors, especially holders of federal debt, appreciated the way the Republican taxes tended to produce budget surpluses in the 1870s, reduced the debt, helped to contract the money supply, and eased the return to the domestic gold standard in 1879.[23]

---

[23] One estimate is that debt retirement and interest payments accounted for as much as half of the rise of the share of national economic product

High tariffs also seemed to benefit workers, who commonly feared competition from lower-wage labor in Europe, Latin America, and Asia and favored tax policies that advanced the prosperity of their industries. Labor support for the high-tariff position of the Republican Party had much to do with its smashing victory in the "critical election" of 1896 and its strong electoral displays, which continued until the Great Depression.

Finally, the high-tariff system received vigorous support from congressional leaders for purely political reasons. They discovered that the tariff system created significant opportunities to reinforce or enhance their power. By making adjustments within the complex and poorly understood web of tax subsidies, they could offer benefits to narrowly defined groups or threaten such groups with penalties, without fear of fatal reprisal from larger publics.

The Republican architects of the tax regime, however, had to face significant partisan resistance to their tax policy, especially after the resumption of serious two-party competition. During the 1870s and 1880s, the Democratic Party challenged Republican power with a biting critique of a central element of the consumption-tax system—the tariff. To some extent, sectional interests drove the Democratic challenge. It was an appeal to the Southerners who received neither the regulatory nor programmatic benefits—Civil War pensions, for example—of the tariffs and excises they paid. But the critique was a more general attack on special privilege, monopoly power, and public corruption—one that harked back to the ideals of the American Revolution and the early republic. The Democrats described the tariff as the "mother of trusts" and, more generally, as the primary engine of a Republican program of subsidizing giant corporations.

devoted to capital formation between the 1850s and the 1870s. See Jeffrey G. Williamson, "Watersheds and Turning Points: Conjectures on the Long-Term Impact of Civil War Financing," *Journal of Economic History*, 34 (September 1974): 636–61.

The Democrats framed their message to appeal to Southerners, to be sure, but also to farmers, middle-class consumers, and owners of small businesses throughout the nation.

In fact, during the 1880s and 1890s, the two competing political parties came to base their economic appeals on sharply conflicting ideological views of the tariff and of taxation in general. In a kind of path-dependent politics initiated by the Civil War crisis, these party identities would have a major influence on revenue policy until World War II. The Republicans' invocation of high tariffs and the Democrats' response had sharply polarized the parties on issues of taxation, which would exacerbate class conflict for nearly a century.[24]

Criticism of the tariff intensified during the depression of the mid-1890s. Economic distress stimulated Populists in the West and the South, along with advocates of Henry George's "single tax" scattered throughout urban America, to promote social justice through tax reform. These two movements converged in their efforts to find ways to use the tax system to punish and discourage monopoly power. The Populists championed a progressive tax on the profits of corporations and the incomes of the wealthy. Single taxers, inspired by Henry George's (1839–97) best-selling *Progress and Poverty* (1880), advocated shifting all taxation to a property tax on the monopoly profits embedded in the price of land—the "unearned increment" in the value of land that resulted from its location rather than its use. This tax would have to be state and local, however, because of the Constitution's requirement that the federal government allocate a "direct" tax, like a property tax, to the states according to the distribution of population (rather than the distribution of property values or "unearned increments"). The single

---

[24] On the partisan and ideological nature of the tariff debates, see Tom E. Terrill, *The Tariff, Politics, and American Foreign Policy, 1874–1901* (Westport, Conn.: Greenwood Press, 1973), especially 210–17.

taxers often supported the progressive tax at the federal level while seeking radical reform of the property tax at the state and local levels.[25]

The new grassroots pressure began to change the politics of federal taxation. During the Civil War, Republican leaders had exercised a great deal of discretion in crafting the income tax. To be sure, they had developed the income tax in anticipation of sectional and class resistance to a federal property tax. But they had designed the income tax without any group's insistence that they do so. And, after the war, they set their own timetable for its demise. In contrast, when Congress began to seriously reconsider income taxation during the early 1890s, it did so primarily in response to popular pressure. Moreover, Congress then faced numerous proposals for a high degree of progression, and the proposers' arguments had a sharp, radical edge.

Central to the appeal of a highly progressive income tax during the 1890s was the claim that it would both reallocate fiscal burdens according to ability to pay and also help restore a virtuous republic free of concentrations of economic power. The rhetoric was, in a sense, conservative; it directed attention to the values of the early republic. What was potentially radical about the movement for progressive income taxation was its content: the goal of raising the government's revenues primarily or even entirely from the largest incomes and corporate profits. The radical advocates of income

---

[25] The traditional "progressive" scholarship placed a great deal of emphasis on the importance of such grassroots pressure by farmers in shaping the inception of the federal income tax. See, e.g., Elmer Ellis, "Public Opinion and the Income Tax, 1860–1900," *Mississippi Valley Historical Review* 27 (September 1940): 225–42. For Henry George's views, see his *Progress and Poverty* (London: J. M. Dent and Sons, 1976). On the career and influence of George, see Charles A. Barker, *Henry George* (New York: Oxford University Press, 1955); and W. Elliot Brownlee, "Progress and Poverty: One Hundred Years Later," *National Tax Association Proceedings* (1979): 228–32.

taxation argued that their tax would not touch the wages and salaries of ordinary people but would instead attack unearned profits and monopoly power. The tax would, its proponents claimed, redress the wealth and power maldistribution that was responsible for the evils of industrialization. Those who believed they had faced expropriation would now do the expropriating.

Thus, support for a radical progressive income tax had far more to do with the search for social justice in an industrializing nation than with the quest for an elastic source of revenue. The tax became an integral part of democratic statism—a radical program of invoking instruments of government power to create a more democratic social order. This redistributional aspect of democratic statism was a major theme uniting some of the important legislative initiatives undertaken by the federal government before World War II. It was, in part, a new kind of liberalism—a realignment of classic nineteenth-century liberalism and the commonwealth tradition of early republicanism, which included a distrust of commerce. Democratic statists like the Populists and the single taxers regarded themselves as applying the ideals of the American Revolution to the new conditions of industrial society. Although the strategy remained one of liberating individual energies by providing a social order of abundant opportunity, the tactics had changed. To these new liberals, the state had become a necessary instrument and ally, not an enemy. They designed their tax program to restructure the market-driven machinery for distributing income and wealth.[26]

---

[26] For a discussion of the meaning of democratic statism and its relationship to progressive income taxation, see W. Elliot Brownlee, "Economists and the Formation of the Modern Tax System in the United States: The World War I Crisis," in *The State and Economic Knowledge: The American and British Experiences*, ed. Mary O. Furner and Barry E. Supple (Washington, D.C.: Woodrow Wilson Center Press, and Cambridge: Cambridge University Press, 1990), 401–35. Democratic statism also had an expression in the regulatory taxation of individual and corporate behavior. In this regard,

During the severe economic depression of the mid-1890s, the
pressures for progressive tax reform from Western and Southern
Populists became strong enough to begin a shift in the position of the
leadership of the Democratic Party. A contributing factor was the
decline of foreign trade and tariff revenues during the depression.
This enabled the Democrats to embrace a proposal for a new tax
while still calling for the shrinkage of swollen Republican programs.
Democrats took control of both houses of Congress in 1893, and
their leaders in the House from the South and the West, including
Benton McMillin of Tennessee, who chaired the Ways and Means
Subcommittee on Internal Revenue, enacted an income tax in 1894
as part of the Wilson-Gorman Tariff. They sensed an opportunity
to use tax issues for a major realignment of the two political parties
along sectional and class lines, and they debated the income tax
with unprecedented agrarian ferocity.[27]

Hostility from Northeastern Democrats, as well as the opposition of most Republicans (including leaders, such as Senator John
Sherman of Ohio and Senator Justin Morrill of Vermont, who had
supported the Civil War income tax), limited the tax's progressivity. Within both parties, leaders recalled how effective the Civil

---

after the turn of the century, reformers built on the precedents of alcohol and
tobacco taxation and used the federal taxing power to regulate grain and
cotton futures, the production of white phosphorous matches, the consumption of narcotics, and even the employment of child labor. See R. Alton Lee,
A History of Regulatory Taxation (Lexington: University Press of Kentucky,
1973).

[27] For suggestions of this kind, see Charles V. Stewart, "The Federal In-
come Tax and the Realignment of the 1890s," in *Realignment in American
Politics: Toward a Theory*, ed. Bruce A. Campbell and Richard J. Trilling
(Austin: University of Texas Press, 1980), 263–87. Stewart also describes
the way in which political parties, in building consensus, moderated the con-
tent and rhetorical tone of income-tax proposals after 1896. See Stewart,
"The Formation of Tax Policy in America, 1893–1913" (Ph.D. dissertation,
University of North Carolina at Chapel Hill, 1974).

War income tax had been in reaching the incomes of the nation's wealthy families. Although Congress reproduced many of the technical features of the Civil War income tax and set a somewhat lower rate on incomes and profits (2 percent), it also introduced several changes that reflected rising popular enthusiasm for taxing the rich. It established a much higher personal exemption ($4,000), thus focusing the tax more directly on very wealthy individuals. It also defined as taxable income any personal property acquired by gift or inheritance. Finally, it applied the 2 percent tax to the income of business corporations (with income defined as revenues above operating expenses, including interest indebtedness). This tax embodied the assumption that the federal government ought to tax corporations according to a "benefit" theory of taxation as well as the principle of ability to pay. Americans had begun to regard corporate taxation as an especially important vehicle for both taxing the rich and assaulting special privilege.

The 1894 tax was short-lived. In 1895 the Supreme Court, in *Pollock v. Farmers' Loan and Trust Co.*, voided the income tax of the Wilson-Gorman Tariff. The Court argued that the income tax was a direct tax and that—because the federal government had failed to allocate the tax across states according to population—the tax was unconstitutional.[28] The *Pollock* decision raised a significant

---

[28] Modern scholarship has modified an older "progressive" interpretation of the Pollock decision as a conspiratorial act of judicial fiat. For that view, see Robert G. McCloskey, *The American Supreme Court* (Chicago: University of Chicago Press, 1960), 140–41, and Sidney Ratner, *Taxation and Democracy in America* (New York: Wiley, 1967), 193–214, among others. The best current discussion of the role of the Court is Stanley, *Dimensions of Law in the Service of Order*, 136–75. Stanley argues that the Court was engaged in a kind of Jacksonian attack on the dominant role of Congress in "statist capitalism." Consistent with his interpretation is Morton Horwitz's argument that the Pollock decision was a logical culmination of a process that established an "anti-redistributive principle" as "part of the very essence of the constitutional law of a neutral state." See Morton J. Horwitz,

institutional barrier to progressive taxation, but it also stimulated some support for income taxation. Populists and Democrats from the South and the West now attacked the Court and found that their audiences responded enthusiastically. Democrats began to introduce constitutional amendments that would permit income taxation, and in 1896 the Democratic Party formally endorsed income taxation. This was the first time a major party had done so.

But the Democrats went down to a decisive defeat in 1896, and the Republican Party's leaders believed the results proved that they did not need to confront any pressure for progressive tax reform.[29] When Republicans faced the problem of financing the Spanish-American War in 1898, they had recovered the power to neutralize the Democratic thrust for income taxation. Republicans were willing to accept, however, a progressive but modest tax on estates.

Enthusiasm for the taxation of estates or inheritances had grown even more rapidly than the popularity of income taxation. In 1888, the economist Richard T. Ely captured the spirit of proposals for estate taxation when he wrote that a progressive tax on estates would be consistent with the "Jeffersonian" principle of "the abolition of hereditary distinctions and privileges." Jefferson and "other founders" of the republic, he wrote, aimed "to force each one to rely on his own exertions for his own fortune, desiring to give to

The Transformation of American Law, 1870–1960: The Crisis of Legal Orthodoxy (New York: Oxford University Press, 1992), 19–27.

[29] For suggestions of the influence on tax policy of what political scientists call "critical elections" on tax policy, see Susan B. Hansen, *The Politics of Taxation: Revenue without Representation* (New York: Praeger, 1983). Hansen rests heavily on these elections, which produced long-term realignments of party loyalty, for explaining the timing of major shifts in tax policy, but the fit is very loose. Among the critical elections, only the 1860 (and possibly 1980) election was followed by an immediate shift in tax regimes; the 1896 election confirmed the existing regime rather than ushering in a new one; and the introduction of the World War I regime was not associated with a critical election.

all as nearly as practicable an equal start in the race of life." Between 1890 and 1900, eighteen states adopted inheritance taxes. In contrast to the progressive income tax, the progressive estate tax won some support from the nation's wealthiest citizens. Some of them, like Andrew Carnegie, expressed idealistic motives. To others, estate taxation may have seemed less threatening than income taxation. For this reason, in 1898 the Republican leadership was willing to enact a federal estate tax even though the top rate was high, reaching 15 percent. But Republicans regarded the measure as temporary. They left it in place for a time after the Spanish-American War to fund the suppression of the Huks (in the Philippines) and U.S. intervention in the Boxer Rebellion. But the tax was repealed in 1902.[30]

During the next fifteen years, support for income taxation grew gradually. The gains were most marked across rural America but especially strong in the Midwest and the West. Republican leaders like Robert M. La Follette of Wisconsin discovered that income taxation was one of those reform issues that attracted and held voters to the alignment the party had crafted in 1896. Presidents Theodore Roosevelt and William Howard Taft both recognized this support and made vague gestures on behalf of a graduated income tax (in 1906 and 1908, respectively). But popular backing for income taxation grew too in the urban Northeast; both Republican and Democratic leaders found that the tax had begun to appeal to their constituents.

Important to the new support for federal income taxation was the formation of an urban-rural alignment of middle-class citizens who favored state and local tax reform. The economic depression of the 1890s, which was followed by accelerating demands for

---

[30] On the estate tax enacted during the Spanish-American War, see Ratner, *American Taxation*, 234–37. For Ely on inheritance taxation, see his *Taxation in American States and Cities*, 312–20.

services from state and local governments, accentuated the flaws in general property taxation. Both farmers and middle-class property owners in towns and cities resented how their tax burdens grew as a consequence of the inability of local and state governments to use general property taxation to reach intangible personal property. And these groups became interested in the adoption of new taxes—such as income, inheritance, and corporate taxes—as replacements for state property taxes.[31] Small property owners, both rural and urban, increasingly believed that income taxes would help restore the progressiveness lost in the administrative collapse of the Jacksonian general property tax under industrial conditions.[32] Ely, the economist who most vigorously championed reform of state general property taxation, captured the essence of the new reform program. In the 1880s, he wrote: "Some way must be contrived to make owners of . . . new kinds of property, who include most of our wealthiest citizens, pay their fair share of taxes." His solution was for states to adopt the income tax, "the fairest tax ever devised."[33]

The states, however, were very slow to adopt the new, alternative taxes, and industrial states were especially slow in adopting income taxes. No state adopted a modern income tax until 1911, when Wisconsin did so. The Wisconsin tax pioneers finessed the administrative problems by collecting most of the revenues from

---

[31] For an example of early advocacy for replacing personal property taxation with state income taxation, see Ely, *Taxation in American States and Cities*, 287–311.

[32] See David P. Thelen, *The New Citizenship: Origins of Progressivism in Wisconsin, 1885–1900* (Columbia: University of Missouri Press, 1972), 202–22; Yearley, *Money Machines*, 193–250; John D. Buenker, *Urban Liberalism and Progressive Reform* (New York: W. W. Norton, 1973), especially 103–17; and Morton Keller, *Regulating a New Economy: Public Policy and Economic Change in America, 1900–1933* (Cambridge, Mass.: Harvard University Press, 1990), 208–15.

[33] Ely, *Taxation in America States and Cities*, 140, 288.

corporations, which faced a stringently administered 6 percent tax on their profits. Manufacturers accounted for about two-thirds of the corporate burden. But the tax slowed the pace of industrial investment in Wisconsin by increasing the cost of capital to Wisconsin manufacturers significantly above the levels faced by their competitors located elsewhere in the Great Lakes states.

Political leaders in the other Great Lakes states and in industrial states elsewhere regarded the damage to industry in Wisconsin as a cautionary tale. Massachusetts and New York did not adopt income taxes until they faced the fiscal problems imposed by World War I, and not until they were confident that they could build the administrative machinery required to assess and collect a tax based primarily on individual incomes rather than corporate profits. Most industrial states did not enact income taxes until the revenue crisis created by the Great Depression.[34]

Nonetheless, the debates promoted widespread interest in any approach, including the adoption of income taxes, that might rebalance the equity of the tax system. In addition, the sluggish progress of income taxation at the state level increasingly convinced middle-class citizens that it would be desirable to enact the tax at the federal level.

---

[34] W. Elliot Brownlee, "Income Taxation and the Political Economy of Wisconsin, 1890–1930," *Wisconsin Magazine of History* 59 (summer 1976): 299–324; Brownlee, *Progressivism and Economic Growth: The Wisconsin Income Tax, 1911–1929* (Port Washington, N.Y.: Kennikat Press, 1974), and Brownlee, "Income Taxation and Capital Formation in Wisconsin, 1911–1929," *Explorations in Economic History* 8 (September 1970): 77–102. For challenges to my views on Wisconsin's tax, see John O. Stark, "The Establishment of Wisconsin's Income Tax," *Wisconsin Magazine of History* 71 (autumn 1987): 27–45; Stark, "Harold M. Groves and Wisconsin Taxes," *Wisconsin Magazine of History* 74 (spring 1991): 196–214; and John D. Buenker, *The History of Wisconsin*, vol. 4, *The Progressive Era, 1893–1914* (Madison: State Historical Society of Wisconsin, 1998).

During the ferment over tax issues at the state and local levels, some defenders of the wealthiest property owners joined in support of federal income taxation. They concluded that the tax might help take the wind out of the sails of more radical tax measures at the state and local levels. The most influential among these conservatives was a group of urban economists and attorneys who were tax experts. Edwin R. A. Seligman of Columbia University and Charles J. Bullock of Harvard University led them in promoting income taxation, on the one hand, and in moderating the rhetoric used to justify the tax, on the other. As early as 1894, Seligman had argued that the point of the tax was to "round out the existing tax system in the direction of greater justice." Such language helped shift the discourse over taxation from a focus on the salvation of industrial America to an emphasis on a moderate redistribution of the tax burden.[35]

Conservative support for moderate income taxation might be described as expressing a kind of "corporate liberalism" or "progressive capitalism." More generally, this vision, developing in tension with democratic statism, influenced not only the development of income taxation but also the ideas of the so-called progressive movement. Reformers of this more conservative persuasion wanted to bring a greater degree of order to industrial society and to strengthen national institutions, just as did the democratic statists. But in contrast to the democratic statists, "progressive capitalists" or "corporate liberals" looked with admiration on the efficiency of the modern corporation. Government regulation, including taxation, was desirable only if it served to protect the investment system.[36]

---

[35] Edwin R. A. Seligman, "The Income Tax," *Political Science Quarterly* (1894): 610.

[36] Exemplary discussions of corporate liberalism are Mary Furner, "Knowing Capitalism: Public Investigation and the Labor Question in the Long Progressive Era," in *The State and Economic Knowledge*, ed. Furner and

By 1909, there were enough insurgent Republicans in Congress who supported a graduated income tax to force action. A diverse group of representatives and senators from both parties supported the immediate enactment of such a tax. Congressman Cordell Hull, a first-term Democrat who represented the same Tennessee district as had Benton McMillin, noted changes in the composition of the Supreme Court and found it "inconceivable" that the nation "had a Constitution that would shelter the chief portion of the wealth of the country from the only effective method of reaching it for its fair share of taxes."[37] A bipartisan group hammered out a proposal, but they had to limit the tax's progressiveness to generate enough support. Senator Nelson Aldrich, the chair of the Senate Finance Committee, proved resourceful in both preserving Republican Party union and blunting the thrust toward income taxation. He worked closely with President Taft to persuade the insurgents to accept a modest corporate income tax, and to describe it as "a special excise tax" in order to protect it from the thrust of the *Pollock* decision. He also worked to submit the Sixteenth Amendment to the Constitution, legalizing a federal income tax, to the states for ratification. Aldrich and the Northeastern Republicans recognized the growing popular support for income taxation but hoped that the measure would fail.

Ratification prevailed in 1913, much to the surprise and consternation of stand-pat conservatives.[38] The process of ratification succeeded in part because of two other campaigns. One was a revival

Supple, 241–86, and Martin J. Sklar, *The Corporate Reconstruction of American Capitalism, 1890–1916* (Cambridge: Cambridge University Press, 1988).

[37] Cordell Hull, *The Memoirs of Cordell Hull* (New York: Macmillan, 1948), vol. 1, 49.

[38] The standard source on the ratification movement is John D. Buenker, *The Income Tax and the Progressive Era* (New York: Garland, 1985).

of the single-tax movement. Beginning in 1909, soap magnate Joseph Fels, who had converted to Henry George's faith in the single tax, began to finance campaigns for constitutional reforms permitting classification of property for the purpose of taxation (and thus high rates of taxation on the "site value" of land) and local option in taxation. Although the campaigns won no significant electoral victories except in Oregon in 1910, they awakened the interest of the urban middle class in using the income tax to redistribute wealth.[39] The campaigns also convinced more wealthy property owners that they needed moderate reform as a defensive measure, and their support was important to the crucial victory of ratification in New York in 1911. The other set of campaigns was the presidential election of 1912. As a consequence of the campaigns of Woodrow Wilson, Theodore Roosevelt, and Eugene Debs, popular enthusiasm for federal policies designed to attack monopoly power reached an all-time high.

In 1913, bipartisan support for income taxation was broad, and the Democrats controlled Congress. Nonetheless, the income-tax measure they enacted was only modest. To some extent, this was because the leaders of both parties were cautious and wanted to maximize support for income taxation within the Northeast, where they feared the tax would be unpopular, and thus maintain party unity. To a greater extent, it was because the nation's political leaders, as well as the general public, were unsure of how much redistribution they wanted the new tax instrument to accomplish. Wilson urged caution on Furnifold M. Simmons, chair of the Senate Finance Committee. "Individual judgments will naturally differ," Wilson wrote, "with regard to the burden it is fair to lay upon incomes which run

[39] On Joseph Fels's campaigns see Arthur P. Dudden, *Joseph Fels and the Single-Tax Movement* (Philadelphia: Temple University Press, 1971), 199–245, and Arthur N. Young, *The Single Tax Movement in the United States* (Princeton, N.J.: Princeton University Press, 1916), 163–83.

above the usual levels."[40] Moreover, the supporters of income taxation were themselves uncertain how income ought to be defined or how the income tax would work administratively.

Finally, virtually none of the income-tax proponents within the government believed that the income tax would become a major, let alone the dominant, permanent source of revenue within the consumption-based federal tax system. Certainly the advocates of income taxation who were hostile to the protective tariff hoped that the tax would succeed and expedite the reduction of tariffs. But they doubted that the new revenues would be substantial. And the idea that the tax would enable the federal government to grow significantly was far from the minds of the drafters of the 1913 legislation.

To be sure, Congressman Hull, who was the primary drafter of the 1913 legislation, wanted to make certain that the federal government would have access to the income tax in wartime; he believed that the federal government could make the tax, as an emergency measure, even more productive than it had been during the Civil War. But for Hull, as well as for the other income-tax enthusiasts, the revenue goals of the tax were far less important than the desire to use the tax to advance economic justice.[41]

---

[40] Woodrow Wilson to Furnifold M. Simmons, September 4, 1913, in *The Papers of Woodrow Wilson*, ed. Arthur S. Link (Princeton, N.J.: Princeton University Press, 1978), vol. 28, 254.

[41] Jordan A. Schwartz has cited Cordell Hull's emergency-revenue argument in claiming that "anticipation of war made the income tax a war tax." See Schwartz, *The New Dealers: Power Politics in the Age of Roosevelt* (New York: Alfred A. Knopf, 1993), 14. There is no evidence, however, that Hull expected war in 1910, when he made the cited comment, and there is much evidence that Hull was then primarily interested in a redistribution of tax burdens. For Hull's own description of his important role in federal tax reform before World War I, see Hull, *Memoirs of Cordell Hull*, 45–74. Between 1894 and 1913, when champions of income taxation referred to the possible need to levy it in wartime, they were usually buttressing their legal

Consequently, the Underwood-Simmons Tariff Act of 1913, which reestablished the income tax, was less progressive and less ambitious in its revenue goals than the Civil War legislation or even the legislation of 1894. The act established the "normal" rate of 1 percent on nearly all personal and corporate income. The act set a high exemption ($3,000 for single taxpayers) that excused virtually all middle-class Americans from the tax. The act also established a graduated surtax up to 6 percent, but this did not come into play for incomes under $20,000. The wealthiest American families paid marginal rates ranging between 1 and 7 percent—substantially lower than those they had faced during World War I. The act also exempted interest income earned by owners of state and local bonds.[42] And it exempted dividends up to $20,000 from the personal income

arguments for the constitutionality of the federal tax. See, e.g., the dissenting opinion of Justice John Marshall Harlan in *Pollock v. Farmers' Loan and Trust Company*, 158 U.S. 601, 15 S.Ct. 673, 39 L.Ed. 1108 (1895), and Edwin R. A. Seligman, "The Proposed Sixteenth Amendment to the Constitution," in Seligman, *Income Tax*, 627–28 (Seligman first published this part of his essay in 1910). Historians have only rarely claimed that the architects of the Sixteenth Amendment or the 1913 legislation expected the tax to produce major additions to federal revenue. The leading examples are Ben Baack and Edward J. Ray, who claim that the passage of the 1913 income tax "signaled voters that the federal government had the wherewithal to provide something for everybody." See Baack and Ray, "The Political Economy of the Origin and Development of the Federal Income Tax," in *Emergence of the Modern Political Economy: Research in Economic History, Supplement 4*, ed. Robert Higgs (Greenwich, Conn.: JAI Press, 1985), 121–38.

[42] Some proponents of the legislation went further by arguing that the Constitution itself protected owners of state and local bonds from federal taxation. They referred to the case of *Collector v. Day* (1870), in which the Supreme Court had ruled that Article 10, taken together with *McCulloch v. Maryland*, rendered unconstitutional the federal taxation of the salaries of state judicial officers. The Court's position on the issue became known as the doctrine of reciprocal intergovernmental immunity—the doctrine that the Constitution shields the federal government and state governments from discriminatory taxes on each other's activities.

tax. Thus, the act attempted a partial integration of corporate and personal taxes, limiting the double taxation of corporate earnings to the portion of those earnings received as dividends by the richest Americans.

In the first several years of the income tax, only about 2 percent of American households paid taxes. Meanwhile, the tariff and the taxation of tobacco and alcohol remained the most productive sources of revenue. The tariff, in fact, became even more productive, because the 1913 reduction of tariff rates by the Wilson administration stimulated trade and increased revenues. If it had not been for the mobilization for World War I, the major consequence of the passage of the income tax in 1913 might have been the protection of the regime of consumption taxation inherited from the Civil War.

2

The democratic-statist tax regimes,
1916–1941

By the time of World War I, the forces of industrialization had abundantly fueled democratic pressures for the federal government to enter the arena of direct taxation and assume some of the responsibility that state and local governments had undertaken for ameliorating social tensions over the uneven distribution of wealth. At the same time, mature industrialization, which included the flowering of modern corporations and of sophisticated financial intermediaries, had created much of the organizational capability necessary for implementing a direct tax on the incomes of corporations and wealthy individuals. But even so, the federal government would have been slow to adopt income taxation without the play of historical contingency. Without the intervention of the United States in World War I and the management of that intervention by the leaders of the Democratic Party, the development of federal taxation would have proceeded far more incrementally. It almost certainly would have relied much more heavily on the taxation of consumption.

As it was, the highly contingent politics of mobilizing for World War I drove the creation of a democratic-statist tax regime. That regime, with its steeply progressive tax rates and its tax base consisting of the incomes of corporations and wealthy individuals, provided the core of wartime finance. The regime then endured and survived the return to "normalcy" after World War I. The democratic-statist thrust of federal taxation weakened under the economic and political pressures that the highly progressive rate structure created for carving out loopholes. But in a contingent fashion, another national emergency—this one economic, in the form of the Great Depression—intervened. Once again, the leadership of the Democratic Party was in a position to manage the crisis, and the administration of Franklin D. Roosevelt resumed the democratic-statist restructuring of the federal tax system that had begun during World War I. Following that approach, the New Deal launched a new tax regime.

THE WORLD WAR I SYSTEM

The financial demands of World War I, set in the context of redistributional politics, accelerated tax reform far beyond the leisurely pace that corporate liberals would have preferred. In fact, the wartime crisis produced a brand-new tax regime—one that was close to the ideals of democratic statists. This new tax system, the most significant domestic initiative to emerge from the war, probably would not have taken the form it did had the United States not entered the war.[1]

---

[1] On the financing of World War I, see W. Elliot Brownlee, "Wilson and Financing the Modern State: The Revenue Act of 1916," *Proceedings of the American Philosophical Society* 129 (1985): 173–210; Brownlee, "Economists and the Formation of the Modern Tax System in the United States: The World War I Crisis," in *The State and Economic Knowledge: The American and British Experiences*, ed. Mary O. Furner and Barry E. Supple (Washington, D.C.: Woodrow Wilson Center Press, and Cambridge: Cambridge University Press, 1990); and Brownlee, "Social Investigation and Political Learning in the Financing of World War I," in *The State and Social Investigation in Britain and the United States*, ed. Michael J. Lacey and Mary O. Furner (Washington, D.C.: Woodrow Wilson Center Press, and Cambridge: Cambridge University

The tax-reform process began in 1916 when President Wilson and Secretary of the Treasury William G. McAdoo made the single most important financial decision of the war. They chose to cooperate with a group of insurgent Democrats in arranging wartime financing on the basis of highly progressive taxation. Led by Congressman Claude Kitchin of North Carolina, who chaired the Ways and Means Committee in the House of Representatives, the insurgent Democrats attacked concentrations of wealth, special privilege, and public corruption. Kitchin exploited the influence of the Ways and Means Committee. The insurgents were able to insist that if preparedness, and later the war effort, were to move forward, they would do so only on the financial terms of the insurgents. They embraced taxation as an important means to achieve social justice according to the humanistic ideals of the early republic. Redistributional taxation then became a major element of the Wilson administration's program for steering between socialism and unmediated capitalism.[2]

Press, 1993), 323–64. See also Jerold L. Waltman, *Political Origins of the U.S. Income Tax* (Jackson: University Press of Mississippi, 1985). For a different interpretation of World War I finance, see economist Charles Gilbert, *American Financing of World War I* (Westport, Conn.: Greenwood Press, 1970). Gilbert was interested in World War I finance as an example of how democracies tend to abstain from the kind of taxation that would promote strategic mobilization with the least inflation and disruption of productive capacity: taxation transferring purchasing power from consumers to the government. "War finance," Gilbert wrote, "is and always has been a victory of expediency over economics" (p. 236). Gilbert's characterizations of tax institutions are similar to those of the political scientists described as pluralists. Herbert Stein presented a more positive view of McAdoo's Treasury but offered one similar criticism of its approach to taxation. Stein suggested that the Treasury was unwilling to pay the political costs of devising a tax program focused on discouraging "nonessential production." See Herbert Stein, *Government Price Policy in the United States during the World War* (Williamstown, Mass.: Williams College, 1939), 78–84, 124.

[2] Southern sectionalism reinforced the class-based populism of Claude Kitchin. Some political science scholarship has stressed the crippling effect

The war provided an opportunity for Democratic progressives to focus the debate over taxation on one of the most fundamental and sensitive economic issues in modern America: What stake does society have in corporate profits? More specifically, the question became one of whether the modern corporation was the central engine of productivity, which tax policy should reinforce, or whether it was an economic predator, which tax policy could and should tame. The outcome of the debate was that the nation embraced a new tax system: "soak-the-rich" income taxation.[3]

Thus, during the period of crisis—one in which the pressure of fighting a modern war coincided with powerful demands to break the hold of corporate privilege—Wilson and the Democratic Party turned Republican fiscal policy on its head. They embraced a tax policy that they claimed—just as the Republicans had for their tariff

of post–Civil War Southern sectionalism, and the associated hostility toward the federal government, on the development of a modern state. But this scholarship does not discuss progressive federal income taxation, which, if anything, this sectionalism (expressed in the careers of Claude Kitchin and Cordell Hull) promoted during World War I. See Richard Bensel, *Sectionalism and American Political Development, 1880–1980* (Madison: University of Wisconsin Press, 1984); Bensel, *Yankee Leviathan: The Origins of Central State Authority in America, 1859–1877* (Cambridge: Cambridge University Press, 1990); and Jill Quadrango, *The Transformation of Old Age Security: Class and Politics in the American Welfare State* (Chicago: University of Chicago Press, 1988). Historians are well aware of the general significance of the Southerners who were in the Wilson administration or among his supporters in Congress, but no one has systematically examined their ideas on government. The best analyses are Arthur S. Link, "The South and the 'New Freedom': An Interpretation," *American Scholar* 20 (1950–51): 314–24; and George B. Tindall, *The Emergence of the New South, 1913–1945* (Baton Rouge: Louisiana State University Press, 1967), 1–60.

[3] A contrasting view of the importance of redistributional impulses is John Witte's. In explaining the crucial Revenue Act of 1916, he stresses the "dictates of war" and asserts that "there is little evidence of an independent interest in redistributing income through the tax system." See Witte, *The Politics and Development of the Federal Income Tax* (Madison: University of Wisconsin Press, 1985), 81–82.

system—would sustain a powerful state and economic prosperity. But the Democrats' new tax policy was one that assaulted, rather than protected, the privileges associated with corporate wealth.

The Democratic tax program, which was implemented in the wartime Revenue Acts, transformed the experimental, rather tentative income tax into the foremost instrument of federal taxation. The Revenue Act of 1916 imposed the first significant tax on personal incomes, doubled (to 2 percent) the tax on corporate incomes, and introduced an excess profits tax of 12.5 percent on munitions makers. It rejected a broadly based personal income tax— one falling most heavily on wages and salaries—and focused on the taxation of the wealthiest families. Among the provisions of the 1916 legislation was the elimination of the personal exemption for dividends. Thus, the act deliberately introduced the double taxation of corporate earnings distributed as dividends. In effect, the 1916 legislation embraced the concept of using the corporate and personal income taxes as two different means of taxing the rich. The architects of the Revenue Act of 1916 intended to implement on one hand, through the personal income tax, an "ability-to-pay" philosophy and on the other hand, through corporate taxation, a "benefit" theory of taxation.[4]

The Democratic tax program of 1916 also introduced federal estate taxation. The primary congressional champion of the estate tax was Cordell Hull, who believed that the direct taxation of estates would compensate in part for the failure of the general property tax to reach personal property. In other words, the federal government

---

[4] W. Elliot Brownlee, "Wilson and Financing the Modern State: The Revenue Act of 1916," *Proceedings of the American Philosophical Society* 129 (1985): 173–210. On the sympathy of leading figures in the Wilson administration for benefit approaches to taxation, see Brownlee, "Social Investigation and Political Learning in the Financing of World War I," in *State and Social Investigation in Britain and the United States*, ed. Lacey and Furner, 335–37.

would tax accumulated personal property at death, rather than rely on state and local governments to collect a wealth tax throughout an individual's lifetime. George F. Peabody—a wealthy, influential ally of Woodrow Wilson—supported the estate tax for similar reasons. He pointed out that jurisdictional problems made high estate taxation impractical for states, and he saw the estate tax as a practical alternative to the kind of aggressive, Henry George–style property taxation that he preferred in principle. Estate taxation, he said, presented "a way to restore [the] unearned increment without giving a shock to the general conscience by suggestion of 'confiscation.'" Under the 1916 legislation, estates larger than $50,000 paid a progressive tax that increased from a minimum of 1 percent to a maximum of 10 percent (on estates larger than $5 million).[5]

In 1918, only about 15 percent of American families had to pay personal income taxes, and the tax payments of the wealthiest 1 percent of American families accounted for about 80 percent of the revenues from the personal income tax. Even without taking into account the incidence of the corporate income tax on the rich, this wealthiest 1 percent of taxpayers paid marginal tax rates ranging from 15 to 77 percent and effective rates averaging 15 percent, having increased from 3 percent in 1916.[6] Similarly, the richest

---

[5] Cordell Hull, *The Memoirs of Cordell Hull* (New York: Macmillan, 1948), vol. 1, 80; Hull, "Speech in Defense of the Revenue Act of 1916," Papers of Cordell Hull, Library of Congress; George Foster Peabody to Warren Worth Bailey, March 22, 1916, Papers of Warren Worth Bailey, Mudd Library, Princeton University; Sidney Ratner, *American Taxation: Its History as a Social Force in Democracy* (New York: W. W. Norton, 1942), 354–58.

[6] Effective rates are the average percentages of taxable income paid in income taxes by categories of taxpayers. The rates take into account the effect of both marginal rates of taxation and offsetting deductions and exemptions. On the effective rates on the richest 1 percent of households in the twentieth-century United States, see W. Elliot Brownlee, "Historical Perspective on U.S. Tax Policy toward the Rich," in *Does Atlas Shrug? The Economic Consequences of Taxing the Rich*, ed. Joel B. Slemrod (New York and Cambridge,

Americans accounted for almost all the estate taxes paid. Wartime legislation raised the maximum estate tax rates to 25 percent (on estates larger than $10 million) but did not lower the exemption or increase the minimum tax rate. Consequently, only slightly more than 1 percent of decedents paid any estate taxes.[7]

Finally, the Democratic program of finance embraced the concept of taxing corporate "excess profits." The Revenue Act of 1917 increased the tax on corporate incomes to 6 percent and expanded the excess-profits tax on munitions makers to a graduated tax on all business profits above a "normal" rate of return. The rates of taxation were graduated progressively by rates of return on invested capital. In 1917, the tax rates ranged from 20 percent on profits above the "normal" rate of return to 60 percent on profits earned by more than a 33 percent rate of return. The Revenue Act of 1918 doubled the basic corporate income tax to 12 percent and further increased excess-profits taxation. The act reduced the number of tax rates from six to two but increased the lowest rate to 30 percent and the top rate to 65 percent (on profits earned by more than a 20 percent rate of return). The excess-profits tax accounted for

Mass.: Russell Sage Foundation and Harvard University Press, 2000), especially p. 45 on the rates during World War I. Because they ignore the incidence of corporate income taxation on the rich, these estimates seriously understate the effective rates. Richard Kasten et al. estimated that in 1980, for example, the corporate income tax might have increased the effective rate of all federal taxes on the top 1 percent of households from 28.7 percent (assuming that all of the corporate tax fell on labor income) to 34.9 percent (assuming that all of the corporate tax fell on capital income). See Richard Kasten, Frank Sammartino, and Eric Toder, "Trends in Federal Tax Progressivity, 1980–1993," in *Tax Progressivity and Income Inequality*, ed. Joel Slemrod (Cambridge: Cambridge University Press, 1994), 21.

[7] For the percentages of decedents who were more than twenty-five years of age and whose estates paid estate taxes, 1922–1977, see Carole Shammas et al., *Inheritance in America: From Colonial Times to the Present* (New Brunswick, N.J.: Rutgers University Press, 1987), 128–29.

about two-thirds of all federal tax revenues during World War I and added to the tax burden that the personal income tax imposed on the rich. Only the United States and Canada among the belligerents taxed excess profits in this way, and only the United States placed excess-profits taxation at the center of wartime finance.

Excess-profits taxation turned out to be responsible for most of the tax revenues raised by the federal government during the war. Taxes accounted for a larger share of total revenues in the United States than in any of the other belligerent nations, despite the fact that by the end of 1918 the daily average of war expenditures in the United States was almost double that in Great Britain and far greater than that in any other combatant nation.[8]

The income tax with excess-profits taxation at its core outraged business leaders. Redistributional taxation, along with the wartime strengthening of the Treasury (including the Bureau of Internal Revenue, the forerunner to the Internal Revenue Service), posed a long-term strategic threat to the nation's corporations. Those most severely threatened were the largest corporations, which believed their financial autonomy to be in jeopardy. In addition, the new tax system empowered the federal government, as never before, to

---

[8] A comprehensive explanation of differences among the belligerents in their reliance on taxation would have to incorporate economic constraints as well as political culture. The explanation would have to recognize, for example, that while Great Britain financed somewhat less of its war costs through taxation (roughly 29 percent as against 37 percent for the United States), Britain's war costs were about 21 percent larger than those of the United States. Gerd Hardach provides limited international comparisons regarding war finance. See Hardach, *The First World War, 1914–1918* (Berkeley: University of California Press, 1977), 150–55. The source behind most of Hardach's figures is Harvey E. Fisk, *The Inter-Ally Debts: An Analysis of War and Post-War Public Finance, 1914–1923* (New York: Bankers Trust Company, 1924). The most careful accounting of American war costs remains Edwin R. A. Seligman, *Essays in Taxation* (New York: Macmillan, 1921), 748–82.

implement egalitarian ideals. No other single issue aroused as much corporate hostility to the Wilson administration as did the financing of the war. Wilson's longtime supporters within the business community, among them Bernard Baruch, Jacob Schiff, and Clarence Dodge, bitterly attacked his tax program within the administration and often quietly supported Republican critics. This conflict between advocates of democratic-statist, soak-the-rich taxation on the one hand and business leaders on the other hand would rage for more than two decades.

Despite the damage to business confidence, the Wilson administration and congressional Democratic leaders moved forward with excess-profits taxation with almost no attention to the complaints of Baruch and other business critics. The Democratic leaders did so in part because they shared Kitchin's ideal of using taxation to restructure the economy according to nineteenth-century liberal ideals. They presumed that the largest corporations exercised inordinate control over wealth and that a "money trust" dominated the allocation of capital. For Wilson and McAdoo, the tax program, with its promise to tax monopoly power and break monopoly's hold on America's entrepreneurial energy, seemed to constitute an attractive new dimension to Wilson's "New Freedom" approach to the "emancipation of business." Thus, wartime public finance was based on the taxation of assets that democratic statists regarded as ill gotten and socially hurtful, comparable to the rents from land monopolies that Henry George and his followers had wanted to tax. In fact, both Wilson and McAdoo entertained explicit single-tax ideas as they developed their tax-reform program.[9]

[9] Wilson, however, had far greater suspicion of the administrative state than did McAdoo. In 1916, because of that suspicion, Wilson may well have been attracted to using taxation, rather than administrative regulation, to tackle the "monopoly problem." As the war wore on, and as he was unable to resist the growing influence of business within the wartime bureaucracy, Wilson became even more attracted to the antimonopoly potential of excess-profits

Party government also played a crucial role in the decision of the Wilson administration. Wilson and McAdoo knew they could have easily engineered passage of a much less progressive tax system— one relying more heavily on consumption taxes and taxation of middle-class incomes—in cooperation with Republicans and a minority of conservative Democrats. They were confident in their ability to administer such broad-based taxes effectively. But they regarded mass-based taxation as a betrayal of the principles of their party. After all, the Democratic Party had strong traditions of representing the disadvantaged, of hostility to a strong central government as the instrument of special privilege, of opposition to the taxation of consumption, and of support for policies designed to widen access to economic opportunity. A failure to adopt a highly progressive and "reconstructive" tax program would have had serious consequences for Wilson and McAdoo. They would have bitterly divided their party. They would have spoiled their opportunities for attracting Republican progressives to their party. And they would have destroyed their strong partnership with congressional Democrats—a partnership that both leaders regarded as necessary for the effective advancement of national administration.[10]

Closely related to the Wilson administration's tax program was its sale of war bonds to middle-class Americans. Rather than tax

taxation. But no scholar has fully explored the linkages between Wilson's approach to the taxation of business and his overall relations with business. Consequently, the issue of whether or not Woodrow Wilson's ideas and policies, considered comprehensively, represent democratic statism or corporate liberalism lies beyond the scope of this book. The best study of Wilson and business during the war is Robert D. Cuff, *The War Industries Board: Business–Government Relations during World War I* (Baltimore: Johns Hopkins University Press, 1973).

[10] For a discussion of the sustained hostility toward special privilege within the Democratic Party, see Robert E. Kelley, *The Transatlantic Persuasion: The Liberal-Democratic Mind in the Age of Gladstone* (New York: Alfred A. Knopf, 1969).

middle-class Americans at high levels, the Wilson administration employed a voluntary program to mobilize their savings, a strategy that McAdoo called "capitalizing patriotism." He attempted to persuade Americans to change their economic behavior: to reduce consumption, increase savings, and become creditors of the state. He hoped that after the conclusion of the war, middle-class bondholders would be repaid by tax dollars raised from corporations and the wealthiest Americans. He intended to adopt the opposite, from a distributional standpoint, of the kind of debt retirement that had followed the Civil War.

Selling the high-priced bonds directly to average Americans on a multibillion-dollar scale required marketing campaigns far greater in scope than those used anywhere else in the world. Largely through trial and error, the Wilson administration pioneered a vast array of state-controlled national marketing techniques, including the sophisticated analysis of national income and savings. Financing by the new Federal Reserve system, which Secretary McAdoo turned into an arm of the Treasury, was important, but not as much as McAdoo's efforts to shift private savings into bonds. In the course of managing and promoting four "Liberty Loans," McAdoo and the Treasury expanded the federal government's and the nation's knowledge of the social characteristics of capital markets. The Treasury team used information gathered by its own systematic investigations, armed itself with modern techniques of mass communication, and placed its loans deep in the middle class—far deeper than it had during the Civil War or than European governments had in World War I. In the third Liberty Loan campaign (conducted in April 1918), at least half of all American families subscribed. Thus, the new public finance regime installed by the Wilson administration encompassed a revolution in borrowing strategy as well as tax policy.

The Wilson administration also tried to keep middle-class taxes down while guaranteeing business access to capital by adopting a

statist or administrative approach to converting capital to the conduct of the war. Benjamin Strong, the governor of the New York
Federal Reserve Bank, described the choice confronting the Treasury as a choice between "one school believing that economy could
and should be enforced and inflation avoided through establishing
higher [interest] rate levels" and "the other school" believing "that
economy must be enforced through some system of rationing, or
by consumption taxes, or by other methods more scientific, direct,
and equitable than high-interest rates." The Treasury's plan relied
on the latter approach: to borrow capital at low rates and then develop new government machinery that would guarantee American
business adequate access to capital into the postwar period.

As part of this policy element, Secretary McAdoo led an effort to
gain control of the nation's capital markets. Beginning in late 1917,
when he became concerned about the difficulties that the railroads
and other utilities were having in financing wartime expansion, he
led in devising proposals for centralized control that resulted in the
formation of the Capital Issues Committee of the Federal Reserve
Board, the creation of the War Finance Corporation, the federal
takeover of the nation's railroad system, and his appointment as
director general of the railroads. Outside the Treasury, he pressed
Wilson, other members of the Cabinet, and Congress to increase the
federal government's control over prices and the allocation of capital, and to coordinate and centralize all wartime powers through
instruments even more powerful than the War Industries Board.

The new public finance regime had broad and significant administrative implications. The complex and ambitious program of taxing and borrowing required a vast expansion of the Treasury's administrative capacity. A major arm of the Treasury was the Bureau
of Internal Revenue (BIR), whose personnel increased from 4,000 to
15,800 between 1913 and 1920 and which underwent a reorganization along multifunctional lines, with clear specifications of responsibilities and chains of command. One of the BIR's most demanding

chores was administering the excess-profits tax. In the process of interpreting, selling, explaining, and assessing the new business tax, the Treasury created a modern staff of experts—accountants, lawyers, and economists.

Much of this bureaucracy also implemented the new individual income tax by processing the huge volume of information on individual taxpayers. This flow of information resulted from an "information at the source" provision in the Revenue Act of 1916, which required corporations to report on salaries, dividends, and interest payments. In short, the Treasury built a class of mediators—defining themselves as experts—whose task was to reconcile the goals of the corporation and affluent individuals with the needs of the state. But under McAdoo's leadership, the Treasury undertook far more than a "broker-state" balancing of contesting interest groups; it enhanced the power of the state to advance economic justice and the war.

McAdoo assembled an exceptionally capable team to manage the Treasury. The team employed "businesslike" methods and demonstrated intellectual flexibility and entrepreneurship. Lacking an adequate civil service, McAdoo fashioned within the Treasury the kind of organization one political scientist has called an "informal political technocracy," or a "loose grouping of people where the lines of policy, politics, and administration merge in a complex jumble of bodies." This was an early example of what would become a typical expression of America's unique form of a "higher civil service."[11] For example, within this new bureaucracy, Assistant Secretary Russell C. Leffingwell supervised all aspects of Treasury operations, negotiated with Congress, and, as a former partner and bond specialist in the New York law firm of Cravath & Henderson,

---

[11] See Hugh Heclo, "The State and America's Higher Civil Service," paper delivered at Woodrow Wilson International Center for Scholars Conference on the Role of the State in Recent American History, October 23–24, 1982.

forged connections with the most powerful elements of the business community as well as with Benjamin Strong and the Federal Reserve Board. Daniel C. Roper, who served as BIR commissioner, was a seasoned federal bureaucrat with friends in many agencies and an influential figure in the national Democratic Party. Crucial in assisting Leffingwell and Roper was Yale University economist Thomas S. Adams, who served as principal tax adviser and who led in drafting legislation, tying together the administering of old laws and the formulating of new ones. John Skelton Williams, comptroller of the currency, helped maintain McAdoo's ties with more radical antibusiness progressives and made McAdoo seem, by contrast, conservative and reasonable to many business leaders.

The Treasury group did far more than administer new taxing and borrowing programs. It also served as the Wilson administration's primary instrument for learning about financial policy and its social implications, for shaping the definition of financial issues and administration programs, and for mobilizing support for those programs. The Treasury group developed a significant degree of autonomy. It became the means for McAdoo to form and dominate networks linking together competing centers of power within the federal government and linking the government with civil society. Because McAdoo had formed such a group, he was able to design and implement a financial policy with clear social objectives. Under his leadership, the Treasury avoided falling under the control of competing centers of power within the government and of other groups outside. The Treasury escaped the disarray that befell much of the Wilson administration's mobilization effort.

Wilsonian democratic statism finally succumbed to a business counterattack. In 1918, corporate leaders and Republicans found an opening when President Wilson tried to make a case for doubling taxes. Using vigorous antitax, antigovernment campaigns throughout the nation, and anti-Southern campaigns in the West, Republicans gained control of Congress. Then, in 1920, they rode to a presidential victory during the postwar economic depression. The Democratic Party of Woodrow Wilson had failed to do what the Republican Party of Abraham Lincoln had done—establish long-term control of the federal government and create a new party system.

Although it had been defeated politically, the Wilson administration had proven that the U.S. state, despite its weakness, was capable of fighting a sustained, capital-intensive war. The key was popular support. Critically important both to building popular support and to mobilizing resources on a vast scale was the method of finance: progressive taxation and the sale of "the war for democracy" to the American people through bond drives. Both instruments proved to be critical steps in increasing political authority for the federal government—in increasing its ability, through democratic politics, to acquire resources for national defense and the waging of war. The shaping influence of democratic values on mobilization explained the federal government's success in adopting coercive and statist means for financing the war.

The freewheeling debate over federal tax options continued during the postwar period. Because the federal government had now acquired substantial experience in creating a modern income-tax system, and because tax experts had become more influential within the federal government, the scope of the debate widened. It encompassed not only the reform of income taxation but also the adoption of a variety of new taxes: sophisticated general sales taxes (including a value-added tax), expenditure taxation, undistributed-profits taxation, and federal regulatory taxes.[12]

The Republicans who assumed control of both the presidency and the Congress in 1921 approached tax reform as a means to roll back Wilsonian democratic-statism. Under the leadership of

---

[12] On the history of federal regulatory taxation, narrowly defined, see Lee, *History of Regulatory Taxation.*

Secretary of the Treasury Andrew Mellon, one of the wealthiest men in America, the Republicans blocked new soak-the-rich legislation and attacked the most redistributional parts of the wartime tax system.[13]

In the process, the Republicans granted substantial, across-the-board tax reductions to corporations and to the nation's wealthiest individuals. In 1921, they abolished the excess-profits tax, dashing Claude Kitchin's hopes that the tax would become permanent. In addition, they made the nominal rate structure of the personal income tax less progressive. The primary goal was to make that tax be less burdensome on the rich. In 1921, the Republicans cut the top marginal rate on the rich by one-third, from 73 to 58 percent. They reduced it further in 1926 and 1928 so that in 1928 the top marginal rate fell to 25 percent. Also, Republicans attacked the estate tax. They were unable to eradicate it, as Mellon had hoped to do, but in 1926 they did succeed in reducing the top rate from 25 to 20 percent and in increasing the exemption from $50,000 to $100,000. As a consequence, by 1918 the percentage of decedents paying federal estate taxes had shrunk by half, to about 0.5 percent.[14]

At the same time, the Republicans busied themselves opening new loopholes. Beginning in 1921, in response to intense lobbying, they installed a wide range of special tax exemptions and

---

[13] In 1924, Andrew Mellon paid more income tax ($1.9 million) than all but three other Americans. (Those three were John D. Rockefeller Jr., Henry Ford, and Edsel Ford.) Mellon was a relative newcomer to the ranks of the nation's superrich. Only a decade earlier, he (and the Fords, as well) had not been counted among the nation's wealthiest fifty citizens. Stanley Lebergott, *The American Economy: Income, Wealth and Want* (Princeton, N.J.: Princeton University Press, 1976), 169–71. For a discussion of the largest income-tax payers in 1923 and 1924, as made public by a provision in the Revenue Act of 1923, see Albert W. Atwood, *The Mind of the Millionaire* (New York: Harper & Brothers, 1926), 253–56.

[14] Shammas et al., *Inheritance in America*, 128.

deductions, which the highly progressive rate structure of the income tax made valuable to wealthy taxpayers. The Revenue Act of 1921 introduced the preferential taxation of capital gains at a rate of 12.5 percent for assets held longer than two years (this rate held until 1934). That act also introduced a variety of deductions, such as oil- and gas-depletion allowances, that favored particular industries. The effect of these provisions on the taxation of the rich was to cut their effective rates nearly in half. By 1923, the effective rate on the richest 1 percent of American families had fallen to less than 8 percent, and it remained at this general level through the rest of the decade. It would have fallen even further if the economic growth of the 1920s had not pushed the less-rich households within the top 1 percent into higher tax-brackets.[15]

Mellon argued that these tax reductions, especially on wealthy Americans and corporations, were necessary to stimulate economic expansion and restore prosperity. He argued, in effect, that rich Americans responded to high taxes in three different ways, all of which damaged the nation's economic health. Those who paid the taxes might become discouraged and reduce their entrepreneurial effort. Those who were able to pass on the taxes to consumers raised the general cost of living. And, those who avoided taxes by, for example, investing in tax-exempt bonds, moved their capital into less productive avenues. Slashing the highest marginal tax rates would, Mellon claimed, encourage the rich to invest at higher rates and in more productive enterprises, thereby enhancing economic efficiency. In short, Mellon declared that there was a trade-off between progressivity and equity, and he recommended sacrificing progressivity on behalf of growth.

On one occasion, Mellon's interest in promoting growth led him to try to close off a significant loophole in the tax code—the

[15] Brownlee, "Historical Perspective on U.S. Tax Policy toward the Rich," 45.

complete or partial exemption from personal income taxation of interest payments from the government bonds issued during four wartime Liberty Loans and the postwar Victory Loan. Mellon proposed a constitutional amendment removing the tax deductibility of all government securities. He was concerned that the deductibility encouraged wealthy taxpayers to invest in tax-exempt government bonds, thereby drawing capital away from investments that would be more stimulative of economic growth. Congress, however, received great pressure from the beneficiaries of this loophole and did not follow Mellon's recommendation.[16]

Along with the regime of highly progressive taxes created by World War I came enhanced power for the tax-writing committees of Congress. During the 1920s, legislators on these committees discovered how much influence they wielded through the incremental, relatively invisible consideration of valuable loopholes. Although they did not use the term, the legislators had discovered the political appeal of "tax expenditures." They could establish what amounted to new expenditure programs by creating pockets of privilege within the tax code. In turn, they won or maintained the

---

[16] For Andrew Mellon's progrowth arguments, see Andrew W. Mellon, *Taxation: The People's Business* (New York: Macmillan, 1924), especially 93–107 and 127–38. For a discussion of the significance of Mellon's policies, see Ronald Frederick King, "From Redistributive to Hegemonic Logic: The Transformation of American Tax Politics, 1894–1963," *Politics and Society* 12, no. 1 (1983): 1–52, and *Money, Time & Politics: Investment Tax Subsidies in American Democracy* (New Haven, Conn.: Yale University Press, 1993), 104–11. King argues that Mellon invoked a "hegemonic tax logic" that was finally victorious in the Kennedy-Johnson tax cuts of 1964. No one has ever demonstrated that the Mellon tax cuts actually stimulated economic growth, but two economists have argued persuasively that the postwar lowering of the marginal rates at the top reduced tax avoidance through the purchase of tax-exempt securities. See Gene Smiley and Richard H. Keehn, "Federal Personal Income Policy in the 1920s," *Journal of Economic History* 55 (June 1995): 285–303.

support of powerful, wealthy groups or individuals while avoiding the political costs associated with raising taxes. Just like the system of protective tariffs before it, the federal income tax had become an instrument to advance special privilege.

To exert and reinforce their new power, the congressional tax-writing committees won approval in the Revenue Act of 1926 to create the Joint Committee on Internal Revenue Taxation (JCIRT), which would become the Joint Committee on Taxation in 1976. Congress originally charged the JCIRT with investigating avenues to simplify the law and with improving its administration, and the JCIRT's professional staff did increase the tax-writing committees' technical capabilities. But the JCIRT immediately became primarily a vehicle for enhancing the influence of the committees' senior members.[17]

The Republicans were tempted to go even further in their tax reforms. But Secretary Mellon moderated the reactionary assault by leading a struggle within the Republican Party to protect income taxation from those who wanted to replace it with a national sales tax. He helped persuade corporations and the wealthiest individuals to accept *some* progressive taxation and the principle of "ability to pay." This approach would, he told them, demonstrate their civic responsibility and defuse radical attacks on capital by recognizing the popular support that soak-the-rich taxation had gathered. Thus, while shrinking the state, Republican leaders took care to preserve progressive estate and personal income taxes. And these leaders also supported retaining the basic corporation income tax; they held it

---

[17] On the formation of the JCIRT, see Roy G. Blakey and Gladys C. Blakey, *The Federal Income Tax* (London: Longmans, Green, 1940), 542–43, 546–48. See also Donald R. Kennon and Rebecca M. Rogers, *The Committee on Ways and Means: A Bicentennial History, 1789–1989* (Washington, D.C.: U.S. Government Printing Office, 1989), 330–33; and Thomas J. Reese, *The Politics of Taxation* (Westport, Conn.: Quorum, 1980), 61–88.

at the World War I rate of about 12 percent. Mellon went so far as to advocate providing a greater reduction in taxes on "earned" than on "unearned" income, and the Revenue Act of 1924 included such a provision. "The fairness of taxing more lightly incomes from wages, salaries, or from investments is beyond question," Mellon asserted. "In the first case, the income is uncertain and limited in duration; sickness or death destroys it and old age diminishes it; in the other, the source of income continues; the income may be disposed of during a man's life and it descends to his heirs." Thus, he helped to preserve a revenue system that, even in its weakened form, advanced social justice.[18]

Mellon's strategy was what might be described as the pursuit of enlightened self-interest—as corporate liberalism, in contrast to Woodrow Wilson's democratic statism. Mellon received crucial support for his approach from the tax-writing committees of Congress, which wanted to preserve the political influence they found they could exert under a progressive system of income taxation.

Mellon also strengthened the World War I tax system by protecting and rationalizing the influence of the Treasury. Most important, he promoted the passage of the Budget and Accounting Act of 1921, which drew on the 1911 reports of the Taft Commission to create the first national budget system. The act established presidential responsibility for preparing a comprehensive budget rather than simply assembling and transmitting departmental requests. It created two important agencies: the Bureau of the Budget (located inside the Treasury) to assist in budget preparation, and the General Accounting Office (as an arm of Congress) to conduct independent audits of the federal government.[19]

---

[18] Mellon, *Taxation*, 56–57.

[19] On the movement to establish a national budget system, see Charles Stewart III, *Budget Reform Politics: The Design of the Appropriations Process in the House of Representatives, 1865–1921* (Cambridge: Cambridge

At the same time, Mellon attempted to strengthen the Treasury by transforming it into a "nonpartisan" agency. In his 1924 book, *Taxation: The People's Business* (which was actually written largely by his expert assistant secretaries), he explained, "Tax revision should never be made the football either of partisan or class politics but should be worked out by those who have made a careful study of the subject in its larger aspects and are prepared to recommend the course which, in the end, will prove for the country's best interest."[20]

Mellon was interested in more than scientific policymaking. His main goal was to insulate the Treasury from pressure from Democratic Congresses. He wanted to ensure that the Treasury operated within the confines of conservative assumptions about the state and corporate power, and within a political framework that advanced the Republican Party. Consequently, when he approached tax cutting during the postwar reconversion and downsizing of government, he rejected the advice of Thomas S. Adams, who was the primary tax adviser in the Mellon Treasury.

If the federal government was to dismantle its wartime system of taxation, Adams believed, it should take the opportunity to replace the system with an economically efficient income tax or a progressive spendings tax, that is to say, a tax on "unnecessary or surplus consumption." Adams began to despair of income taxation, concluding that it contained "incurable inequalities and inconsistencies" and had "reached a condition of inequality the gravity of which could scarcely be exaggerated." He advocated eliminating the excess-profits tax and reducing the rate of progression, but he urged avoiding the kind of special deductions that Mellon had introduced. In addition, Adams favored the integration of corpo-rate and individual income taxation. But rather than follow Adams's lead, Mellon chose to recommend tax cutting that created privileged groups and industries while providing protection to Republican ad-ministrations and Congresses against the charge that they favored the abolition of progressive taxation.[21]

Mellon's tax program consolidated the flow of income-tax rev-enues into the Treasury. The portion of general revenues provided to the federal government by indirect taxes (largely the tariff) fell from almost 75 percent in 1902 to about 25 percent in the 1920s; meanwhile, income-tax revenues increased, accounting for nearly 50 percent of the federal government's general revenues. As had been the case in World War I, income-tax revenues proved to be more abundant than the Treasury experts had forecast, and the Republican administrations enjoyed substantial, growing budget surpluses until the onset of the Great Depression.

The large revenues from income taxation provided the basis for the expansion of federal domestic programs and for the political re-inforcement of the World War I tax system. During the 1920s, the federal government expanded its programs of grants-in-aid, which it had begun in 1914 with the support of the Smith-Lever Act for agri-cultural extension. This grant system provided federal funding that included matching requirements, formulas for distribution among the states, and monitoring of states' expenditure plans. Highway programs were the major beneficiaries; as early as 1921, roughly 40 percent of all highway funding came from the federal govern-ment, on the basis of the Federal Aid Road Act of 1916.

Just as had been the case after the Civil War, state and local governments welcomed this new federal funding. The federal rev-enues helped state and local governments satisfy demands for public

---

[21] For a discussion of Adams's analysis, see Brownlee, "Economists and the Formation of the Modern Tax System in the United States," 430–31.

services, especially schools and roads, and relieve pressure on their tax systems. State governments became the most swiftly growing level of government during the 1920s, and they replaced their crumbling systems of state property taxation with new arrays of sales taxes (e.g., gasoline taxes), user charges (e.g., motor vehicle fees), and special taxes on corporations and incomes. In 1902, states were getting about 53 percent of their tax revenues from property taxation; by 1927, they raised only about 23 percent from that source. Of the new taxes, those on sales, especially on gasoline, were the most dynamic. Sales taxes increased as a share of state tax revenues from 18 percent in 1902 and 1913 to 27 percent in 1927 and to 38 percent in 1932.

The Republican administrations and Congresses of the 1920s had shifted ground within the World War I tax regime. Soak-the-rich taxation remained, but with progressiveness reduced, major loopholes added, and its sharp anticorporate edge dulled. As a consequence of the path-dependent nature of the development of the tax regime initiated by U.S. involvement in World War I, the income tax conveyed very mixed messages about the nature of wealth and civic responsibility in America.

Without the wartime crisis, the growth of the federal government almost certainly would have been slower and reliant on some combination of tariff revenues, sales taxes, and low-rate taxation of personal and corporate incomes or spending. That system might have been as riddled with inconsistencies, departures from horizontal equity, and theoretical confusion as was the highly progressive tax system that emerged during and after the World War I crisis. But in contrast to the system that probably would have emerged from a more incremental process, the system for financing World War I substantially raised the stakes of conflict over tax policy. Along with highly progressive taxation came opportunities both to undertake massive assaults on wealth and corporate power and to carve out lucrative enclaves of special privilege within the tax code.

These high stakes helped keep taxation at the center stage of politics through World War II.

THE GREAT DEPRESSION AND THE NEW DEAL
TAX REGIME

The Great Depression—the nation's worst economic collapse—produced yet another tax regime. Until 1935, however, Depression-driven changes in tax policy consisted of ad hoc quests for short-term economic stimulation and revenue growth rather than efforts to seek comprehensive tax reform. Until then, both the Republican administration of Herbert Hoover and the Democratic administration of Franklin Roosevelt put economic recovery and budgetary considerations ahead of any other concerns while making fiscal policy. Both administrations stressed the need for tax policies that would maintain the confidence of the business community.

In the first phase of its fiscal policy, the Hoover administration, working with Congress, extended the scope of corporate liberalism to include fiscal activism. Judged by the standards of the day, Hoover was an activist in the manipulation of tax rates to stimulate investment and reduce unemployment. He began his innovative program soon after the stock market crash in 1929. He managed to cut taxes payable in 1930, called on state and local governments (and public utilities as well) to increase capital outlays, and during 1930 and the first half of 1931 pushed up the federal public works budget, financing projects such as the building of Boulder Dam (begun in 1928 and completed in 1936).

As a result of Hoover's policy and supportive congressional action, federal fiscal policy took a distinctly expansive turn between 1929 and 1931. Even if the economy had been operating at full employment in 1931, and thus had retained a large base for income taxation, the budgetary surplus of $1 billion in 1929 would have become a large deficit—roughly $3 billion by 1931. (This figure is known as the "full-employment deficit," or the revenue deficit that would have been attained had the economy been operating at full employment.) Not until 1936 was the full-employment deficit as large, and not until World War II was the rate of change in the deficit as substantial in an expansionary direction.[22]

In October 1931, however, the Federal Reserve system produced a monetary contraction that severely limited the ability of the nation's banking system to meet domestic demands for currency and credit. Hoover feared that continued deficit spending would increase competition between government and private borrowers, raise long-term interest rates, and inhibit private investment. He also believed that wavering confidence in the dollar within foreign quarters stemmed in part from the persistent deficits of his administration. Reducing the deficits, he was convinced, would diminish the gold flow and thus relieve international pressure on the Federal Reserve Board to tighten the monetary screws. Consequently, in December 1931, he invoked a new phase of his fiscal policy—the phase that has tended to predominate in the public's memory. He asked Congress for tax increases that promised to raise revenues by one-third, and he and his new secretary of the treasury, Ogden Mills, suggested enacting a general sales tax.[23]

[22] The purpose of using the full-employment deficit as a measure of federal fiscal policy is to eliminate the effects on the federal deficit of variations in national income. These variations cause the tax base to rise or fall independently of variations in rates of taxation and obscure the intention of fiscal policy. Thus, even if the federal government did nothing in the face of a depression—that is to say, if the federal government did not change its tax and spending policies—the increase in the deficit that resulted from a declining tax base would suggest that the government had adopted a counter-cyclical fiscal policy. For the full-employment deficit (surplus) data, see E. Cary Brown, "Fiscal Policy in the Thirties: A Reappraisal," *American Economic Review* 46 (December 1956): 857–79.

[23] The best description of the development of Hoover's fiscal policy is Herbert Stein, *The Fiscal Revolution in America* (Chicago: University of Chicago

The severity of the Depression and the unpopularity of deficits led many congressional Democrats, including Speaker of the House John Nance Garner and all but one of the members of the Ways and Means Committee, to support a general sales tax. But a group of Democratic insurgents in the House, led by Robert L. Doughton of North Carolina (the only member of the Ways and Means Committee to oppose the sales tax), and Fiorello La Guardia of New York, challenged the House leadership. Doughton described the tax as a violation of "ability to pay" and as a measure that would undercut the plans of some state governments to enact general sales taxes. He and the insurgents worried that the general sales tax might replace the income tax as the centerpiece of the federal tax system, just as Garner's patron, the publisher William Randolph Hearst, intended. The insurgents won the support of most House Democrats and blocked the general sales tax. Doughton privately described the outcome as "the greatest victory ... achieved for the common people since the days of Woodrow Wilson."

In the end, the Revenue Act of 1932, enacted with bipartisan support, imposed the largest peacetime tax increases in the nation's history. It created some new federal sales taxes (e.g., on gasoline, electricity, refrigerators, and telephone messages) but increased revenues mainly by raising personal and corporate income-tax rates across the board and by reducing income-tax exemptions. The act raised the top marginal rate from 25 to 63 percent and thus nearly restored it to World War I levels. In addition, the act dramatically increased estate taxes by cutting the exemption in half

Press, 1969), 6–38. See also William J. Barber, *From New Era to New Deal: Herbert Hoover, the Economists, and American Economic Policy, 1921– 1933* (Cambridge: Cambridge University Press, 1985). Both scholars pay close attention to the role of ideas and actors inside the federal government in shaping tax policy.

(down to $50,000) and more than doubling the maximum rate (to 45 percent). In 1934, as a consequence of the 1932 act, some economic recovery in 1933–34, and loophole closing in the Revenue Act of 1934, the effective income tax rate on the rich rose to about 11 percent, which was higher than at any time during the years of Republican "normalcy."[24]

Taxation was not a central issue in the critical election of 1932, but the politics of the Revenue Act of 1932 may have advanced the career of Franklin D. Roosevelt. Speaker Garner's support of the general sales tax damaged his candidacy for the Democratic presidential nomination, and almost all the congressional insurgents backed Roosevelt's candidacy. Voters who were upset over the large tax increases may well have blamed them on Hoover and the Republicans.[25]

[24] On the effective rates, see Brownlee, "Historical Perspective on U.S. Tax Policy toward the Rich," 51. Among the congressional efforts at loophole closing in 1932 was a request that the Treasury establish systematic procedures for corporations to calculate their depreciation deductions. The Treasury responded by requiring straight-line depreciation for income-producing property. See William T. Hogan, *Depreciation Policies and Resultant Problems* (New York: Fordham University Press, 1967), 7–8. See also chapter 3, note 25, below. The 1934 act retained the preferential taxation of capital gains, but increased the tax rate and made it progressive. For example, the act taxed gains from assets held between two and five years at 60 percent of the personal tax rates, or at marginal rates that ranged between 3 and 36 percent, rather than the previous flat rate of 12.5 percent. See Blakey and Blakey, *Federal Income Tax*, 586–88. This approach to taxing capital gains remained in place through World War II, although the Revenue Act of 1938 cut the percentage of long-term capital gains subject to personal income taxation from 60 to 50. See Bureau of Internal Revenue, *Statistics of Income for 1946, Part I* (Washington, D.C.: U.S. Government Printing Office, 1946), 50–56, 420–23.

[25] For the quotations from Robert Doughton, and for an excellent description of the congressional consideration of the Revenue Act of 1932, see Walter K. Lambert, "New Deal Revenue Acts: The Politics of Taxation" (Ph.D. dissertation, University of Texas, Austin, 1970), 1–103. See also Jordan

In the first 100 days of his administration, Roosevelt moved beyond Hoover's corporate liberalism to apply the coercive power of government to the tasks of relief and economic recovery. It may have been a high-water mark for democratic statism, but not for the implementation of tax principles in the democratic-statist tradition. This was true despite the fact that, like Woodrow Wilson before him, Roosevelt was personally devoted to *both* balanced budgets and redistributional taxation. In the 1932 campaign, Roosevelt had pledged to balance the federal budget, which for three years Hoover's administration had been unable to do. In 1933, Roosevelt warned Congress that "too often in recent history liberal governments have been wrecked on the rocks of loose fiscal policy." He also personally opposed general sales taxes, which he regarded as "the last word in foolishness," and favored soak-the-rich taxation—shifting the tax burden to the wealthiest individuals and corporations according to their "ability to pay."[26] Moreover, he recognized the large constituency that the Depression had created for the sort of tax reform—redistributional and anticorporate—undertaken by the Wilson administration. Nonetheless, in contrast with the early phase of Wilson's financing of World War I, Roosevelt's early New Deal brought no progressive fiscal innovations.[27]

A. Schwarz, "John Nance Garner and the Sales Tax Rebellion of 1932," *Journal of Southern History* 30 (May 1964): 162–80.

[26] In 1932, after his election, Roosevelt outlined his views on sales taxation through a letter from Felix Frankfurter to Walter Lippmann. See Max Freedman, ed., *Roosevelt and Frankfurter: Their Correspondence, 1928–1945* (Boston: Little, Brown, 1967), 68. On Roosevelt's opposition to sales taxation in the transition of 1932–33, see Frank Freidel, *Franklin D. Roosevelt: Launching the New Deal* (Boston: Little, Brown, 1973), 53.

[27] A very different view of Roosevelt and his program can be found in the work of historian Mark Leff, who argues that Franklin D. Roosevelt looked only for symbolic victories in tax reform. See Mark H. Leff, *The Limits of Symbolic Reform: The New Deal and Taxation* (Cambridge: Cambridge University Press, 1984). Walter Lambert found no evidence that Roosevelt

For Roosevelt, the Depression posed massive problems that Wilson had not faced in the expansive years of 1916 and 1917. These problems were both political and economic. Because the Great Depression had shrunk the tax base, a serious effort at pay-as-you-go financing of expensive New Deal programs would have required massive increases in tax rates or the introduction of substantial new taxes. Both Roosevelt and Congress disliked having to pick the losers in the political game of increasing taxes. Both feared, in particular, that a democratic-statist tax policy would arouse business opposition to innovative New Deal programs and pave the way for a conservative counterattack on the New Deal if economic recovery failed. On this score, they had learned from Wilson's experience. Roosevelt, who had been the Democratic candidate for vice president in 1920, remembered all too well the success of the Republican backlash against Wilsonian taxation during the economic troubles of 1918–20. Also worrisome—though of less consequence to Roosevelt and Congress—were the possible economic effects of democratic-statist taxation. They acknowledged that if they raised income and corporate taxes sufficiently to balance the budget in the short run, they might run the risk of worsening the economic depression by undermining business confidence and investment.

Finally, Roosevelt faced an important institutional barrier to a democratic-statist tax policy. Twelve years of Republican leadership had built a Treasury staff that was unenthusiastic about undertaking the work of devising new progressive taxes. Roosevelt's long-term secretary of the treasury, Henry Morgenthau Jr., did not take office until January 1934, and his immediate deputies needed several years to rebuild a capability within the department for advancing

favored a radical distribution of tax burdens, but he did find a deep ethical commitment to the principle of "ability to pay." See Lambert, "New Deal Revenue Acts," passim. See also W. Elliot Brownlee, "Taxation as an X-Ray," *Reviews in American History* 14 (March 1986): 121–26.

democratic-statist reform. Meanwhile, Roosevelt instructed him to leave the proposal of new taxes to Congress and, in particular, to the Ways and Means Committee, now under Doughton's leadership.

During the New Deal's first two years, the combination of Roosevelt's hostility to sales taxation and progressive initiatives on the part of Congress produced modest increases in income taxes and loophole-closing reforms. The National Industrial Recovery Act imposed a 5 percent tax on dividends and a small excess-profits tax; it also tightened provisions for deducting business and capital losses. The Agricultural Adjustment Act added a tax on food processing. In addition, other acts restored the earned-income tax credit, slightly increased the progressiveness of income-tax rates, and raised capital-gains taxes.[28]

During these years, however, Congress and the Roosevelt administration relied less heavily on tax increases than on automatic revenue increases that resulted from the interaction of existing taxes (enhanced by the Hoover administration's Revenue Act of 1932) and from the economic recovery that began in 1933. The repeal of Prohibition was especially timely. Liquor taxes were still on the books and were far more popular among Democratic voters than general sales taxes or other excises. Between 1933 and 1936, revenues from alcohol taxes increased by almost $500 million. In 1936, special excise taxes, led by the increases in liquor taxes and levies on tobacco and gasoline consumption, produced about $1.5 billion, which was more than 40 percent of federal tax collections and larger than the $1.4 billion raised by income taxes in that year. (In 1936, only about 2 million American households—out of 32 million— owed any federal income tax; the personal income tax accounted for less than half of income-tax collections.) In addition, Roosevelt and Congress allowed federal deficits to grow—from $2.6 billion

[28] On the importance of the sales-tax issue during the first year of the New Deal, see Freidel, *Franklin D. Roosevelt*, 51–59, 446–51.

in 1933 to $4.4 billion in 1936, more than 40 percent of federal expenditures. During his first term, in every annual budget message, Roosevelt asserted that the deficits would disappear along with the Depression.[29]

In 1935, Roosevelt decided that political and economic conditions favored a resumption of a democratic-statist tax policy. Most important, the growing "Thunder on the Left," particularly Huey Long's "Share Our Wealth" movement, opened the way for vigorous redistributional taxation designed to remedy flaws in the nation's economic structure. Moreover, Roosevelt had gained confidence in the prospects for economic recovery and was less worried about a business backlash. And Morgenthau had finally established the required infrastructure of professional expertise within the Treasury.[30]

Morgenthau's staff contained a group of law professors, including General Counsel Herman Oliphant and Roswell Magill. Magill, a tax expert from Columbia University, directed a comprehensive survey of the federal tax system in preparation for a reform initiative. The monetary economist Jacob Viner also advised Morgenthau

---

[29] For an analysis of the trends of the various federal revenue sources during the Great Depression, see John M. Firestone, *Federal Receipts and Expenditures during Business Cycles, 1879–1958* (Princeton, N.J.: Princeton University Press, 1960), 36–54.

[30] The following account of the making of tax policy within the Roosevelt administration through World War II draws heavily on John Morton Blum, *From the Morgenthau Diaries: Years of Crisis, 1928–1938* (Boston: Houghton Mifflin, 1959), 297–337, 439–51; Blum, *From the Morgenthau Diaries: Years of Urgency, 1938–1941* (Boston: Houghton Mifflin, 1965), 22–30, 278–318; and Blum, *From the Morgenthau Diaries: Years of War, 1941–1945* (Boston: Houghton Mifflin, 1967), 33–78. Blum's still stands as the best general treatment of this subject. Also valuable is Randolph Paul, *Taxation in the United States* (Boston: Little, Brown, 1954), 168–406. See as well Lambert, "New Deal Revenue Acts," for excellent details on the relationship between the Roosevelt administration and Congress.

on tax issues, and Carl S. Shoup, Roy Blough, and Lawrence H. Seltzer—all economists who specialized in public finance—worked closely with Magill. Central to their work was an intensified effort to study the distributional effects of taxation at all levels of government.[31]

At the end of the summer of 1934, Magill and his Treasury colleagues had presented Morgenthau with recommendations designed to raise new revenues and attack concentrations of wealth; in December, Morgenthau had forwarded the proposals to the White House. In developing a tax proposal for Congress, Roosevelt drew assistance from his close adviser Felix Frankfurter, who since the outset of the New Deal had been urging the president to use the taxing power to attack bigness in business. Roosevelt and Frankfurter used the Treasury recommendations to craft an ambitious program of radical tax reform, which Roosevelt presented to Congress in June. Roosevelt told Harold Ickes, the secretary of the interior, that the speech was "the best thing he had done as President."[32]

---

[31] The most important study of tax incidence undertaken during the 1930s was the unpublished analysis of economist Louis Shere; see "The Burden of Taxation," unpublished memorandum, U.S. Department of the Treasury, Division of Research and Taxation, 1934. For an excellent survey of the modern measurement of tax burden in the United States, see B. K. Atrostic and James R. Nunns, "Measuring Tax Burden: A Historical Perspective," in *Fifty Years of Economic Measurement: The Jubilee of the Conference on Research in Income and Wealth*, National Bureau of Economic Research Studies in Income and Wealth, vol. 54, ed. Ernest R. Berndt and Jack E. Triplett (Chicago: University of Chicago Press, 1990), 343–408.

[32] On the significance of Frankfurter's interest in this tax legislation, see Ellis Hawley, *The New Deal and the Problem of Monopoly: Study in Economic Ambivalence* (Princeton, N.J.: Princeton University Press, 1966), 344–59. Hawley, however, concludes that the Revenue Acts of 1935 and 1936 were "relatively innocuous" (p. 359). Harold Ickes's discussion of the 1935 tax measure is in the June 19, 1935, entry in his diaries, in the Harold L. Ickes Papers, Library of Congress.

Roosevelt proposed a graduated tax on corporations to check the growth of monopolies, a tax on the dividends that holding companies received from corporations they controlled, surtaxes to raise the maximum income-tax rate on individuals from 63 to 79 percent, and an inheritance tax, to be imposed in addition to federal estate taxation. In his message to Congress, he explained that accumulations of wealth meant "great and undesirable concentration of control in relatively few individuals over the employment and welfare of many, many others." Moreover, "whether it be wealth achieved through the cooperation of the entire community or riches gained by speculation—in either case the ownership of such wealth or riches represents a great public interest and a great ability to pay." But Roosevelt's goal was not a simplistic redistribution of wealth and power. Later that year, he explained to a newspaper publisher that his purpose was "not to destroy wealth, but to create a broader range of opportunity, to restrain the growth of unwholesome and sterile accumulations and to lay the burdens of Government where they can best be carried." Thus, he justified his tax-reform program in terms of both its inherent equity and its ability to liberate the energies of individuals and small corporations, thereby advancing recovery. For Roosevelt, there was no trade-off between growth and progressiveness.[33]

During his 1935 initiatives, and throughout the peacetime New Deal, Roosevelt was able to count on the support of Robert Doughton, who served as chair of the House Ways and Means Committee from 1933 until 1947. (Counting a second term, from 1949 to 1953, he was the longest serving chair of the committee in its history.) Doughton's support was often decisive in Congress, where Senator Pat Harrison of Mississippi, chair of the Senate

---

[33] For the Roosevelt quotations, see Arthur M. Schlesinger Jr., *The Age of Roosevelt: The Politics of Upheaval* (Boston: Houghton Mifflin, 1960), 328; and Lambert, "New Deal Revenue Acts," 259–60.

Finance Committee, and other conservative Southern Democrats often opposed New Deal tax reform. Doughton at times had his doubts about the more sophisticated New Deal tax proposals, and he resisted large tax increases of any kind. He privately complained in 1935 that "we have had too many theories in key places under this administration." But he believed in the justice of shifting the distribution of taxes away from the "poor, weak, and humble," who—he was certain—paid a higher percentage of their incomes in taxes than did the wealthy. And ever since he had begun his service in Congress in 1911, he had put party loyalty and the need to establish a record of Democratic leadership first.[34]

Doughton and many of his Southern colleagues may have had reservations about big government, but for them taxing the rich became an effective expression of community values. Even one of the most conservative Southerners, John Rankin of Mississippi, supported taxing the rich. In 1932, he told a group of disabled World War I veterans that he was for "taxing profits of the last war in order to take care of the deficit, care for our disabled veterans, redistribute the wealth of the nation, and lift the burden of taxation from those least able to bear it." He then invoked the symbolism of Andrew Mellon. "I am told," Rankin declared, that he "has an income of $30 million a year. If I had my way we would put a wound stripe [the World War I equivalent of a purple heart] on his purse big enough to be seen from Pittsburgh to Philadelphia."[35]

---

[34] For suggestions as to the significance to the early New Deal of Doughton in particular and Southern members of Congress in general, see Tindall, *Emergence of the New South*, 607–13. Pat Harrison was less energetic and effective than Doughton, but he was able to kill Roosevelt's proposal for the taxation of inheritances in 1935. The Doughton quotations are from Lambert, "New Deal Revenue Acts," 297 and 226.

[35] For the quotation from John Rankin, see U.S. Congress, *Proceedings of 11th National Convention of Disabled American Veterans of the World War*, House Doc. 50, 72nd Congress, 1st Session, p. 16. On Rankin, see

Led by Doughton, Congress gave Roosevelt much of the tax reform he wanted. The Revenue Act of 1935, joined with economic recovery, pushed households into higher tax brackets and raised effective rates on the rich by nearly 50 percent. In 1936, the effective rate paid by the richest 1 percent of taxpayers increased to 16.4 percent, higher than during any year of World War I, and in fact the highest level it had ever reached. It remained roughly at that level until 1940, when economic recovery pushed enough taxpayers into higher marginal rates to increase the effective rate even further, to more than 20 percent. The Revenue Act of 1935 also pushed up the maximum rate of estate taxation to 70 percent. By 1938 this change, along with the 1932 amendments to the estate tax, returned the share of decedents paying federal estate taxes to the level (1.2 percent) that had been reached in 1925 and raised the average tax per estate (in constant dollars) to more than triple the level of 1925.[36]

Offsetting the progressiveness of Roosevelt's income-tax reforms, however, was the regressiveness of the payroll taxes that were enacted in 1935 as a central part of the Social Security system.[37] The

Frank Freidel, *FDR and the South* (Baton Rouge: Louisiana State University Press, 1965), 80–81. For a stimulating analysis of conservative support for various aspects of the New Deal, including taxation, see Theodore J. Lowi, *The End of the Republican Era* (Norman: University of Oklahoma Press, 1995), 130–35.

[36] On the effective rates, see Brownlee, "Historical Perspective on U.S. Tax Policy," 51. On the rates of estate taxation, see Shammas et al., *Inheritance in America*, 128.

[37] For histories of the adoption of Social Security told from the perspectives of experts within the Roosevelt administration, see Edwin E. Witte, *The Development of the Social Security Act: A Memorandum on the History of the Committee on Economic Security and Drafting and Legislative History of the Social Security Act* (Madison: University of Wisconsin Press, 1963); and Arthur J. Altmeyer, *The Formative Years of Social Security: A Chronicle of Social Security Legislation and Administration, 1934–1954*

incongruity might suggest that Roosevelt was little more than a cynical manipulator of the powerful symbolism of taxation. But Roosevelt conceived of Social Security as an insurance system. He thought of the taxes paid by middle-class people as premiums that established investments. Thus, in his mind, taxpayers received the benefits for which they had paid. Roosevelt's concept was shared by much of the American public, and it lent the payroll tax a popularity that gave it an edge in winning a narrow victory in 1935. Roosevelt's leadership—including his support of the social-insurance experts who favored funding through payroll taxes—was largely responsible for the victory of old-age insurance.[38]

In addition, Roosevelt realized that the insurance principle worked to protect the system from conservative counterattack. As he put it, "With those taxes in there, no damn politician can ever scrap my social security program." He succeeded, probably beyond his wildest expectations, in protecting Social Security. In addition, the benefit formula of even the initial Social Security program had a progressive dimension. In 1939, Roosevelt and Congress firmly established a progressive benefit formula and introduced pay-as-you-go financing.[39]

(Madison: University of Wisconsin Press, 1968). See also Theron F. Schlabach, *Edwin E. Witte: Cautious Reformer* (Madison: University of Wisconsin Press, 1969).

[38] For a history of the financing of Social Security that stresses the importance of Roosevelt's role in 1935, see Edward D. Berkowitz, "Social Security and the Financing of the American State," in *Funding the Modern American State, 1941–1995: The Rise and Fall of the Era of Easy Finance,* ed. Elliot Brownlee (Washington, D.C.: Woodrow Wilson Center Press, and Cambridge: Cambridge University Press, 1995), 149–94.

[39] One historian of the origins of Social Security describes the 1939 changes as designed to "speed up the creation of vested interests in the program, create coalitions of beneficiaries whose interests were coincidental with those of the bureaucracy, and eliminate the potential discipline of a funded system."

Roosevelt believed that the passage of the Revenue Act of 1935 meant that he would not have to request any further new taxes until after the presidential election of 1936. But in early 1936, the Supreme Court invalidated the processing tax of the Agricultural Adjustment Act, and Congress overrode Roosevelt's veto of a bonus bill for World War I veterans. Both events threatened a substantial increase in the federal deficit.

In response, Morgenthau again recommended an undistributed-profits tax, a revenue-raising measure that Roosevelt had previously ignored. Morgenthau's proposal was to eliminate the existing taxes on corporate income, capital stock, and excess profits and to replace them with a tax on retained earnings—the profits that corporations did not distribute to their stockholders. A firm's tax would be graduated according to the undistributed proportion of its profits. Magill's team of experts had discovered this idea when digging into the Treasury archives for inspiration. They had discovered Thomas S. Adams's 1919 proposal for an undistributed-profits tax, which he had favored as a replacement for excess-profits taxation.[40]

Morgenthau and his Treasury staff held the view that the measure would fight tax avoidance. Corporations, they were convinced, deliberately retained profits to avoid the taxation of dividends under the individual income tax. They noted that the Revenue Act of 1932 had restored the marginal rates of taxation on the wealthiest 1 percent of the nation's families to almost World War I levels. They believed that an undistributed-profits tax was necessary to make those rates effective.[41]

See Carolyn L. Weaver, *The Crisis in Social Security: Economic and Political Origins* (Durham, N.C.: Duke University Press, 1982), 112.

[40] For evidence of Adams's influence, see Louis Shere, assistant secretary of the Treasury, to Robert M. Haig, March 6, 1936; Robert Murray Haig Papers, Butler Library, Columbia University.

[41] Office of Tax Analysis, U.S. Department of the Treasury, "Tax Revision Studies, 1937," vol. 4, "Undistributed Profits Tax," National Archives.

Further, the Treasury staff believed that the measure would fight the concentration of corporate power. They were convinced that the largest corporations had the power to retain shares of surpluses greater than those retained by small companies. The surpluses, they were certain, gave large corporations an unfair competitive advantage by reducing the need to borrow new capital. Moreover, the Treasury claimed that the tax would promote recovery. Oliphant and Morgenthau believed that large corporations saved excessively or reinvested their surpluses unwisely. The undistributed-profits tax would provide a powerful incentive for such corporations to distribute their profits to their shareholders. Those shareholders, in turn, as Oliphant and Federal Reserve Board chair Marriner Eccles stressed, would spend some portion of their dividends and thus stimulate the economy.

Roosevelt endorsed the undistributed-profits tax in a message to Congress in March and received support, in principle, from the Ways and Means Committee. But the administration faced the hostility of the Senate Finance Committee and its staff, which feared revenue loss and preferred retaining the existing corporate income taxes while adding a small flat tax on undistributed earnings. In June 1936, Congress passed a graduated tax on undistributed profits, despite heavy business lobbying against Roosevelt's proposal and intense wrangling over widely divergent revenue estimates. Morgenthau intervened in the negotiations between the House and the Senate and had much to do with the outcome. Because of Senate objections, the graduation was less severe than the Treasury had wanted, but Congress retained the basic corporate income tax. The new tax had five steps on undistributed earnings, rising from 7 to 27 percent.

The new corporate tax posed the greatest threat to the autonomy of corporate finance since the passage of the excess-profits tax during World War I. In July, Secretary of the Interior Ickes talked with industrialist Harry F. Guggenheim and concluded, "The fundamental policy issue today is taxation." The increases in the higher brackets, "taxing surpluses in corporation treasuries, and fear of further increases," Ickes wrote, had made "a bitter enemy out of practically everyone" among the "very rich."[42]

The threat to the rich from new legislation was all the more acute because Morgenthau and Roosevelt vigorously prosecuted tax evaders and tried to close loopholes used by tax avoiders. They launched their most spectacular crusade in 1934, when the Treasury prosecuted its former secretary, Andrew Mellon, for tax evasion, claiming that he owed more than $3 million in back taxes and penalties. They chose Mellon as their special target because he seemed to represent the power of financial capitalism, its ability to shape national policy in its interest, the transmogrification of the tax system into an agency of special privilege, and the abuses of Republican government during the 1920s. Morgenthau told the government prosecutor, "I consider that Mr. Mellon is not on trial but Democracy and the privileged rich and I want to see who will win."[43]

Mellon won in court; a grand jury refused to indict him, and in 1937 the Board of Tax Appeals (BTA) found him innocent of tax evasion. But he lost the public relations battle. The BTA also said he had made errors that happened to be in his favor and added that he owed $400,000 in back taxes. And the BTA went even further, using the Mellon case to publicize the loopholes in the tax code. The BIR commissioner pointed out that as secretary of the treasury, Mellon had solicited from the BIR "a memorandum setting forth the various ways by which an individual may legally avoid tax."[44] It turned out that Mellon had used five of the ten methods detailed in the memorandum, as well as several others he had devised on his own.

---

[42] See the July 27, 1936, entry in the Harold Ickes Diaries, Ickes Papers.
[43] Blum, *Morgenthau Diaries: Years of Crisis*, 324–25.
[44] Blum, *Morgenthau Diaries: Years of Crisis*, 325.

In the spring of 1937, the outcome of the Mellon case, coupled with a $600 million shortfall in tax revenues—a deficit that
Treasury analysts blamed on tax avoidance—led Morgenthau and
Roosevelt to seek remedial legislation. At the same time that the
Treasury systematically investigated tax avoidance, Roosevelt won
the support of the chairs of the tax-writing committees for creating
the Joint Committee on Tax Evasion and Avoidance (JCTEA), with
power to acquire the names of tax avoiders from the Treasury. With
staff assistance from Thurman Arnold, whom the Treasury had borrowed from the Department of Justice, Treasury witnesses invento-
ried loopholes and identified sixty-seven "large, wealthy taxpayers"
who had used the device of incorporation to reduce their taxes. The
press zeroed in on Alfred P. Sloan, the president of General Motors,
who had incorporated his yacht. Sloan explained, "While no one
should desire to avoid payment of his share [of taxes,] neither should
anyone be expected to pay more than is lawfully required."[45]

Until the JCTEA's investigation, the public had only rarely had
access to information about individual income tax returns. Virtually
the only period had been between 1923 and 1926, when congressional progressives such as George Norris and Robert La Follette
had succeeded in making public information the taxes paid by the
nation's wealthiest taxpayers. In 1937, before the JCTEA's creation,
Roosevelt wanted to make public the identities of very wealthy individuals who avoided taxes through loopholes. Morgenthau tried to
convince him that this might be illegal, but he nonetheless provided
his boss with names and data. When he settled on the idea of establishing the JCTEA, Roosevelt finally gave up the idea of using his
office to publicize data from the tax returns of the rich. Nonetheless, he passed on some information to administration figures Jim
Farley and Homer Cummings, perhaps hoping that they would leak
them to the press.[46]

[45] Blum, *Morgenthau Diaries: Years of Crisis*, 335.
[46] For this episode, see Blum, *Morgenthau Diaries: Years of Crisis*, 327–37.

The disclosures by the joint committee persuaded Congress to pass, unanimously, the Revenue Act of 1937. The measure increased taxation of personal holding companies, limited deductions for corporate yachts and country estates, restricted deductions for losses from sales or exchanges of property, reduced incentives for the creation of multiple trusts, and eliminated favors for nonresident taxpayers. These increases, coupled with those undertaken the year before, raised tax rates high enough to create a full-employment surplus—the revenue surplus that would have been attained had the economy been operating at full employment. (This was the only year in which New Deal fiscal policy created a full-employment surplus rather than a deficit.)

The economic recovery, which had cut the rate of unemployment in half by 1937, encouraged Roosevelt to plan an even more intense reform program in 1938. He intended to increase the undistributed-profits tax, establish a graduated tax on capital gains, and tax the income from federal, state, and local bonds.

These ambitious plans, more than any other dimension of the New Deal, aroused fear and hostility among large corporations. They correctly viewed Roosevelt's tax program as a threat to their control over capital and their latitude for financial planning. The tax program, along with other New Deal measures, may well have contributed significantly to the exceptionally low level of private investment during the 1930s and even, by depressing business expectations, to the severity of the Recession of 1937–38. Such antimonopolist New Dealers as Ickes went so far as to charge that capitalists had conspired and gone "on strike" in response to New Deal taxes.[47]

---

[47] On the causes of the Recession of 1937–38, see Kenneth D. Roose, *The Economics of Recession and Revival: An Interpretation of 1937–38* (New Haven, Conn.: Yale University Press, 1954), especially 10–12 and 209–16, where Roose discusses the effects of the undistributed profits tax.

There is no evidence of such a conspiracy, but business leaders did enter the political arena and search for support outside the business community. In 1938, they found Roosevelt vulnerable, weakened by two major errors: reinforcing the recession of 1937–38 and opening in 1937 the disastrous fight to restructure the Supreme Court. Some Northeastern Democrats, led by Bernard Baruch and Joseph P. Kennedy, broke with the president and argued that tax cuts were necessary to restore business confidence. They agreed with Senator Pat Harrison, who declared in December 1937 that Roosevelt's tax program had "retarded progress and contributed to the unemployment situation."[48]

In 1938, a coalition of Republicans and conservative Democrats, working through the tax-writing committees, took advantage of Roosevelt's mistakes to try to block any more New Deal tax reform. Roosevelt fought back, denouncing at a Jackson Day dinner the businessmen "who will fight to the last ditch to retain such autocratic control over the industry and finances of the country as they now possess." But conservative Democrats had gathered enough strength to push through Congress, over the opposition of Ways and Means Committee chair Robert Doughton, a measure that gutted the tax on undistributed profits and discarded the graduated corporate income tax. Roosevelt, respecting the strength of the opposition, decided not to veto the bill. Instead, he allowed the Revenue Act of 1938 to become law without his signature and denounced it as the "abandonment of an important principle of American taxation"—taxation according to ability to pay. In 1939, Congress wiped out the undistributed-profits tax and formally eradicated the brief episode of radical tax reform.

Schumpeter also stressed the role of that tax; see Schumpeter, *Business Cycles* (New York: McGraw-Hill, 1939), 1038–40. On the conspiracy charges, see Leff, *Limits of Symbolic Reform*, 212–13.
[48] For the Harrison quotation, see Lambert, "New Deal Revenue Acts," 422.

Roosevelt's defeats in 1938 and 1939 also signaled a reassertion of congressional power over the shape of revenue legislation. From then on until the end of World War II, the congressional tax-writing committees carefully maintained their control over the initiation of tax policy. The influence of Morgenthau and his Treasury advisers had waned; they were able to influence Congress decisively only when Roosevelt was able to mobilize public opinion.

The New Deal program of tax reform ended in the late 1930s, but Roosevelt and Congress had already ushered in a new tax regime, composed of a strengthened soak-the-rich component, an expanded taxation of consumption, and the new Social Security taxes. The Roosevelt administration did not redistribute income through taxation to any great extent, but overall the tax system had become somewhat more progressive. And Roosevelt's income-tax reform program had conditioned Americans to expect that significant tax increases would be accomplished by raising taxes on the wealthy and on corporations. Whatever its redistributional limitations, the new system dramatically enhanced the federal government's revenue capacity. Despite the fact that in fiscal 1941, economic recovery had not yet restored full employment, federal tax collections—led by Social Security taxes, consumption taxes, and corporate income taxes—had more than doubled; collections had increased from $2.9 billion in 1929 to $7.4 billion in 1941.

The expansion of this federal tax capacity found a welcome audience in state and local governments, just as it had during the post–Civil War era and the 1920s. The early 1930s had been especially traumatic for state and local leaders, and they generally applauded the reduced pressure on their tax systems. Local governments had faced sharply increased relief obligations but suffered declining property-tax revenues, soaring rates of default, and even popular revolts, including a tax strike in Chicago. States had provided growing subventions for local governments by increasing sales taxes and reducing spending on highways and schools.

State constitutions, however, limited deficit finance, and new state and municipal bonds were extremely difficult to market. As the Depression worsened in 1931 and 1932, state and local governments found it impossible to conduct business as usual and still balance their budgets. They adopted more drastic economies, scaled back total expenditures in 1931, and sharply contracted spending in 1933 and 1934. State and local governments had pushed up tax rates every year between 1929 and 1933, and they maintained those high levels until 1936, when they raised them even further.

State governments also increased the scope and rates of their sales taxes until, in 1940, they were raising most of their funds through such levies. By 1940, consumer taxes—on gasoline, tobacco, liquor, soft drinks, and oleomargarine—produced $1.1 billion, and the new general retail-sales taxes, which thirty-three states adopted between 1932 and 1937, produced $500 million. Meanwhile, local governments increased their effective rates of property taxation.

In its latter stages, the New Deal did much to strengthen state and local revenue systems through a massive, complex system of intergovernmental transfers—which accounted for more than 10 percent of state and local revenues by the end of the New Deal—and through the promotion of taxpaying. A key example of such promotion was the work of the Home Owners' Loan Corporation, which required borrowers to pay off back taxes as a condition for receiving subsidized mortgage loans.[49]

---

[49] Economist John J. Wallis argues that New Deal programs "explain" the relative decline of local governments and the sustained growth of state governments during the 1930s. See Wallis, "The Birth of Old Federalism: Financing the New Deal, 1932–1940," *Journal of Economic History* 44 (March 1984): 139–59. David Beito argues that tactics such as those of the Home Owners' Loan Corporation were part of a larger strategy to undermine traditional, virtuous resistance to taxpaying. See Beito, *Tax Payers in Revolt: Tax Resistance during the Great Depression* (Chapel Hill: University of North Carolina Press, 1989).

The demise of New Deal tax reform was part of a larger col-lapse of any political effort to develop a comprehensive, democratic-statist program. The New Deal had thrust the federal government into new zones, but the American public had not embraced a coher-ent theory that would justify the greatly expanded state. Instead, the various groups that the New Deal had served tended, on the one hand, to embrace the capitalist order and, on the other, to appreci-ate the particular benefits they had received. These groups wanted the rewards of capitalism but expected the federal government to protect them from substantial risks in the marketplace and, when social discord became too severe, to broker agreements with ri-val entities. For example, these agreements might involve favored treatment in the tax code for particular groups through special ex-emptions or deductions. But such agreements did not encompass far-reaching tax reform—which could have produced broad shifts in the distribution of taxation.

The Roosevelt administration's innovation of the broker state was associated with an assumption of a greater responsibility to promote economic recovery through such fiscal mechanisms as cut-ting taxes, increasing expenditures, and expanding deficits. But this assumption of responsibility was slow, erratic, and still highly in-complete when the United States entered World War II.[50]

It is true that, judging by *actual* deficits, the Roosevelt adminis-tration's fiscal policy might be interpreted as one of consistent, more and more vigorous promotion of economic recovery through deficit spending. However, the deficits were often unintentional results of a depressed tax base and were always unwelcome to Roosevelt. In fact, only about half of his administration's deficits resulted from de-liberate policy decisions. Roosevelt and Morgenthau never intended

[50] The following account of the development of Roosevelt's fiscal policy draws from the sources cited previously and from Stein, *Fiscal Revolution in America*, 39–196, which remains the best general treatment of the subject.

the deficits to be a permanent feature of the nation's system of public finance.[51]

During Roosevelt's first term, in 1933 and 1935, he and Congress adopted an expansionary fiscal policy. But the stimulus was only modest. Because of his and Morgenthau's persistent efforts to balance the budget, his first-term fiscal policy was no more expansive than Hoover's between 1929 and 1931. In fact, his policy was more conservative than Hoover's. In contrast to Hoover, Roosevelt had succeeded in liberating monetary policy from Federal Reserve control and in creating an expansive money supply. Consequently, he did not face Hoover's problem: that increased deficits were likely to drive up interest rates to the point of discouraging borrowing.

Roosevelt certainly had not chosen to seek salvation in the prescriptions of John Maynard Keynes, who in *The Means to Prosperity* had urged Depression governments to stimulate private investment through the vigorous use of deficits. Recalling a visit with Roosevelt in 1934, Keynes remarked that he had "supposed the president was more literate, economically speaking." Roosevelt remembered that Keynes "left a whole rigmarole of figures." Roosevelt added, "He must be a mathematician rather than a political economist."

In 1938, after both tax reform and economic recovery had faltered, Roosevelt did adopt a more reformist fiscal policy—moving it toward a Keynesian position. Near the end of the recession of 1937–38, Roosevelt launched an energetic new spending program that was unaccompanied by significant tax increases. Consequently,

---

[51] The stimulus of the deficits pales even further in the light of state and local fiscal policy. State and local governments enacted such large tax increases between 1933 and 1939 that they would have had huge budget surpluses if the economy had been at full employment. The state and local full-employment surpluses were large enough to offset the expansive effects of federal deficits in all but two of those seven years.

the full-employment surplus became a full-employment deficit, and it surged upward in 1938 and 1939.

The influence of Keynesian ideas on Roosevelt's fiscal policy, however, was still only indirect; Roosevelt had not become a convert. He had shifted policy largely because he had decided to abandon tax reform. He recognized that conservative opposition to the New Deal had grown too strong for him to seek significant tax increases or to pursue economic recovery through his preferred means, redistributional tax reform. Moreover, Roosevelt could not ignore the strong indications that restrictive fiscal policy had contributed to the sharp downturn in 1937–38. Consequently, he listened more closely to a group of government officials— scattered across the Works Progress Administration, Department of Agriculture, and Federal Reserve—who had become more partial to deficits and had begun to discover, in the work of Keynes, a rationale for their political position.

There is no evidence that the members of this group—Harry Hopkins, Henry Wallace, and Marriner Eccles—ever convinced Roosevelt to share their view that permanent deficits would be necessary to achieve and maintain full employment. However, Roosevelt did adopt a Keynesian argument to justify his shift in tax policy. In 1938, he explained to Congress that his large increases in expenditures, unaccompanied by tax increases, would add "to the purchasing power of the Nation."

During the years of economic recovery immediately before Pearl Harbor, economists within the federal government intensified the advancement of Keynesian ideas. Some, like Alvin Hansen, were senior economists who learned Keynes's concepts late in their careers but used his ideas to order their long-standing beliefs that economic stagnation was inevitable without permanent deficits or drastic income redistribution. Others were weaned on *The General Theory of Employment, Interest, and Money*, which appeared in 1936. These economists staffed agencies such as the Division of Industrial

Economics within the Department of Commerce, the Bureau of the Budget (including the Office of Statistical Standards, created in 1939), and the National Resources Planning Board. Within the Treasury, the economist Harry Dexter White and Lawrence H. Seltzer, chief economist in the Research Division, began to promote and apply Keynesian ideas.

All these economists, and their colleagues outside government, had a significant effect on expert advisers throughout the Roosevelt administration. These experts included many of the lawyers who advised Morgenthau within the Treasury. As early as 1937, Magill argued for budget balancing over a number of years: "The effects of borrowing will be stimulating to the national economy," he explained. Oliphant was even more explicitly Keynesian. And the New York tax lawyer Randolph Paul, who took over the Tax Division in late 1941 and became general counsel in mid-1942, was the most vigorous in pressing Keynesian ideas upon Morgenthau.

Keynesian ideas, however, had achieved only limited success by the time the United States entered World War II. Within the Treasury, Morgenthau never abandoned his desire to balance budgets on an annual basis, although he encouraged argument over this point among his expert advisers. Within the administration at large, Keynesian advocates had succeeded in establishing a consensus on only two vague propositions. The first was that the federal government should avoid adopting restrictive fiscal policies (e.g., the Hoover administration's tax increase of 1932 and Roosevelt's expenditure cuts of 1937) during a recession or depression. The second was that the federal government should expand spending programs during an economic reversal. But the Roosevelt administration had not translated these ideas into a clearly defined strategy of spending and deficits; nor had it created a federal agency to specify reliable techniques and magnitudes.

The Roosevelt administration had, however, taken important steps toward the centralization of budgetary authority. In 1939, the

Reorganization Act created the Executive Office of the President, transferring to it the Bureau of the Budget (from Treasury) and the National Resources Planning Board (from Interior) and establishing within it the Office of Emergency Management. For public consumption, Congress emphasized the act's goal of reducing expenditures through coordination and elimination of overlapping agencies, but its primary purpose was to enhance presidential control over a greatly expanded executive branch. Thus, at the same time that the Roosevelt administration edged toward the embrace of deficit spending as a positive good, it moved toward a more self-conscious use of the federal budget as an instrument of national policy.

By the end of the 1930s, democratic statism had played out as the determining force in the development of federal taxation. But the tax regime instituted by Franklin Roosevelt's New Deal was still very much in place, although it had become less ambitious in its redistributional scope than between 1935 and 1938. To President Roosevelt and some of his advisers, it seemed that another world war—an intervention managed once again by a Democratic administration—would be the occasion for renewed victories for democratic statism.

3

The era of easy finance, 1941–1980

World War II, like the great national emergencies before it, created opportunities for public finance reforms that had clear social intent and organizational coherence. As had been the case during World War I and the Great Depression, decisive presidential leadership contributed significantly to the creation of a new tax regime. The administration of President Franklin D. Roosevelt—motivated by a concern for social justice as well as by the threat to the nation's security—shaped the enactment of a wartime tax regime and then exercised initiative in using the media to persuade Americans to accept it.

After the war, this new tax regime proved even more resilient than the World War I regime had been during the 1920s. At the core of the new regime was a broad-based income tax. Because of this broad base, economic growth and long-term inflation enabled the federal government to garner increasing revenues from the new regime. Until the late 1970s, the new regime funded the expansion of both domestic and foreign programs while enabling the federal government to reduce corporate and excise taxes and to avoid the politically damaging process of increasing tax rates.

107

THE FORMATION OF THE TAX REGIME

As Americans prepared to enter World War II, President Roosevelt and the congressional leadership assumed that mobilization would be on a much greater scale than during World War I and that the inflationary pressures would be even more severe. As a consequence, the nation's leaders quickly reached a bipartisan consensus favoring large tax increases. These increases would finance a major portion of the war and, at the same time, control inflation by discouraging consumers from bidding up prices in competition with the government. Therefore, the leaders of both political parties assumed that wartime tax increases would be even larger than during World War I. Despite the consensus, the political process of adopting this new fiscal policy was neither smooth nor direct. The specific taxes and the level of taxation employed turned out to be matters of severe contention.

The war presented Roosevelt with another opportunity to resuscitate democratic-statist tax reform. Like Woodrow Wilson and William McAdoo in 1916–17, Roosevelt and Secretary of the Treasury Henry Morgenthau Jr. set out to finance a large fraction of the costs of war with taxation and to use taxes that bore heavily on corporations and upper-income groups.

The president began to prepare for financing mobilization as early as 1939, and he focused more on the issue of tax structure than on the level of taxation. He talked widely about the need for excess-profits taxation; in the summer of 1940, he proposed such a tax, to be steeply graduated, on both individuals and corporations. Roosevelt, the Treasury, the Ways and Means Committee of the House of Representatives, and Senate liberals such as Robert M. La Follette Jr. all favored a World War I–style tax on profits above a minimum rate of return. Senator Pat Harrison (Mississippi) and other conservative Democrats, however, opposed this and had the power to prevail. In the Second Revenue Act of 1940, passed in October, they established a graduated tax on excess profits, reaching a maximum of 50 percent, but provided a generous credit based on prewar profits. Secretary of the Interior Harold Ickes complained that this was "abandoning advanced New Deal ground with a vengeance," but Roosevelt decided not to challenge the power of Congress by accusing it of having sold out to big business.[1]

In 1941, following the passage of the Lend-Lease Act, the Roosevelt administration faced growing inflationary pressures. In response to those pressures, as well as to the need for new revenues, Roosevelt and Morgenthau now supported lowering the exemptions from personal income and thus restraining consumption. But they did not abandon reform. Morgenthau proposed taxing away all corporate profits above a 6 percent rate of return, as well as increasing surtaxes on personal income, increasing the base for gift and estate taxes, and increasing excise taxes on beer, tobacco, and gasoline. Roosevelt made it clear he favored a massive elimination of personal income-tax deductions by switching to the taxation of gross income. But in the Revenue Act of 1941, Congress once again rejected most of the reform measures. The act's major provisions consisted of lower exemptions and higher tax rates on upper-middle-class families.

After Pearl Harbor, Morgenthau and Roosevelt resumed their bid for public support of tax reform. "In this time of grave national danger, when all excess income should go to win the war," Roosevelt told a joint session of Congress in 1942, "no American citizen ought to have a net income, after he has paid his taxes, of more than $25,000."[2] But opposition to radical war-tax proposals grew even stronger in the face of the revenue requirements of full mobilization.

---

[1] In June, Roosevelt had favored a graduated tax on all profits in excess of 4 percent; June 9 and August 10, 1940, entries in Harold Ickes Diaries, Ickes Papers.

[2] *Congressional Record*, 78th Congress, 1st Session, vol. 89 (Washington, D.C.: U.S. Government Printing Office, 1942), 4448.

One source of opposition came from a diverse group of military planners, foreign policy strategists, financial leaders, and economists. Throughout the turbulence of the 1920s and 1930s, these experts had marshaled the economic lessons of World War I and its aftermath. Now, this collection of experts wanted to mobilize even greater resources, to do so more smoothly and predictably, and to reduce inflationary pressures. They promoted a policy of mass-based taxation. They favored a general sales tax or an income tax that produced most of its revenue from wages and salaries—one that would build on the successful performance of Social Security taxation. One of the leading experts was Russell C. Leffingwell, who had been assistant secretary of the treasury during World War I and a partner in J. P. Morgan and Company since the early 1920s. He urged Morgenthau to avoid steep excess-profits taxation and to instead adopt "taxes widely spread on all the people." An income tax that not only was broad based but also taxed people "to the very limit of endurance" was the core of successful war finance, he wrote to Morgenthau.[3]

The second source of opposition to Roosevelt's and Morgenthau's radical wartime tax proposals came, in sharp contrast to Wilson's situation during World War I, from Democrats in both Congress and the administration itself. Many Democratic members of Congress, especially the leadership of the Senate Finance Committee, shared the verdict of *Time* magazine, which warned that the kind of plan that Morgenthau proposed would put corporations in a "weakened financial position to meet the slump and unemployment that [would] come with peace." This same fear of postwar depression led Federal Reserve chair Marriner Eccles, Budget Director Harold Smith, Office of Price Administration Director

---

[3] Leffingwell to Morgenthau, October 2, 1941, and June 11, 1942, Russell C. Leffingwell Papers, Yale University Library. This was part of an extensive wartime correspondence between Leffingwell and Morgenthau.

Leon Henderson, and Vice President Henry Wallace to support the sales-taxation approach to war finance. Morgenthau complained that his opponents had forgotten about the "people in the lower one-third." He noted, "I can get all my New Dealers in the bathtub now."[4]

In the summer of 1942, Morgenthau, on the recommendation of Randolph Paul and Roy Blough, tried to bridge the gap between the administration and Congress by proposing the adoption of a sharply graduated tax on spending that would be designed to raise large revenues and restrain consumption while increasing progressiveness. Adoption of such a spendings tax would have been by far the most radical departure in U.S. tax policy since 1916. The congressional tax-writing committees regarded this proposal as too radical economically and too threatening to the influence they enjoyed as gatekeepers for the complex exemptions and deductions in the income tax. Roosevelt recognized the power of the committees, and regarded the spendings tax as a bargaining tool for defeating a general sales tax and for making the income tax more progressive. The president decided not to support Morgenthau, explaining that "I always have to have a couple of whipping boys."[5]

In October, Congress finally agreed to a few progressive concessions and settled on the income tax as the centerpiece of wartime finance. One of the concessions was increasing the rate of excess-profits taxation to 90 percent, but Congress rejected the World War I method of determining excess profits, made the tax explicitly a temporary measure, and taxed only incorporated businesses. The committees also protected major loopholes favoring the wealthy and provided less than half the revenues that Roosevelt had requested.

[4] John Morton Blum, *From the Morgenthau Diaries: Years of War, 1941–1945* (Boston: Houghton Mifflin, 1967), 35.
[5] Blum, *Morgenthau Diaries: Years of War*, 48.

The Revenue Act of 1942 represented agreement between Congress and Roosevelt on what became the core of a new tax regime—a personal income tax that was both broadly based and progressive. The act made major reductions in personal exemptions, establishing the means for the federal government to acquire huge revenues from the taxation of middle-class wages and salaries. At the same time, the imposition of a surtax that was graduated from 13 percent on the first $2,000 to 82 percent on taxable income over $200,000 raised the marginal rates of taxation on personal income taxes higher than at any other time in the history of the income tax in the United States.

The highly progressive income tax, coupled with the defeat, once again, of general sales taxation, was the major payoff from Roosevelt's earlier tax-reform campaigns, which had established widespread public expectations that any significant new taxes would be progressive. At the same time, Roosevelt and many New Deal legislators hoped to be able to distribute much of the new revenue in progressive fashion. They believed that a mass-based income tax would be the best way to ensure a permanent flow of revenue to federal programs of social justice.

Roosevelt continued his reform fight to make the income tax even more progressive, to tax corporations more heavily, and to shift revenue raising from borrowing to taxation, but he suffered two major defeats in 1943. The first was over withholding.

In 1943, to accelerate the flow of tax revenues into the Treasury and thus restrain inflation, the Treasury proposed adopting a system for withholding taxes through monthly payroll deductions or quarterly payments. The federal government had already employed such a system of "collection at the source" during the Civil War (and again between 1913 and 1916) in an effort to replicate the administrative accomplishments of the British income tax. As early as 1911, the State of Wisconsin had employed a comprehensive system of acquiring "information at the source" from corporations to assess individual income taxes owed by salaried managers and skilled workers. More recently, the federal government had achieved great success with a "collection-at-the-source" administrative system for Social Security taxes. Edwin E. Witte, who served as executive director of Roosevelt's Committee on Economic Security, which drafted the Social Security Act of 1935, had become intimately familiar with the Wisconsin system during his years as chief of Wisconsin's Legislative Reference Library. He may well have drawn from that experience in championing payroll taxation. By mid-1940, the Bureau of Old-Age Benefits had processed, without the benefit of electronic computers, more than 312 million individual wage reports forwarded by the Bureau of Internal Revenue (BIR) and had posted more than 99 percent of them to more than 50 million individual employee accounts.[6]

The proposed collection system would keep taxpayers current rather than allow them to pay the year after the taxes were incurred. Also, it would expedite taxpaying by citizens, such as most industrial workers, who had no experience in filing income-tax returns. Further, withholding promised to make it possible, for the first time, to vary income-tax rates and collections in an effective countercyclical fashion. The Keynesians within the Treasury had supported withholding at the source for that reason. Adoption of the plan meant, however, that during 1943 taxpayers would pay both their 1942 and their 1943 obligations.

---

[6] Arthur J. Altmeyer, *The Formative Years of Social Security* (Madison: University of Wisconsin Press, 1963), 86–87. In 1916, the Wilson administration abandoned "collection at the source" in favor of Wisconsin's "information at the source." The Wilson administration was responding to pressure from large corporations, which received no compensation for their administrative costs, and was concerned that corporations were undercollecting individual income taxes. See W. Elliot Brownlee, "Wilson and Financing the Modern State: The Revenue Act of 1916," *Proceedings of the American Philosophical Society* 129 (1985): 196–67.

One of the first to oppose the double payment was Beardsley Ruml, chair of the New York Federal Reserve Bank and treasurer of R. H. Macy and Company. He launched a radio and press campaign to challenge the Treasury. He favored withholding but proposed the forgiveness of 1942 taxes to ease the pinch in 1943. Ruml's plan gained public support, but Roosevelt defended the Treasury, telling the chair of the Ways and Means Committee, "I cannot acquiesce in the elimination of a whole year's tax burden on the upper income groups during a war period when I must call for an increase in taxes... from the mass of people."[7] After some modest concessions to Roosevelt, Congress adopted the Ruml plan in the Current Tax Payment Act of 1943.

The second defeat for Roosevelt's wartime tax program occurred in the Revenue Act of 1943. Led by the tax-writing committees, Congress rejected the Treasury's advice and passed legislation providing for only modest tax increases ($2.3 billion versus the $10.5 billion requested by the Treasury) while creating a host of new tax favors for business, especially the mining, timber, and steel industries. Roosevelt denounced the bill as "not a tax bill but a tax relief bill, providing relief not for the needy but for the greedy."[8] He vetoed the bill. But for the first time in history, Congress overrode a presidential veto of a revenue act. Alben Barkley, the Democratic majority leader in the Senate, described Roosevelt's veto message as a "calculated and deliberate assault upon the legislative integrity of every member of Congress."[9] Ickes hoped that Roosevelt would go "to the people with his case against the Congress" for enacting "a vicious bill designed to protect the rich at the expense of

[7] Blum, *Morgenthau Diaries: Years of War*, 63.
[8] *Congressional Record*. 78th Congress, 2nd Session, vol. 90 (Washington, D.C.: U.S. Government Printing Office, 1943), 1958–59.
[9] Blum, *Morgenthau Diaries: Years of War*, 76.

the poor."[10] But the humiliating defeat convinced Roosevelt that he had to accept the structure of income taxation without further complaint. His defeats in 1943 essentially ended the conflict, which had begun during World War I between business and progressive advocates, over "soak-the-rich" income taxation.

Under the new tax system, the number of individual taxpayers grew from 3.9 million in 1939 to 42.6 million in 1945, and federal income-tax collections during the period leaped from $2.2 billion to $35.1 billion. By the end of the war, nearly 90 percent of the members of the labor force submitted income-tax returns, and about 60 percent of the labor force paid income taxes. In 1944 and 1945, individual income taxes accounted for roughly 40 percent of federal revenues, whereas corporate income taxes provided about a third—only half their share during World War I. Mass taxation had become more important than class taxation.

Despite the focus on the development of mass-based income taxation and the congressional defeats of Roosevelt's efforts to make the new income-tax system more progressive, the wartime legislation did increase dramatically the rates of taxation of America's rich through the personal income tax. Wartime revenue acts increased the marginal rates of taxation to levels ranging from 50 to more than 90 percent throughout the war. The substantially higher marginal rates, coupled with wartime inflation, produced effective rates that, from 1942 through 1945, were more than 40 percent, or roughly twice the effective rate achieved in 1940. In 1944, the effective rate on the rich reached an all-time high of nearly 60 percent, or almost four times the highest level achieved during World War I.[11]

---

[10] February 26, 1944, entry, Harold Ickes Diaries, Ickes Papers.

[11] W. Elliot Brownlee, "Historical Perspective on U.S. Tax Policy toward the Rich," in *Does Atlas Shrug? The Economic Consequences of Taxing the Rich*, ed. Joel B. Slemrod (New York and Cambridge, Mass.: Russell Sage Foundation and Harvard University Press, 2000), 60.

The rates were high enough so that, even with the broad base of taxation, in 1945 the richest 1 percent of households produced 32 percent of the revenue yield of the personal income tax.[12]

At the same time, the federal government came to dominate the nation's revenue system. In 1940, the federal income tax had accounted for only 16 percent of the taxes collected by all levels of government; by 1950, it produced more than 51 percent of all collections. The installation of the new regime was the most dramatic shift in the nation's tax policies since 1916.

In making the new individual income tax work, the Roosevelt administration relied heavily on voluntarism by encouraging the self-reporting of income.[13] Roosevelt, Morgenthau, and the congressional leadership all were reluctant to impose a highly coercive system of assessment and collection. To be sure, payroll withholding was coercive, but it was popular in that it spread out payments over twelve months, reducing the pain of taxpaying, and it did not reach self-employed and many salaried workers.

The federal government won middle-class political support for, and compliance with, the new income tax in part because of the structure of the tax. General deductions (e.g., for interest on home mortgages and for payments of state and local taxes) sweetened the new tax system for the middle class. Moreover, middle-class taxpayers preferred the mass-based income tax to a national sales tax, which many corporate leaders favored and promoted. Furthermore, fear of a renewed depression made the middle-class public

---

[12] Bureau of Internal Revenue, U.S. Department of the Treasury, *Statistics of Income for 1945, Part I* (Washington, D.C.: U.S. Government Printing Office, 1951), 71.

[13] Scholars often call reliance on self-reporting an example of American exceptionalism in taxation. For international comparisons of income-tax administration, see Arnold J. Heidenheimer, Hugh Heclo, and Carolyn T. Adams, *Comparative Public Policy: The Politics of Social Choice in Europe and America* (New York: St. Martin's Press, 1975), 235–42.

more tolerant than it had been during World War I toward taxation that was favorable to corporations and corporate privilege. This leniency may have seemed naive to radical New Dealers, but it expressed a widely shared commitment to the pursuit of enlightened self-interest.

The new regime of mass taxation also succeeded because of the popularity of the war effort. It was less necessary to leverage popular support and sacrifice for the war by enacting a highly redistributional tax system. More so than in World War I, Americans concluded that their nation's security was at stake and that victory required both personal sacrifice through taxation and indulgence of the corporate profits that helped fuel the war machine.

But the Roosevelt administration believed that the new withholding system and the fundamental popularity of the new income tax were not enough to make mass-based taxation effective. The administration concluded that it had to go beyond shaping the tax code in ways that compelled or encouraged compliance. It had to persuade the public that the tax was fair, convenient, and for a necessary purpose. Roosevelt and Morgenthau invoked the extensive propaganda machinery at their command in a campaign to convince the millions of new taxpayers to pay tax obligations. The Treasury, its BIR, and the Office of War Information launched a massive propaganda effort, invoking the same calls for civic responsibility and patriotic sacrifice that the Wilson administration had crafted so effectively during the bond campaigns of World War I.

The Roosevelt administration made full use of the instruments of mass communication in promoting conscientious taxpaying. The Treasury commissioned Irving Berlin to write a song for the effort entitled "I Paid My Income Tax Today." The Treasury sent recordings of the song to radio stations and asked Danny Kaye to perform it in New York night clubs. The Treasury also commissioned a Walt Disney animated short, "The New Spirit," starring Donald Duck. Having been informed by the radio that it is "your privilege, not just your duty . . . to help your government by paying your tax and paying it promptly," Donald gathers the supplies (including a bottle of aspirin) necessary to fill in his return. He finds the job easier and, with the exemptions and credits for his three nephews, less painful than he anticipated. The message was that the average citizen would find the new income taxes easy to pay. The film ends with Donald traveling to Washington to pay his tax in person, and to see how tax revenues are transformed into the arsenal of democracy. In early 1942, more than 32 million people in 12,000 theaters watched "The New Spirit."[14]

In the campaigns on behalf of mass-based income taxation, the Roosevelt administration demonstrated the power of presidential leadership. The administration persuaded at the same time as it coerced. Thus, during World War II, as well as in World War I and even in the Civil War, a liberal-democratic state demonstrated the fiscal power of a trusting and wealthy public. That trust, nurtured

---

[14] On the income-tax advertising campaigns, see Carolyn C. Jones, "Class Tax to Mass Tax: The Rise of Propaganda in the Expansion of the Income Tax during World War II," *Buffalo Law Review* 37 (1989): 685–737; Jones, "Taxes to Beat the Axis: A Comparison of American and British Income Tax Publicity during World War II," paper prepared for presentation at the Tenth International Economic History Congress, Louvain, Belgium, June 12, 1990; and Jones, "Mass-Based Income Taxation: Creating a Taxpaying Culture, 1940–1952," in *Funding the Modern American State, 1941–1995: The Rise and Fall of the Era of Easy Finance*, ed. W. Elliot Brownlee (Washington, D.C.: Woodrow Wilson Center Press, and Cambridge: Cambridge University Press, 1996), 108–48. These campaigns ought to be set in the context of all of the propaganda efforts by the Roosevelt administration. Mark Leff has usefully suggested viewing such campaigns as part of the "politics of sacrifice." But as in his study of New Deal tax policy, Leff neglects the substantial, as opposed to a purely symbolic, interest of Roosevelt and Morgenthau in increasing the sacrifice of corporations and the wealthy; Leff, "The Politics of Sacrifice on the Home Front in World War II," *Journal of American History* 77 (March 1991): 1296–1318.

by the federal government, permitted and encouraged the adoption of income taxation, which is, along with property taxation, the most coercive and statist means of raising revenue. Perhaps only the liberal-democratic states can impose coercive taxation in a sustained fashion—and still survive in the long run. In any event, the U.S. government overcame any structural weaknesses during World War II, just as it had during the two earlier emergencies of the Civil War and World War I. In a fiscal sense, the adoption of mass-based income taxation during World War II—and the victory of a taxpaying culture—represented a triumph for both the republican virtue and the national strength the framers of the Constitution had sought to advance.

Because of the buoyant revenues produced under the new tax regime, during the last two years of World War II the federal government covered roughly half of its expenditures with tax revenues. In addition, the federal deficit, after increasing from $6.2 billion in 1941 to $57.4 billion in 1943, held steady at about the 1943 level for the remainder of the war. These were impressive feats, because the wartime expenditures represented a more massive shift of resources from peacetime endeavors than had been the case during World War I. The average level of wartime federal expenditures, which increased from 1942 through 1945, amounted to roughly half the national product—more than twice the average ratio during World War I. In addition, the shift of resources was faster and more prolonged. At the same time, the fact that the federal government had hitched taxation more firmly to expenditure needs and dramatically broadened the tax base helped restrain wartime price inflation.

SURVIVAL OF THE REGIME AFTER THE WAR

The winning of World War II and a postwar surge of economic prosperity, which followed so closely on the heels of the Great

Depression, all helped produce a popular, bipartisan consensus of support for sustaining the basic policy shifts undertaken during the Roosevelt administration. One expression of this consensus was the congressional passage of the Employment Act of 1946. This act was a formal commitment by the federal government to what was believed to have been Roosevelt's implicit fiscal policy; in fact, the act captured three important elements of the policy.

First, the act declared the federal government's central responsibility for managing the level of employment. Second, by creating the Council of Economic Advisers and charging it with the development of an annual published report (*The Economic Report of the President*), the act established that the president and the public should have economic advice that was expert and independent. And third, it formally embodied a central objective of the New Deal: to embrace human values as the context for setting and evaluating fiscal policy. The institutional framework was in place for the proactive manipulation of the federal budget on behalf of economic stability.

Like Roosevelt's real fiscal policy, however, the act provided policymakers with little guidance on the substance of fiscal policy. It failed to make a government guarantee of full employment, it restricted countercyclical actions to only those consistent with other economic objectives, and it avoided a specific definition of appropriate policy. Keynesian ideas had won a larger audience during World War II, but public finance experts sharply disagreed over the content of countercyclical policy. Some regarded the conjunction of great deficits and dramatic economic expansion as proof that deficits had not only produced the economic expansion of World War II, ending the Great Depression, but were also required for sustained prosperity in peacetime. Other experts, such as the leadership of the Committee for Economic Development (CED), which represented businesspeople interested in Keynesianism, had a more conservative view. In 1947, the CED issued a statement on fiscal policy, *Taxes and the Budget*, which accepted deficits during recessions but advocated budget surpluses during times of high employment and stable rates of taxation.[15]

In the realm of tax policy, the World War II emergency institutionalized a new tax regime. It had three elements: (1) a progressive but mass-based personal income tax for general revenues; (2) a flat-rate tax on corporate income, also for general revenues; and (3) a regressive payroll tax for social insurance. Although some important differences remained between the two major political parties, both insisted on maintaining the central characteristics of the World War II revenue system and eschewing both progressive assaults on corporate financial structures and the regressive taxation of consumption. For the first time since the early nineteenth century, the two political parties agreed on the essential elements of the nation's fiscal policy.

The general decline of partisanship after World War II no doubt contributed to the convergence of the two parties on fiscal policy. The convergence on tax policy involved acceptance by the Republican Party of higher levels of taxation of corporate profits and large incomes, levels that the business community had regarded as unconscionable at the time World War II ended. In the immediate postwar years, Republicans accepted marginal rates of personal income taxation on the rich that were as high as during World War II. The postwar tax on corporate incomes reached a peak of 52 percent, which held until 1964; thereafter, until 1986, it was usually either 46 or 48 percent.

The convergence of the two parties, however, was more the product of a shift in direction by the Democratic Party. In the postwar era, Democrats largely abandoned taxation as an instrument to mobilize class interests. Southern Democrats, who had constituted a significant force within the Democratic party on behalf

---

[15] On the 1947 report of the CED, see Herbert Stein, *The Fiscal Revolution in America* (Chicago: University of Chicago Press, 1969), 220–40.

of soak-the-rich taxation, fell under the sway of neoclassical economics and its approach to tax policy. During the 1950s and 1960s, it was the fiscal conservatism of House Ways and Means chair Wilbur Mills (Democrat-Arkansas), rather than the Populism of Claude Kitchin and Robert Doughton (both Democrats–North Carolina), that guided the Southern Democrats who shaped tax policy in Congress.[16] Northeastern Democratic leaders, including those with close ties to organized labor, also abandoned soak-the-rich taxation. The Democratic tax politics that Joseph P. Kennedy and Bernard Baruch had pioneered during the 1930s now prevailed. Given the buoyancy of revenues under the World War II tax regime, Democrats had no need to consider significant tax increases, and thus had no need to justify them by calls to soak the rich. If their commitment to vertical equity was ever in question, they could point to the highly progressive tax system they implemented during World War II and preserved after the war.

During the 1950s, the Democratic congressional leadership accepted revisions of the personal income tax reducing the effective rates of taxation on the rich to roughly 25 percent.[17] Such rates were high by pre–World War II standards, but about half of the peak rates of effective taxation during the war. Presidents John F. Kennedy and Lyndon B. Johnson continued to support tax reforms, such as the taxation of capital gains at death, but they were careful not to push too hard for the reforms, for fear of seeming to threaten increasing the cost of living or putting expansion at risk. They also advocated a variety of selective tax cuts favoring the wealthy by

---

[16] For an analysis of Wilbur Mills's career that emphasizes his commitment to neoclassical analysis of taxation, see Julian E. Zelizer, *Taxing America: Wilbur D. Mills, Congress, and the State, 1945–1975* (Cambridge: Cambridge University Press, 1998). On the underlying transformation of Southern society, see Earl Black and Merle Black, *Politics and Society in the South* (Cambridge, Mass.: Harvard University Press, 1987), 3–72.

[17] Brownlee, "Historical Perspective on U.S. Tax Policy," 61.

hawking "supply-side" benefits, much as Andrew Mellon had done during the 1920s. In 1964, Congress responded to Johnson's call for a tax cut "to increase our national income and Federal revenues" by slashing taxes in the face of large deficits.[18] The Council of Economic Advisers, also committed to "growthmanship," actively supported the 1964 cuts, which reduced capital-gains taxes and allowed more generous depreciation allowances. Most liberals regarded the 1964 tax cuts as a victory for aggressive countercyclical stimulation of demand; they also embraced a supply-side rationale for the cuts, particularly those that reduced the marginal rates on the rich.

Democrats thus assisted the Republican Party in finishing the job it had begun during the 1920s: taking both the partisan sting and the redistributional threat out of taxation. The shift in the tax policy favored by the Democratic Party was part of its more general shift—one begun after 1937, accelerated during World War II, and completed in the Kennedy-Johnson era—away from democratic statism and toward corporate liberalism. This line of thinking had expanded its intellectual ambit, and its political potency, by incorporating Keynesian countercyclical policies. Kennedy and Johnson invoked Keynesian ideas as part of a strategy to win business support for their tax-reform program.[19]

[18] Public Papers of the Presidents of the United States, *Lyndon B. Johnson, 1963–1964* (Washington, D.C.: U.S. Government Printing Office, 1965), book 1, 9–10.

[19] The scholarly literature on the Kennedy-Johnson tax programs has become impressive in depth and scope. See, e.g., Ronald King, *Money, Time and Politics: Investment Tax Subsidies and American Democracy* (New Haven, Conn.: Yale University Press, 1993), 151–319; Cathie Jo Martin, *Shifting the Burden: The Struggle Over Growth and Corporate Taxation* (Chicago: University of Chicago Press, 1991); Martin, "American Business and the Taxing State: Alliances for Growth in the Postwar Period," in *Funding the Modern American State*, ed. Brownlee, 354–407; Stein, *Fiscal Revolution in America*, 372–453; John Witte, *The Politics and Development of the*

The bipartisan consensus ushered in an era of buoyant public finance that lasted until the 1980s. The tax policies and political actions that produced the era were nearly invisible, usually well removed from the contested turf of partisan politics.

Democrats and Republicans generally reached a consensus over the need to support effective income-tax administration, and they kept issues surrounding tax administration out of politics. During the presidency of Harry Truman, both Democratic and Republican leaders saw withholding as crucial to the success of the income tax. They supported ensuring adequate funding for the BIR, including its efforts to punish employers that refused to withhold taxes.

The Truman administration shifted enforcement emphasis from the tax dodges of established fortunes to the "tax chiseling" of those who had profited during wartime and the period of prosperity following the war. In a 1947 *Collier's* article, Undersecretary of the Treasury A. L. M. Wiggins described how the BIR had sent 128 revenue agents to a farming community in Minnesota to examine bank accounts, store accounts, government payments, crop yields, and the records of grain and cattle buyers. Wiggins reported that the BIR had collected more than $5 million in additional taxes and penalties from farmers in that community. The Treasury and the BIR did not reveal that—although they were increasing the efforts to audit individuals—efforts such as the Minnesota investigation were unusual. They wanted those tax dodgers—who were, in the words of George Schoeneman, the commissioner of internal revenue, "a tragic group of otherwise respectable individuals"—to fear apprehension and punishment.

Federal Income Tax (Madison: University of Wisconsin Press, 1985), 155–75; and Julian Zelizer, "Learning the Ways and Means: Wilbur Mills and a Fiscal Community, 1954–1964," in *Funding the Modern American State*, ed. Brownlee, 290–353.

To that end, Wiggins and Schoeneman exaggerated the BIR's efficiency. In 1949, Schoeneman told the readers of *American Magazine* that "you see, it's almost impossible to deceive our investigators, because most of them are generally familiar with every type of dodge ever attempted, and if they run across what appears to be a new one, they can look into the files and find it's been tried before." The Treasury had used propaganda to stress patriotic values during World War II. In the postwar era, it used the mass media to deliver threats. Fear of the BIR (renamed the Internal Revenue Service in 1953), combined with the political popularity of the individual income tax, led to what was, by worldwide standards, an unusually high level of taxpayer compliance.[20]

An equally central but more veiled element of the era of easy finance was an expansive system of Social Security. With remarkably little public debate, and with bipartisan agreement, the federal government embraced a policy of steadily raising Social Security tax rates. Roosevelt's institutional legacy was part of the reason for the success of Social Security proponents in raising taxes during peacetime. His strategy of earmarking tax revenues for Social Security helped defeat pluralist hostility to increasing taxes.

Crucial as well to the expansion of Social Security was a policy network that formed around the Social Security experts who were in government. A professionally diverse set of experts in the Social Security Administration, including Arthur Altmeyer, Robert Ball, and Wilbur J. Cohen, not only provided substantial intellectual contributions to the analytical understanding of Social Security but

[20] A. L. M. Wiggins, "They Can't Fool the Internal Revenue Man," *Collier's*, September 1947; George Schoeneman, "Tax Cheaters Beware!" *American Magazine*, February 1949. On the postwar enforcement efforts, see Jones, "Mass-Based Income Taxation." We do not have a scholarly history of the Internal Revenue Service and the BIR, but for a very useful reference work, see Shelley L. Davis, *IRS Historical Fact Book: A Chronology, 1646–1992* (Washington, D.C.: U.S. Government Printing Office, 1992).

also acted as policy entrepreneurs. These experts created a network of allies elsewhere in the government and beyond, within the public at large. This "Social Security crowd" began defending the system against political threats during the 1930s and 1940s. Some of the threats came at the hands of Keynesian economists who criticized the system's accumulation of funds as deflationary. The Social Security network advanced programs incrementally, but in 1950 it also engineered a major expansion of program coverage (including, for the first time, self-employed persons) and payroll taxation. In the next decade, the network won strong bipartisan and congressional support, including that of Mills, for their accomplishments and for further expansion of the system.

Increases in the tax base, as well as higher tax rates, boosted Social Security revenues. Steady and often dramatic economic growth—defined as growth in productivity—meant that payroll taxation tended to produce greater per capita levels of tax revenues. Social Security taxes increased from less than 1 percent of gross national product (GNP) in the late 1940s to more than 7 percent by the late 1970s. With this funding, Social Security payments increased from $472 million in 1946 (less than 1 percent of GNP) to $105 billion in 1979 (about 4.3 percent of GNP).[21]

Persistent inflation, as well as economic growth, helped to extend the life of the World War II tax regime. This inflation was another silent source of growing fiscal capacity. Inflation peaked first in the late 1940s, then increased again during the late 1960s and continued to rise throughout the 1970s. This inflation reduced the value of outstanding debt and thereby played a role of unprecedented proportions in financing the federal government. Inflation

---

[21] On the postwar expansion of the Social Security system, see Edward D. Berkowitz, "Social Security and the Financing of the American State," in *Funding the Modern American State*, ed. Brownlee, 149–94.

also produced "bracket creep," or the push of increasing numbers of families into higher tax brackets faster than their real incomes increased. Thus the structure of income-tax rates became substantially more progressive, especially at the higher levels of income. Although the Kennedy-Johnson tax cuts had reduced marginal rates of personal income taxation of the rich, and these rates remained relatively stable until the 1980s, the effective rates of taxation paid by the rich edged up during the 1970s. The rates reached nearly 30 percent, or roughly those that had prevailed immediately before and after World War II.[22]

The same effect, coupled with a failure to increase the personal exemption as rapidly as prices rose, propelled many low-income families into the tax system. By the early 1980s, the portion of the labor force paying taxes had increased to more than 75 percent from the 60 percent reached at the end of World War II.

Meanwhile, the corporate income tax, with a flat rate and hence no bracket creep, became a less dynamic source of revenue. In 1950, individual and corporate income-tax revenues were roughly equal; by 1980, individual income-tax revenues were nearly four times as large as corporate.[23]

Because of unanticipated inflation, the revenue system proved to be far more elastic after World War II than experts had predicted. Economists at the CED, for example, had believed that after the war, federal tax receipts as a share of gross domestic product would fall from the wartime peak of 22 percent to somewhere between 10 and 15 percent. In fact, the tax share of national product dipped

---

[22] Brownlee, "Historical Perspective on U.S. Tax Policy," 61.

[23] For a summary of the operation of postwar individual income tax, including the trends in progressiveness, see Jon Bakija and Eugene Steuerle, "Individual Income Taxation since 1948," *National Tax Journal* 44 (December 1991): 451–75.

below 15 percent only briefly, in 1950. By 1952, it was approaching 20 percent, and ever since it has remained close to or slightly above 20 percent.[24]

The combination of growth in productivity and inflation meant that the federal government often could respond positively to requests for new programs without enacting politically damaging tax increases. The highly elastic revenue system paid for the strategic defense programs of the Cold War and, without any general or permanent increases in income taxation, for the mobilizations for the Korean and Vietnam Wars as well. But the size of the defense budget relative to GNP tended to decline throughout the 1970s, except during the Korean and Vietnam Wars. Thus, the post–World War II increases in federal revenues went largely for the expansion of domestic programs—education, welfare, health services (including Medicare), urban redevelopment, and the channeling of federal revenues to state and local governments through indirect methods such as grants-in-aid and revenue sharing.

The federal government expanded intergovernmental support based on the programs that were developed after the Civil War, after World War I, and during the New Deal. Federal grants declined in importance during the 1940s, increased modestly during the 1950s, and then grew swiftly during the 1960s and 1970s. In these two decades, revenue sharing—federal subsidies to state and local governments without programmatic strings—dominated. By 1974, more than 20 percent of state and local revenues came from federal aid, which amounted to a kind of tax relief to state and local governments. Following World War II, state and local tax receipts had increased even more rapidly than had federal taxes. State and local taxes almost doubled as a share of GNP, rising to almost 10 percent by 1972.

---

[24] The late Herbert Stein provided the information regarding the CED estimates at the end of World War II; Stein to Brownlee, June 20, 1994.

TAX EXPENDITURES AND THE WEAKENING
OF THE REGIME

The inflation-driven increases in revenues also permitted new "tax expenditures"—special preferences offered under the tax code in the form of exclusions, deductions, and credits. Tax expenditures that benefited middle-class taxpayers had accompanied the introduction and expansion of mass-based income taxation during the 1940s and 1950s. After World War II, and the ebbing of patriotism as a factor in income-tax compliance, Congress relied increasingly on tax expenditures and other measures—including the introduction of the income-splitting joint return for husbands and wives and the acceptance of community-property status—to enhance the popularity of the new tax regime. However, a deduction that had been in the tax code since 1913—that for home mortgage interest—also favored the middle class and was one of the most expensive tax expenditure. Other deductions, such as one for accelerated depreciation, which was introduced in 1954, disproportionately favored the wealthy.[25]

During the 1960s and 1970s, tax expenditures became even more popular, and both old and new forms grew relative to conventional expenditures. Politicians became attracted to tax expenditures as a way to accomplish social goals—such as the promotion of homeownership embedded in the deduction of mortgage interest—without having to make large and politically difficult direct expenditures of funds. In other words, many Democratic and Republican

---

[25] On the joint return and community-property status, see Jones, "Mass-Based Income Taxation." For a discussion of how accelerated depreciation for income-producing structures helped turn real estate development into a rewarding tax shelter and may have contributed to an explosion in shopping center construction, see Thomas W. Hanchett, U.S. Tax Policy and the Shopping-Center Boom of the 1950s and 1960s," *American Historical Review* 101 (1996): 1082–1100.

members of Congress found self-serving political benefits in hiding tax programs from public scrutiny. Contributing to the movement as well were taxpaying groups that aggressively sought preferential treatment within the tax code to offset the effects of bracket creep. In turn, the taxpayers and legislators who benefited from the tax expenditures developed a vested interest in increasing the complexity of the process of tax legislation. The tax-writing committees of Congress—the House Ways and Means and the Senate Finance Committees, and their expert staffs—grew in power because they were able to deliver new federal programs, albeit in the form of tax preferences.[26]

Although the general public was slow to recognize the significance of tax expenditures and the political culture of cutting taxes by granting preferences, a group of tax lawyers and economists struggled to expose the inequities resulting from increasing exemptions and deductions. Especially influential were the economist Joseph Pechman and the law professor Stanley Surrey. They drew on a line of economic analysis that had its roots in the arguments of the economists Thomas S. Adams, Robert Murray Haig, and Henry Simons. During the 1920s and 1930s, they had argued that the federal government ought to rationalize the personal income tax by basing it on a comprehensive, economic definition of income—one that measured, in Haig's words, "the money value of the net accretion of one's economic power between two points in time." Adopting Haig's definition for the purposes of income taxation would require the taxing of items such as net capital gains and the income-in-kind that an owner enjoys from an owner-occupied residence.[27]

---

[26] The leading analysis of the bureaucratic complexity of making tax policy, especially within Congress, during the 1960s and 1970s is Thomas J. Reese, *The Politics of Taxation* (Westport, Conn.: Quorum, 1980).

[27] Robert M. Haig, "The Concept of Income," in *The Federal Income Tax*, ed. Robert M. Haig (New York: Columbia University Press, 1921), 7.

Base broadening won a wider audience during World War II, when the CED commissioned Simons to develop a reform program focused on expanding the definition of taxable income. In 1959, Congressman Mills held hearings and published papers that put base-broadening reforms on the agenda of a new fiscal community that coalesced in the late 1950s and early 1960s. By acting as a broker between fiscal experts and the larger political world, Mills promoted coherent policymaking within the complex administrative state created by the New Deal and World War II. As a consequence of the influence of Mills and other experts, the Revenue Act of 1962 contained a few base-broadening reforms, such as restrictions on foreign tax havens, on benefits for cooperatives, and on travel and entertainment deductions.[28]

Beginning in 1967, Surrey, as assistant secretary of the treasury (1961–69), further enhanced the visibility of base broadening.

[28] For a summary of the base-broadening movement, see Joseph A. Pechman, "Tax Reform: Theory and Practice," *Journal of Economic Perspectives* 1 (summer 1987): 11–28. The CED published Simons's program in 1944 as *Committee for Economic Development: A Post-War Federal Tax Plan for High Employment* (New York: Committee for Economic Development, 1944). Simons later published an elaborate version of his plan; see Henry C. Simons, *Federal Tax Reform* (Chicago: University of Chicago Press, 1950). For an assessment of Simons's contributions to tax theory, see Harold Groves, *Tax Philosophers: Two Hundred Years of Thought in Great Britain and the United States*, ed. Donald J. Curran (Madison: University of Wisconsin Press, 1974), 74–85. For the influential hearings sponsored by Wilbur Mills, see U.S. House of Representatives, Committee on Ways and Means, *Tax Revision Compendium: Compendium of Papers on Broadening the Tax Base*, 2 vols. (Washington, D.C.: U.S. Government Printing Office, 1959). On Mills's interest in base-broadening reform, see Zelizer, "Learning the Ways and Means." It should be noted that Pechman lent support to Zelizer's interpretation of Mills by crediting Mills with boosting the cause of comprehensive personal-income taxation. See Pechman, "Tax Reform: Theory and Practice," 12.

He introduced the organizing concept of tax expenditures.[29] This helped him effectively articulate the Treasury's position that the government should pursue social goals openly, through direct expenditures. Surrey, economists within the Treasury, and a string of Treasury assistant secretaries and commissioners of internal revenue who favored base broadening worked in ways that would have pleased Thomas S. Adams. From within the Treasury, they highlighted the massive size of tax expenditures and underscored the kind of economic inefficiencies, distortions, and unfairness that the tax expenditures created. In 1974, the Congressional Budget Act acknowledged the importance of the concept and advanced the debate by requiring the annual publication of a "tax-expenditure budget."

Surrey and the Treasury experts argued, in effect, that the income-tax regime created during World War II had weakened significantly. The federal income tax, because of the relentless carving out of new special preferences, was even further than the mass-based tax of World War II from the ideals of comprehensive income taxation articulated by Simons. And the decay seemed to be accelerating. The Congressional Budget Office later estimated that in 1967, tax expenditures cost the federal government nearly $37 billion (equal to 21 percent of federal expenditures) and that the total cost had soared to $327 billion by 1984 (equal to 35 percent of federal expenditures).

The acceleration of loophole creation was a consequence of economics as well as politics. An increasing rate of inflation had always intensified the search for new loopholes and the exploiting of old ones as ways to offset bracket creep. For example, the huge inflation

---

[29] For a discussion of Surrey's views, including his 1967 proposal of a "tax-expenditure budget," see Stanley S. Surrey, *Pathways to Tax Reform: The Concept of Tax Expenditures* (Cambridge, Mass.: Harvard University Press, 1973).

following World War I, between 1918 and 1920, had led to irresistible pressure for new tax preferences. This is what had so bitterly disappointed Thomas S. Adams. The inflationary pressures of the 1960s and 1970s were not as intense as those following World War I, but they held sway for a much longer period of time. General price inflation peaked in 1980 at 13 percent (when measured by the consumer price index), and the sustained nature of the inflation has led some economic historians to term the episode "the Great Inflation."[30]

In and of itself, this dramatic inflation meant a weakening of the income tax regime. The price increases meant huge, unlegislated tax increases for most individual taxpayers. Bracket creep became bracket leap as inflation vaulted individuals into higher tax brackets, even though their real income had not increased. It was not just the rich and middle class who were affected. Many lower-income people, especially those with dependents, had to pay income tax for the first time as the value of their personal and dependent exemptions and the effective tax-exempt level of income eroded.

During the 1970s, at the same time that inflation soared, the expansion of the economy slowed and economic productivity ceased to grow. This was "stagflation," as it became known, representing the failure of the nation's economic managers to provide either economic growth or price stability. With the consequent stagnation of the income-tax base, whatever growth there was in federal tax revenues came to depend on continued inflation. In 1979, Paul Volcker, the chair of the Federal Reserve System, launched an attack on inflation, but few knew if and when he might succeed. A situation in which the strength of the tax system had perversely come to depend on a dysfunctional and harmful economic phenomenon called out for fiscal reform.

[30] See, e.g., Gary M. Walton and Hugh Rockoff, *History of the American Economy*, 9th ed. (Stamford, Conn.: Thomson Learning, 2002), 626–28.

PATHS TO REFORM

One approach to reform that emerged during the late 1970s was to build on the Treasury investigations and attempt to roll back the surging wave of tax preferences. In the presidential campaign of 1976, Democratic candidate Jimmy Carter advocated this approach. He called the U.S. tax system "a disgrace to the human race" and promised to broaden the base of the income tax by eliminating tax expenditures. But he did not propose rolling back all tax expenditures; he focused on those that favored the rich. As he dealt with the consequences of inflation, he wanted to make the tax system more progressive. Whatever the details of his program might turn out to be when in office, he promised to avoid "a piecemeal approach to change." During his first two years in office, he continued to advocate systematic reduction of tax expenditures. Nonetheless, he found himself embroiled with Congress working on piecemeal change.[31]

The political problem that Carter faced and could not solve was that most congressional leaders, both Republican and Democrat, favored an approach that was philosophically at odds with Carter's. It was to expand, rather than reduce, tax preferences. In addition, in contrast to Carter, they sought to favor the rich. The advocates of this approach had the support of some conservative economists who focused on the effects of the progressive tax system and of bracket creep on the cost of capital. Two such economists were Norman Ture and Paul Craig Roberts, who was an adviser to Representative Jack Kemp (Republican–New York).

Ture and Roberts approved of the way in which many tax expenditures favored investors and savers, who were concentrated in higher income brackets. They embraced this favoritism as a way

[31] On Carter's program for tax reform, see W. Carl Biven, *Jimmy Carter's Economy: Policy in an Age of Limits* (Chapel Hill: University of North Carolina Press, 2002), 198–200.

of offsetting what they regarded as the penalties that the income tax imposed on saving. They argued, for example, that the income tax penalizes savers by taxing twice income earned and saved while taxing only once income earned and spent, and that the income tax taxes capital income twice—at both the corporate and individual levels. And they correctly pointed out that some of the Kennedy-Johnson tax cuts of 1964 had sought to use tax preferences to reduce the cost of capital. In 1975, they provided Kemp with a "supply-side basis" for a bill designed to promote capital formation and enhance productivity through tax subsidies for business investment.[32]

The second approach prevailed during the Carter administration. The president reluctantly signed the Revenue Act of 1978, which provided only minimal tax relief and simplification for individuals but offered significant cuts in capital gains and business taxes. In the process of working out the act, Carter was able to block three other approaches to reform, two of which conservatives favored.

One approach that conservatives favored was an incisively direct solution to bracket creep: the indexing of income tax rates for inflation. A number of economists—including Martin Feldstein of Harvard University and William Fellner of the American Enterprise Institute—advocated this approach. But to most politicians, indexing sounded exceedingly complex and academic, and liberals were generally worried about the consequent loss in revenues. However, in California, an innovative Republican assemblyman, William Bagley, took on the intellectual challenge and led a successful fight to index the state's income tax for inflation. California was the first state to do so. The ex-governor of California, and presidential candidate, was watching his state, which he regarded as a barometer of

---

[32] Paul Craig Roberts, *The Supply-Side Revolution: An Insider's Account of Policymaking in Washington* (Cambridge, Mass.: Harvard University Press, 1984), 31.

national trends. In addition, he was closely following the ideas of conservative economists, including Feldstein. In 1977, Ronald Reagan quickly endorsed indexing the federal income tax. The measure won growing support among Republicans in Congress, but the Carter administration was able to block it.[33]

The second conservative approach that Carter was able to turn back was straightforward, simple, and easy to understand: provide relief to the victims of bracket creep by slashing income tax rates across the board. In 1977, Kemp endorsed deep cuts in income taxes. He first proposed a 30 percent reduction across the board in one year. Then, in July, he joined with Senator William Roth (Republican-Delaware) to spread the cuts over three years—to cut across the board by 10 percent every year, for three years (these became known as the 10-10-10 tax cuts). In October, Reagan also endorsed the Kemp-Roth proposal. The Kemp-Roth plan gained increasing support in Congress, and in 1978 Senator Sam Nunn (Democratic-Georgia) nearly succeeded in including a version in the Revenue Act. Both houses endorsed the Nunn Amendment, but Carter used the threat of a veto to force Congress to drop the supply-side initiative.[34]

---

[33] On the interest of economists in indexing, see "Comments" by Murray Weidenbaum, Martin Feldstein, and Russell Long in "Tax Policy, Summary of Discussion," in *American Economic Policy in the 1980s*, ed. Martin Feldstein (Chicago: University of Chicago, 1994), 228. On Reagan's proposal, see Ronald Reagan, "More About Taxes, January 19, 1977," and "Indexing, June 15, 1977," in *Reagan, In His Own Hand*, ed. Kiron K. Skinner, Annelise Anderson, and Martin Anderson (New York: Free Press, 2001), 273–74.

[34] The best account of the development of the Kemp proposals is Roberts, *Supply-Side Revolution*, 1–33, 69–88. On Reagan's endorsement, see Ronald Reagan, "Taxes, October 18, 1977" in *Reagan, In His Own Hand*, 274–77. As Lou Cannon has suggested, Reagan's endorsement of the Kemp formula to the development of Reagan's tax program came early, fully two years before Reagan (according to Martin Anderson) endorsed Kemp's

In 1977, Kemp and Reagan advanced a startling argument to help justify the drastic nature of the tax they proposed: The cuts would actually reduce budget deficits and thus relieve the upward pressure on prices, including interest rates. This deficit reduction would occur, Kemp and Reagan argued, because of the huge expansion of the tax base produced by American investors and workers invigorated by big cuts in tax rates. Thus, they seemed to embrace what became the most controversial proposition of the supply-side argument for tax cuts: The cuts would not just stimulate productivity; they would also reduce deficits.

Martin Anderson, a central economic adviser in Reagan's first term as president, later claimed that supply-siders were actually moderate in their views, arguing only that tax cutting "would *not lose as much revenue as one might expect*" (emphasis in original). Anderson was correct for most supply-siders—especially among professional economists who leaned toward that view—but not all. And Reagan himself on occasion tended to express true belief in the most extreme view, which implied almost no loss in revenues, even in the initial years. In the radio address in which he endorsed Kemp's program, Reagan declared that the Kemp cuts "would reduce the deficit which causes inflation because the tax base would be broadened by increased prosperity."[35]

specific plan as part of a deal to win Kemp's support for Reagan's presidential bid. See Cannon, *Reagan* (New York: G. P. Putnam's, 1982), 236–37; and Anderson, *Revolution* (San Diego: Harcourt Brace Jovanovich, 1988), 162–63. The total tax cut proposed was a bit smaller than the 30 percent that Kemp and Reagan touted. Because the tax cut program would apply each 10 percent cut to a successively lower rate of taxation, the net tax proposed was about 27 percent. More precisely, the net tax cut percentage, pt, was: $pt = 1 - [(1 - 0.1) \times (1 - 0.1) \times (1 - 0.1)]$.

[35] Ronald Reagan, "Taxes, October 18, 1977" in *Reagan, In His Own Hand*, 274, 277. I have spelled out some of the abbreviations that Reagan used in his original radio scripts. Reagan's commitment to the extreme version of supply-side economics appears to have come more than two or three

The Democratic approach to reform that Carter turned back was that of a few influential Democrats who wished to protect or expand revenues but agreed with the desire of Republicans to reduce the cost of capital and encourage investment. These Democrats proposed replacing the income tax (and Social Security taxes as well) with a new tax—a value-added tax on consumption. For each transaction in the chain of production, the tax would apply a small levy to the value added in that step—the difference between the sale price of the product or service and the cost of the goods and services purchased to create the product or service. France had adopted a value-added tax as early as 1954, and between 1967 and 1973 all the members of the European Economic Community, including Great Britain, adopted it as their standard form of sales taxation.

In 1978, Senator Russell Long, chair of the Senate Finance Committee, proposed this radical transformation of the tax system. Then Representative Al Ullman (Democrat-Oregon), who chaired the House Ways and Means Committee, introduced a concrete plan to move in that direction. For the first time since 1940, Congress looked closely at comprehensively taxing consumption.

years earlier than the briefing on the Laffer curve, by Arthur Laffer, that David Stockman and others believed marked Reagan's conversion just before his 1980 victory in the New Hampshire primary. In 1976, in a newspaper column, Reagan suggested that the tax cuts of presidents Harding and Kennedy had produced increased revenues. Sidney Blumenthal claims that at a dinner in 1977, Reagan told Laffer that he supported supply-side economics. In 1976 and 1977, Reagan may have been reading Jude Wanniski's *Wall Street Journal* editorials promoting Laffer's ideas. See Blumenthal, *The Rise of the Counter-Establishment: From Conservative Ideology to Political Power* (New York: Random House, 1986), 166–67, 190–96; and Stockman, *The Triumph of Politics: How the Reagan Revolution Failed* (New York: Harper & Row, 1986), 258. On the role of Wanniski's editorials, see Roberts, *Supply-Side Revolution*, 27–30, and Anderson, *Revolution*, 148–52.

At the time, Ullman's proposed Tax Reconstruction Act of 1980 was probably the most radical approach to tax reform seriously considered by Congress since World War II. However, liberals, including President Carter, worried about its regressiveness, and conservatives, including business leaders, argued that the new tax would encourage the growth of government. Together, they prevented the bill from coming to a vote. Meanwhile, Oregon's voters, who apparently disliked the prospect of any new taxes, and particularly despised new ones on consumption, ended Ullman's congressional career. Once again, just as at earlier junctures, the federal government stopped short of encouraging savings and investment through the comprehensive taxation of consumption.[36]

Carter's efforts to increase taxation of wealthy Americans and Ullman's campaign for a new tax put them at odds with an antigovernment movement that was gathering real force in 1978. The movement was founded on widespread concerns about the rising costs of government, doubts about the effectiveness of governmental solutions to social problems, dissatisfaction over the quality of public services, and distrust of legislatures. Hostility to taxation gave the movement a policy center.

The antigovernment movement focused at first not so much on federal taxation as on state and local taxation, which taxpayers often felt more directly, and which grassroots organizing could more easily attack. The movement gained its most dramatic expression in a 1978 taxpayers' revolt in California. The basis of the revolt was the fact that during the "Great Inflation," real estate values also rose rapidly, leading to large property-tax increases relative to

---

[36] Only the high-tariff system of the late nineteenth century stands as a possible exception to this pattern. But the central motivation for the tariff system had little to do with the stimulation of savings; it was designed primarily to manipulate international prices of manufactured goods and labor.

income. In a referendum, California voters approved Proposition 13, amending the state's constitution to limit the property-tax rate to 1 percent of market value and to require a two-thirds majority of each house of the legislature to enact any new taxes.

Then, in a number of other states, citizens who had been stimulated by the success of Proposition 13 organized coalitions similar to the one that had formed in California—a combination of homeowners and owners of commercial property trying to reduce their tax bills, conservatives attacking welfare, liberals seeking a more progressive tax system, and people simply striking out at modern life. The measures they framed were not as drastic as Proposition 13, but all were in its spirit and most survived state-level referenda and court challenges.[37]

Presidential candidate Reagan watched the stunning success of the California taxpayers' revolt. He did so as the most important architect of the antigovernment movement and the tax revolt.[38] When he was governor of California (1967–75), he had felt frustrated in his attacks on government. With the success of Proposition 13, however, he became certain that dismal economic conditions had created an opportunity to use tax issues in a popular revolt against the size of government. He decided to make tax reform the core of his economic program in his bid for the presidency in 1980. And he

---

[37] There is a substantial literature on the Proposition 13 movement. See, e.g., Arthur O'Sullivan, Terri A. Sexton, and Steven M. Sheffrin, *Property Taxes and Tax Revolts: The Legacy of Proposition 13* (Cambridge: Cambridge University Press, 1995); Alvin Rabushka and Pauline Ryan, *The Tax Revolt* (Stanford, Calif.: Hoover Institution Press, 1982); and David O. Sears and Jack Citrin, *Tax Revolt: Something for Nothing in California* (Cambridge, Mass.: Harvard University Press, 1982).

[38] The following discussion of Reagan, which continues into the next chapter, draws in part on W. Elliot Brownlee and C. Eugene Steuerle, "Taxation," in *The Reagan Presidency: Pragmatic Conservatism and Its Legacy*, ed. W. Elliot Brownlee and Hugh Davis Graham (Lawrence: University Press of Kansas, 2003), 155–81.

settled on promoting ideas of indexing and across-the-board cuts, following Kemp's proposals, as the core of his tax program.

To some extent, Reagan's tax platform represented traditional Republican tax cutting. He remembered the high rates of the late 1940s that had left him with almost nothing from making additional movies, and he consequently regarded a tax cut for the rich as an effective way of stimulating economic productivity. But his proposal also had a distinct populist dimension. His proposal for major tax cuts across the board, and for indexing, offered significant economic relief to middle- and working-class Americans. He emphasized, in particular, that the deep cuts would directly offset the harsh impact of inflation on standards of living for all income-tax payers, and he promised to retain the progressive income tax.[39] Even though his message was antistatist, Reagan, like Franklin D. Roosevelt, sought to use tax issues to build a new political coalition of workers and consumers.

During his campaign for the presidency, however, Reagan never entertained any intention of pushing beyond indexing or rate cutting to reform the federal tax system in a fundamental way. A nonstarter was base-broadening reform, which he aggressively criticized.[40] As

[39] Reagan was correct about the direction of the tax relief that a rate reduction would offer to those suffering from inflation, but he did not mention the fact that a rate reduction offered a great deal more relief from the effects of inflation to the wealthy than to the poor. An individual who, previous to inflation, had no income tax burden might now begin to pay taxes because of inflation. But a 27 percent tax would pare back only about one-fourth of his increase in taxes. In contrast, someone with almost all of her income in the top tax bracket would have little income subject to "bracket-creep" but would still get a 27 percent cut in taxes.

[40] Another nonstarter for Reagan was a federal consumption tax, like a value-added tax (VAT). Reagan may have understood and been sympathetic to the economic case for consumption taxation, but he was probably aware that some Democrats had begun to smile on VAT forms of consumption taxation as a means for painlessly expanding the welfare state. And he also may have

early as 1975, he had expressed his skepticism about the concept of tax expenditures. In July 1979, he said that the term "tax expenditures" was "the new name government has for the share of our earnings it allows us to keep. You and I," he said, "call them deductions." "All told," he concluded, "our rich . . . Uncle Sam has an eye on about $170 billion that we think is ours." He was focused on the political fact that President Carter and other liberals supported "tax expenditure" reform because they were interested in closing tax loopholes for the rich to make the income tax more progressive and increase its revenue capacity.[41]

Reagan's position on tax expenditures opened the way for corporate lobbyists to shape the agenda of his presidential campaign. During the summer of 1980, they succeeded in inserting a huge tax expenditure into the Reagan program. Their leader was Charls Walker, whose firm represented dozens of industrial clients—members of the traditional Republican elite—who had enormous investments in plant and equipment. Walker persuaded the Republican platform committee to propose a dramatic increase in the allowances to corporations and individuals for the depreciation of tangible assets. The proposal became known as "10-5-3," which was shorthand for the three new depreciation lifetimes for structures (ten years), equipment (five years), and light vehicles (three years).

been aware that an important source of Republican support—the small-business community—was hostile to a VAT. A third nonstarter was the head tax or, in the term more common in the United States, a poll tax. Supply-side economics pointed logically toward them, but they were alien to American political culture. We do not know whether or not Margaret Thatcher, whose later proposal of a small head tax contributed to her political downfall, ever discussed head taxes with Reagan. On the supply-side logic of poll taxes, see C. Eugene Steuerle, *The Tax Decade: How Taxes Came to Dominate the Public Agenda* (Washington, D.C.: Urban Institute Press, 1992), 40.

[41] Ronald Reagan, "Tax Loopholes, May 1975," in *Reagan, In His Own Hand*, 268–70, and "Tax Expenditures, July 27, 1979," in *Reagan, In His Own Hand*, 283–84.

To pay for 10-5-3, Reagan's platform committee dropped entirely the proposal to reform the income tax by indexing the tax rate for individuals, which was of much greater benefit to labor income and the income of the middle class.[42]

This change reflected the primacy within the Reagan camp of pragmatic political concerns, and the decidedly secondary role of any interest in coherent, systematic economic reform. Reagan and his political operatives focused on campaigning for a deep, across-the-board, tax cut that would be easily understood. As a political proposition, the approach was decidedly successful. The tax platform helped Reagan sweep to victory in 1980, and the tax issue became the first vehicle for the Reagan administration to flex its legislative muscles. Ronald Reagan had caught the wave of tax reform that Jimmy Carter had missed.

---

[42] On the role of Charls Walker, see Jeffrey H. Birnbaum and Alan S. Murray, *Showdown at Gucci Gulch: Lawmakers, Lobbyists, and the Unlikely Triumph of Tax Reform* (New York: Random House, 1987), 16–18; Timothy J. Conlan et al., *Taxing Choices: The Politics of Tax Reform* (Washington, D.C.: Congressional Quarterly Press, 1990), 96; and Cathie J. Martin, *Shifting the Burden: The Struggle over Growth and Corporate Taxation* (Chicago: University of Chicago Press, 1991), 47.

Part II

The conservative challenge

4

The "Reagan Revolution," 1980–1986

As the efforts of President Jimmy Carter to reduce tax expenditures had failed in the late 1970s, presidential candidate Ronald Reagan and the Republican Party seized the issue of tax reform. They did so by fanning public hostility to anything resembling new taxes, and in winning popular support for tax reductions. In 1981, when Reagan took charge of the White House, and the Republicans took control of the Congress, they set out to adopt Reagan's campaign platform. By 1986, they had wrought the most significant changes in the income-tax system since World War II, but in 1981 no one foresaw what the actual path of reform would be or what the final accomplishments would look like.

TAX CUTS, DEFICITS, AND TAX INCREASES

When Reagan won the Republican nomination in 1980, his campaign staff quickly turned to the analysis and drafting of tax legislation. He intended to make tax reduction the first major victory for his administration's domestic program. But as he and his staff wrestled with the details of the legislation, they had to cope with the major complication that tax cutting would increase budget deficits.

The advisers disagreed among themselves as to the extent of the deficits. But most agreed that there indeed would be deficits and that unless contained, the deficits would put pressure on capital markets, raise interest costs, possibly increase interest rates, and undermine public confidence in Reagan's program.

Reagan's personal views strongly shaped how the administration implemented his campaign platform. A few weeks after his acceptance speech, his economic advisers met with him, and most, including Alan Greenspan and Charls Walker, advised him that he ought to go slower and take five, rather than three, years to implement the 10-10-10 tax cuts (which, as explained in chapter 3, involved proposing to cut taxes across the board by 10 percent every year, for three years).

When Reagan's economic advisers had made their case, warning him about the deficits, he replied, "I don't care." Walker remembered that they all "nearly fell out of their chairs." Reagan had turned out to be the most extreme populist in the room. The president wanted to cut everyone's taxes, regardless of whether or not any particular economic theory supported him, and regardless of whether or not the cuts worsened the deficit. The president got his way and stayed with the 10-10-10 formula. In general, the president, more than many of his advisers, wanted deep cuts in income taxes, and he did not want the cut focused on businesses and the highest-income individuals. His goal was to exploit broad popular support for a tax cut, pave the way for other policy initiatives, and produce a more profound realignment of voters.[1]

Reagan and his supply-side advisers—Martin Anderson, Paul Craig Roberts, and Norman Ture, among others—may have had another reason for supporting the deep tax cuts. They may have

[1] Charls Walker, "Summary of Discussion," in *American Economic Policy in the 1980s*, ed. Martin Feldstein (Chicago: University of Chicago, 1994), 224–25.

actually *wanted* higher initial deficits to restrain spending, as Senator Daniel Patrick Moynihan (Democrat–New York) once suggested. David Stockman, Reagan's director of the Office of Management and Budget, denied that, and his memory of what was said in the councils of government seems to have been accurate.[2] But Stockman may not have fully understood Reagan's intentions, and conservatives and liberals would generally agree on the simple point that spending is easier when revenues are available than when they are not. Reagan said as much on February 5, 1981, in a national address. He invoked one of his homilies to justify going forward with a tax cut before trying to moderate or roll back spending: "Well," he said, "we can lecture our children about extravagance until we run out of voice and breath. *Or* we can cure their extravagance simply by reducing their allowance."[3]

Republicans controlled both houses of Congress, but even so, the depth of Reagan's tax cuts initially caused serious, bipartisan trouble there for his proposals. But in March 1981, the assassination

[2] In 1986 and again in 1994, David Stockman denied that the deficits were deliberate. See Stockman, *The Triumph of Politics: How the Reagan Revolution Failed* (New York: Harper & Row, 1986), 267–68, and "Comments by David Stockman, Summary of Discussion: Tax Policy," in *American Economic Policy in the 1980s*, ed. Feldstein, 287.

[3] Ronald Reagan, "Economic Speech—Address to the Nation, February 5, 1981," in *Reagan, In His Own Hand*, ed. Kiron K. Skinner, Annelise Anderson, and Martin Anderson (New York: Free Press, 2001), 490. There is evidence, in fact, of the kind of "causal" connection between taxation and expenditure in much of the history of financing the welfare state during the twentieth century. However, this connection had disappeared during the 1970s. See Kevin D. Hoover and Steven Sheffrin, "Causation, Spending, and Taxes: Sand in the Sandbox or Tax Collector for the Welfare State?" *American Economic Review* 82 (March 1992): 225–48. However, this disappearance may simply reflect the growing significance of "tax expenditures" during the 1970s.

attempt on the president intervened. It had the effect of increasing popular support for him and, by extension, whatever tax program he wanted. Congress found the pressure irresistible. Democratic leaders in Congress abandoned caution and launched a frenzied bidding war with Republicans. Together, the two parties decorated their "Christmas tree" bill with a spectacular array of tax shelters. In the bidding, Congress also restored the very expensive indexing of tax brackets. Reagan's crusty and forthright secretary of the treasury, Donald Regan, told Treasury staff: "My favorite part of the tax bill is the indexing provision—it takes the sand out of Congress's sandbox."

To help pay for the enlarged scope of the tax cuts, Congress did pare some reductions in tax rates. The 10-10-10 formula became 5-10-10, providing for a 23 percent, rather than a 27 percent, net reduction in the tax cuts for individuals. And Congress delayed indexing until 1985. The Economic Recovery Tax Act (ERTA) became law in August 1981.[4]

Even the most extreme supply-siders in the Reagan administration agreed that ERTA would slash tax revenues in the short run, and it did. In addition, a recession and reduction in inflation rates were already under way, and they too undercut revenues. Meanwhile, Reagan pushed substantial increases in defense spending. This also added to the deficits that followed ERTA, and they turned out to be the largest, relative to the size of the economy, that the federal government had ever run in peacetime. By fiscal

[4] For the quotation of Regan, see Hoover and Sheffrin, "Causation, Spending, and Taxes," 225. The president's legislative strategy group had come to support the shift to 5-10-10 as a means "of deficit reduction and acceptance of selected other tax reduction proposals necessary to achieve a political majority." See "Meeting of Legislative Strategy Group," May 12, 1981, folder Economic/Budget Policy 5/81, OA 10972, Craig Fuller Files, Ronald Reagan Library (hereafter, RRL).

1984, the deficit had grown to 5.0 percent of gross domestic product (GDP) from 2.8 percent in 1980.[5]

Concern about deficits of this magnitude grew quickly, inside as well as outside the Reagan administration. Politicians and economists who worried about deficits had difficulty in advancing their concerns, in large part because the federal government had much earlier abandoned a disciplined fiscal policy—a fiscal policy conforming to a rule or set of rules governing the size of the federal deficit. The consensus established in the early 1960s within the federal government behind a rule—the rule that tax and spending policies should produce a balanced budget if the economy were operating at full employment—broke down later in that decade. In 1971, Richard Nixon formally abandoned the rule. He wanted to balance the full-employment budget, but competing economic and political objectives forced him to abandon that goal. In 1974, when Herbert Stein convened President Gerald Ford's Council of Economic Advisers, he found that "no one in or out of the government had a credible theory of fiscal policy." By 1981, few in power, even those who worried about deficits, believed, in Stein's words, "that there was some precise, knowable size of the deficit that was consistent with the stability of the economy."[6]

---

[5] Martin Feldstein, "American Economic Policy in the 1980s: A Personal View," in *American Economic Policy in the 1980s*, 47–48.

[6] In an essay that continues his career-long interest in the evaluation of fiscal policy, Stein describes how the federal government, beginning as early as 1965, abandoned a coherent "aggregate rule" for setting countercyclical fiscal policy, including taxes. Stein has concluded that in 1969 he was premature, at best, when he declared, in *The Fiscal Revolution in America*, that "domesticated Keynesianism" had triumphed in 1962–64. In fact, Stein now finds that during the last thirty years, not one of the major approaches to budget balancing has prevailed. During the past thirty years, Stein argues, policymakers have been unwilling "to subordinate their desires for specific tax and expenditure programs to any aggregate goal." The simple

Despite the lack of widely accepted budget rule, the Reagan administration, beginning as early as 1981, took steps to address the deficit problem. The administration had to face the prospect of political embarrassment in the election years of 1982 and 1984 over surging deficits and the upward pressure of those deficits on long-term interest rates, and the downward pressure on the stock market. The political pressure was bipartisan; it included conservatives in the capital markets and supporters of cuts in tax rates who had counted on reduced expenditures to help pay for those changes.[7]

The administration had only one way to reduce or contain the damaging deficits while staying with both the tax cuts and defense buildup. That was to tackle the large, and continuing, growth in mandatory entitlement spending. A few in the White House understood this and were enthusiastic about the prospect, but many were not. In any case, entitlement reform was a slow process, not one that was easily engaged, and not one that could have an immediate,

---

obstacle to coherent fiscal policy, he suggests, is that "people—politicians and private citizens—cared about the ingredients of the budget for other reasons in addition to their cyclical consequences" and that "almost all were opposed to raising taxes most of the time." See Herbert Stein, "The Fiscal Revolution in America, Part II: 1964 to 1994," in *Funding the Modern American State, 1941–1995: The Rise and Fall of the Era of Easy Finance*, ed. W. Elliot Brownlee (Washington, D.C.: Woodrow Wilson Center Press, and Cambridge: Cambridge University Press, 1996), 195–287.

[7] In 1981 and 1982, Paul Volcker played an important role behind the scenes by lobbying the administration, particularly secretary of the treasury Donald T. Regan, to reduce deficits in return for some monetary ease; Regan, *For the Record: From Wall Street to Washington* (San Diego: Harcourt Brace Jovanovich, 1988), 178. Within the administration, Alan Greenspan defended the Federal Reserve and argued that "at root, our problem is that the markets believe that the Federal deficit will continue to hemorrhage, inducing the Federal Reserve to create excessive money supply growth and hence inflation." Alan Greenspan, untitled enclosure, February 1, 1982, folder "Briefing Book for Long-Range Planning Meeting, Camp David, February 5, 1982 (2)," box 1, Richard G. Darman Files, RRL.

significant impact on the budget.[8] The defense buildup was sacrosanct as Reagan's highest policy priority, so in September 1981, less than two months after the passage of ERTA, his administration quietly proposed tax increases, describing them as "revisions in the tax code to curtail certain tax abuses and enhance tax revenues."

At the same time, the Reagan administration worked more closely with the tax-writing committees of Congress, particularly the Senate Finance Committee under Robert Dole (Republican-Kansas). Meanwhile, within Reagan's inner circle of advisers, the power of Chief of Staff James A. Baker, who was the most concerned about deficits, grew, while the influence of Attorney General Edwin Meese, who had the strongest reservations about tax increases, waned. And as the process of increasing taxes unfolded in 1982, a number of supply-siders at Treasury—in particular, Paul Craig Roberts and Norman Ture—left the administration.[9]

President Reagan played crucial roles in shaping the program of tax increases. In part because he was the most enthusiastic supply-sider within his administration, he blocked any dramatic proposals for tax increases. He also blocked any effort to repeal ERTA's cuts in individual tax rates. But he was willing to support the less visible and less universal forms of tax increases—cuts in tax expenditures—in other words, cuts in the complex array of tax deductions, tax exemptions, and tax credits that riddled the tax code. And as he

---

[8] On the lack of focus in the White House on the growth in entitlement spending, see Stockman, *Triumph of Politics*, 161–62.

[9] Regan, *For the Record*, 176–84. See also Stockman, *Triumph of Politics*, 356; Feldstein, "American Economic Policy in the 1980s," in *American Economic Policy in the 1980s*, 51; and Edwin Meese III, *With Reagan: The Inside Story* (Washington, D.C.: Regnery Publishing, 1992), 142–47. On the support of the Reagan administration for a bipartisan approach, see Donald T. Regan to Dan Rostenkowski, July 12, 1982, folder Tax Issues (3), and Kenneth M. Duberstein, "Meeting with Senator William Roth," August 10, 1982, folder Tax Issues (4), OA 14862, Frederick McClure Files, RRL.

supported such cuts, he found the language of tax reform. During the summer of 1982, when the loophole closing encountered resistance in Congress from conservative Republicans, Reagan made one of his longest speeches to the nation on economic affairs and emphasized that "closing off special interest loopholes" would promote "simple fairness" for "every American, especially those in lower income brackets."[10]

The outcome of Reagan's leadership and the bipartisan cooperation were three measures that combined tax increases with structural reform. The first was the Tax Equity and Fiscal Responsibility Act of 1982 (TEFRA), which imposed the first major tax increase during an election year in peacetime since 1932. TEFRA reduced some of the tax benefits for investment, thus starting to reverse the move that ERTA had begun toward a zero or even negative tax rate on income from physical capital.

The second was a reform in financing the Social Security system, which seemed to be unable to support rising levels of benefits. In December 1981, after the administration took political hits for cost-cutting initiatives, Reagan signed an executive order creating the National Commission on Social Security Reform. In the autumn of 1982, the commission reported its recommendations, and in December, under the pressure of the looming deficits, the president decided to support the recommendations. In 1983, a bipartisan group in Congress, working with Social Security loyalists, experts in the Treasury, and the leadership of the Reagan administration, turned the recommendations into a compromise solution, which included a permanent reduction in Social Security benefits,

---

[10] "Text of the Address by the President to the Nation," August 16, 1982, folder Tax Issues (4), OA 14862, Frederick McClure Files, RRL. On the administration's efforts to highlight the base-broadening elements in TEFRA, see "Fact Sheet, The Equity and Fiscal Responsibility Act of 1982," folder Tax Issues (3), OA 14862, Frederick McClure Files, RRL.

an acceleration of previously scheduled increases in rates of Social Security taxation, and an expansion of the tax base through the taxation of benefits.

Once again, Reagan took the position that the federal government was not increasing taxes. The rate increase he accepted was already scheduled to take place in 1990. So he argued that earlier administrations, not his, had increased the Social Security tax rate, and he was merely advancing the timetable. And he concluded that the broadening of the tax base through the taxation of benefits amounted to just a reduction in net benefits. This compromise, coupled with the relatively small numbers of retirees in the 1990s (largely children of the Depression era), produced a strong rate of recovery of the trust fund (at least until a good number of "baby boomers" retired).[11]

The third measure was the Deficit Reduction Act of 1984 (DEFRA, rhyming with TEFRA), which closed additional income-tax loopholes. Taken together, TEFRA and DEFRA raised revenues on the average of $100 billion a year at 1990 levels of income. Increases this big had never been enacted except during major wars. These measures along with the Social Security reforms meant that Reagan had taken major steps backward from his dramatic tax cut of 1981.[12]

CONSIDERATION OF A "FLAT TAX" AND SYSTEMATIC BASE BROADENING

As members of the White House staff investigated and proposed base-broadening measures, both Democrats and Republicans in

[11] See C. Eugene Steuerle, *The Tax Decade: How Taxes Came to Dominate the Public Agenda* (Washington, D.C.: Urban Institute Press, 1992), 61–64.
[12] For an overview of the tax increases in DEFRA, see Steuerle, *Tax Decade*, 64–69.

Congress forced the Reagan administration to discuss as well the introduction of a "flat tax." In its extreme form, such a tax would have eliminated all deductions, exemptions, and credits and replaced the progressive tax structure with a single low rate of tax. It also would have, in effect, converted the income tax into a tax on consumption while maintaining some progressivity by providing a credit or exemption against the first dollars of tax.[13]

Between mid-1981 and mid-1982, members of Congress, including both Democrats and Republicans, introduced about a dozen bills designed to create versions of a flat tax. In May 1982, Secretary of the Treasury Regan told the House of Representative's Ways and Means Committee that he was intrigued by the flat-tax concept. Later that month, Senator Dole, the chair of the Finance Committee, announced that he would hold hearings on the tax, and the press reported that Senator Bill Bradley (Democrat–New Jersey), who was a member of the Senate Finance Committee, would soon join with Congressman Richard A. Gephardt (Democrat-Missouri) in sponsoring legislation that would provide for a tax with flatter rates coupled with a surtax on higher incomes that would replace the top rate of 50 percent with one of 28 percent.

Bradley, inspired in part by Stanley Surrey's earlier reform program, had, in fact, became enthusiastic about broadening the base of income taxation. He had become convinced that the idea made economic sense, and that Democratic sponsorship of such reform would have voter appeal. In 1982, he drew effectively on the advice of experts—such as economists Joseph Minarik of the Congressional Budget Office and Randy Weiss, who was on the staff of the Joint Committee on Taxation—to draft the base-broadening bill. But Democrats on the Finance Committee were reluctant to

---

[13] Even in the extreme version, therefore, the tax was a two-rate tax, with the first rate equal to zero.

undertake a comprehensive attack on tax expenditures, and Bradley found himself an outsider within the committee.[14]

Within the Reagan administration, however, systematic tax reform along base-broadening lines gathered support.[15] Over the Christmas holidays in 1982, during a round of golf, Secretary of State George Shultz pressed the idea upon the president, who, according to David Stockman, saw classic supply-side possibilities. "By the eighteenth hole," Stockman wrote, "the President was convinced this was a way to reduce the deficit without increasing taxes." In Stockman's account, the president pressed the idea on Regan and Meese as a way of both lowering taxes and immediately reducing the deficit. "Soon," Stockman recalled, "everyone around the White House was talking flat tax." Richard Darman, Baker's deputy chief of staff and key adviser for economic matters, recalled that by January 1983, a "faction...favored proposing radical tax reform, replacing the progressive income tax with either a flat tax or a consumed income tax that would exempt net savings and investment from any tax at all."

Stockman, Darman, and Martin Feldstein, the chair of the Council of Economic Advisers from 1982 to 1984, however, all had reservations about moving quickly toward a flat tax. They worried about versions that would increase deficits even further. They questioned the supply-side assumptions of a swift payoff in increased revenues that seemed to drive the president's interest in

---

[14] On congressional interest in the flat tax in 1982, see "Flat-Rate Tax Advanced as Radical Cure for Problems of Existing Revenue System," *Congressional Quarterly*, June 5, 1982, 1331–34.

[15] The following discussion of deliberations within the White House in late 1982 and 1983 draws upon the consistent recollections of David Stockman and Richard Darman. See Stockman, *Triumph of Politics*, 355–65, and Richard Darman, *Who's in Control? Polar Politics and the Sensible Center* (New York: Simon & Schuster, 1996), 118–19.

tax cutting. "They don't actually believe this mumbo-jumbo, do they?" Feldstein asked Stockman after a meeting in which the president pushed the flat tax. Baker and Darman cooled further as they contemplated the political fallout from radical reform along flat-tax lines—reform that would require, for example, repeal of the deduction of interest payments on home mortgages. In addition, the president may have begun to worry about the possibility that the flat tax might increase taxes for "poorer taxpayers," in Secretary Regan's words.[16] In January 1983, as Stockman recalled, "Schultz's original flat tax idea was packed off to Siberia, in this case a 'deep study mode' at Treasury with a view to 'broadening, simplifying and reforming the income tax.'"

"Siberia" turned out not to be all that remote. During the rest of 1983, Secretary Regan and his staff paid serious attention to the adoption of a flat tax or significant broadening of the income base, and the secretary grew increasingly enthusiastic about such reform. He appreciated the virtues of making the tax system more economically efficient. His years on Wall Street as a broker predisposed him to favor tax reform that would remove tax shelters that drew investment capital away from more productive activities. He recalled that he had "chafed under laws that gave the banking industry tax breaks that brokerage firms were denied" and stressed that "when the same concept is extended to entire industries, the results" are "absurd." He was opposed to "industrial policy," whether it came through regulation or through tax expenditures. Moreover, he had become

---

[16] Donald Regan's recollections point to the president's concern about the loss of progressiveness in the flat tax; see Regan, *For the Record*, 198. His recollections are consistent with his comments in "Interview of Donald T. Regan by Alan Murray of the *Wall Street Journal*, Anne Swardson of the *Washington Post*, and Peter Kilborn of the *New York Times*," July 9, 1986, folder Tax Reform 1985 (4), OA 14862, Frederick McClure Files, RRL. In this interview, Regan said that the administration had had reservations about a flat tax because it "would increase taxes for a heck of lot of people."

intrigued by the prospect of further cuts in marginal rates of income taxation. He understood that in the face of the budget deficits, base broadening provided the only means to pay for such cuts.[17]

In December 1983, during a meeting in which the president and his advisers were preparing for the 1984 State of the Union address, Regan seized his moment.[18] He began by shocking the president with the news that in 1982, the president's personal secretary had paid more federal taxes than General Electric, Boeing, General Dynamics, and fifty-seven "other big companies" combined. The president, according to Regan, did not believe him, but the Treasury secretary persisted: "The time has come to do something fundamental about the tax system. It's too complicated, it's grotesquely unfair, and it's a drag on the economy because it discourages competition." The president finally seemed to yield. "I agree, Don," he said. "I just didn't realize that things had gotten that far out of line." Regan believed he had his marching orders "to go full steam ahead with a proposal to overhaul the entire federal structure as to purge it of inequities, plug its loopholes, and lower the rates for individual taxpayers."

Reagan, in fact, was still not convinced. Nor were Reagan's other close advisers. Baker and Darman preferred to focus on deficit reduction, and they questioned the politics of serious base-broadening reform. However, Baker was worried that Democratic presidential candidate Walter Mondale might base his campaign on tax issues, especially if Reagan and Congress had to raise taxes again. Mondale might, Baker believed, run against Reagan's tax increases, past and future, and at the same time, with the support of Senator Bill Bradley, pick up the banner of tax reform that President Carter had dropped. So, Baker concluded, taking up the mantle of tax

---

[17] Regan, *For the Record*, 207; "Interview of Donald T. Regan."

[18] The following account, including the quotations, is based on Secretary Regan's recollections. See Regan, *For the Record*, 196–203.

reformer might prevent the Democrats from outflanking Reagan with a powerfully attractive domestic issue.[19]

Reagan, therefore, laid the groundwork for possibly playing, once again, the role of tax reformer. In his State of the Union speech, he said that he was "asking Secretary of the Treasury Don Regan for a plan...to simplify the entire tax code so all taxpayers, big and small, are treated more fairly." But few took the president seriously. When he said he was not asking for the plan to be delivered until after the election, in December 1984, almost a year later, the Democratic side of the audience broke out in peals of laughter.

Despite the laughter, the momentum for comprehensive base broadening grew during 1984. Public opinion became a crucial factor. Congressional debates over DEFRA raised awareness of the extent to which loopholes had perverted the tax code. So did intense newspaper advertising for tax shelters designed for people at all income levels. And a wide variety of well-publicized studies showed that many corporations with significant income paid little or no taxes. Among these studies was that of a public interest lawyer, Robert McIntyre, a protégé of Ralph Nader. McIntyre, who worked for a labor-funded organization called Citizens for Tax Justice, combed the annual reports of 250 of the nation's largest companies and discovered that more than half of them had paid no federal income tax for at least one year between 1981 and 1983. Public confidence in the fundamental fairness of the federal income tax was rapidly eroding, and public opinion began to push Reagan toward base broadening.[20]

---

[19] On Baker's political concerns, see Feldstein, "American Economic Policy in the 1980s: A Personal View," and Russell Long, "Summary of Discussion, Tax Policy," in *American Economic Policy in the 1980s*, 20, 226; Timothy J. Conlan et al., *Taxing Choices: The Politics of Tax Reform* (Washington, D.C.: Congressional Quarterly Press, 1990), 48–49.

[20] For a description of the growing public awareness of tax shelters for individuals and corporations in 1984, see Jeffrey H. Birnbaum and Alan

Tax reform, nonetheless, did not become a central issue in the 1984 campaign. During the summer, the president's advisers worried that Mondale might propose what Darman described as a "soak-the-rich-end-the-unfair-loopholes-and-hit-the-big-corporations-plan" for reducing the deficit. They worried that the president would be caught between a Mondale initiative and Republican supply-siders who wanted him to rule out any tax increase. But Mondale decided against running as a tax reformer, and he never specified how he would raise taxes. He thereby allowed the Republicans to present a united front on tax policy.[21]

Meanwhile, during 1984, the Treasury accelerated its work on tax reform. Secretary Regan shielded Treasury experts from members of Congress seeking to expand or protect tax expenditures, from the inquiring eyes of the press, and from the interventions of other members of the administration, the experts.[22] This allowed the economic coordinator of the project, C. Eugene Steuerle, Assistant Secretaries for Tax Policy John E. (Buck) Chapoton and Ronald Pearlman, and Deputy Assistant Secretary for Tax Analysis

S. Murray, *Showdown at Gucci Gulch: Lawmakers, Lobbyists, and the Unlikely Triumph of Tax Reform* (New York: Random House, 1987), 11–13.

[21] On Baker and Darman's concerns about Mondale, see W. Elliot Brownlee and C. Eugene Steuerle, "Taxation," in *The Reagan Presidency: Pragmatic Conservatism and Its Legacies*, ed. W. Elliot Brownlee and Hugh D. Graham (Lawrence: University Press of Kansas, 2003), 169–70.

[22] Among those whom Regan kept out of the process were the members of the Council of Economic Advisers (CEA). William Niskanen, who became acting chair of the CEA in July 1984, recalled that he "asked Regan to allow me to participate in these reviews." Regan told him "bluntly that no one outside Treasury would be informed about the developing plan until after the election." The Treasury, Niskanen noted, had "an effective monopoly within the administration over the formulation of tax policy"; Niskanen, *Reaganomics: An Insider's Account of the Policies and the People* (New York: Oxford University Press, 1988), 87.

Charles E. McLure to craft an exceptionally coherent set of reform proposals.

As the project team worked, they developed a powerful sense of mission: that of offering to the nation an income-tax system that would be economically rational and would, at the same time, respond to the drumbeat of populist complaint and help restore the confidence of Americans in their tax system and their government. By the time of the 1984 elections, they had completed and submitted to Secretary Regan a far-reaching set of proposals known as "Treasury I." These proposals implemented Henry Simons's theory of comprehensive income taxation, attacked "tax-code socialism" and "industrial policy in the tax code," attempted to index everything for inflation, and proposed elimination of the investment tax credit and restoration of longer depreciation schedules in exchange for lower tax rates for corporations and individual investors.[23]

Immediately following the 1984 elections, Secretary Regan presented Treasury I to the president. The secretary once again appealed to Reagan's sense of fairness. He asked Reagan how much tax he had paid before he became president. Reagan reported a large figure. "Sucker," Regan replied, and went on to explain: "With the right lawyer and the right accountant and the right tax shelters, you needn't have paid a penny in taxes even if you made more than a million dollars a year—and it would have been perfectly legal and proper." Regan went on to make his point: "The tax system we have now is designed to make the avoidance of taxes easy for the rich and has the effect of making it almost impossible for people who work for wages and salaries to do the same."

The president, however, was still uncertain. The threat from Mondale had ended, and Reagan was now worried about opening

---

[23] On the process for drafting Treasury I, and its provisions, see Brownlee and Steuerle, "Taxation"; and Steuerle, *Tax Decade*, 102–14.

a major offensive against loopholes and taking on the traditional Republican elites who had benefited from them. After the briefing, which lasted for nearly two hours (the longest period that the secretary of the treasury had spent with the president), Reagan still failed to make a firm commitment. But he did give the secretary permission to release the report to the public after Regan pointed out that it was already leaking to the press.[24]

After release, the study commanded wide attention. At first, retreat seemed to be in the air, as interest groups loudly protested. Even Secretary Regan stated that "it was written on a word processor" and could easily be changed.[25] But White House staffers began to notice that Treasury I was receiving enthusiastic publicity as well. And the positive responses were bipartisan. Most of the conservative and liberal press gave the report rave reviews, and support emerged from both conservative and liberal think tanks, including the American Enterprise Institute as well as the Brookings Institution.[26] Meanwhile, savvy advisers like Baker and Darman began to realize that tax reform, which was clearly winning popular support, might fill a void in the presidential agenda. Major domestic policy initiatives had languished after 1981, except for the rather painful political actions in DEFRA, TEFRA, and Social Security reform, for which Congress had provided most of the leadership. But still, the president had not signed on. Then, in January 1985, Baker, the White House chief of staff, and Secretary of the Treasury Regan swapped jobs.

Whatever the reasons for this job swap, it put Regan in a position to push the president harder on tax reform. And Baker and Darman,

---

[24] For a description of the briefing, including the Regan quotation, see Lou Cannon, *President Reagan: The Role of a Lifetime* (New York: Simon & Schuster, 1991), 565–66.

[25] Regan, *For the Record*, 283.

[26] On the cheering by economists, see Conlan et al., *Taxing Choices*, 68–69.

who accompanied Baker to Treasury as deputy secretary, wished to put their mark on a historic tax reform.[27] They had concluded that broad-based tax reform, coupled with even lower tax rates, would help the Republican Party adapt to the structural shifts associated with the growth of industries focused on finance, knowledge, technology, trade, and entertainment. They turned their formidable political skills to the task of what they regarded as domesticating Treasury I. They turned it into Treasury II, a document that was less pure but had a greater chance of enactment.

Regan, Baker, and Darman finally persuaded the president to endorse the principles of Treasury I, which he did in his State of the Union message of January 1985. By May, the president had met with his staff and personally reviewed each key provision of Treasury II.[28] While Reagan was not aware of many of the technicalities, the proposal did have an ingredient necessary to win his support—a further lowering of the top tax rate. And the president was now eager to assume the role of tax reformer. Reagan and his administration had become more interested in promoting unsubsidized competition and tax equity than in protecting traditional corporate bureaucracies and the other beneficiaries of loopholes.[29]

---

[27] In 1996, Darman recalled that before leaving the White House for the Treasury, he had put tax reform on the "top of the domestic list" and that this "made Treasury an exciting and attractive opportunity for me as well as Baker." See Darman, *Who's in Control?* 139–40.

[28] On the president's review of the administration's tax reform measure, see Brownlee and Steuerle, "Taxation."

[29] Assistant Secretary of the Treasury Richard Darman later described the enterprise-favoring elimination of tax expenditures as "tax populism." See Richard G. Darman, "Populist Force Behind Tax Reform Suggests Future Culture Shifts," *Financier* 10 (December 1986): 23–32; and Darman, "Beyond Tax Populism," *Society* 24 (September–October 1987): 35–38.

THE TAX REFORM ACT OF 1986

On May 28, 1985, Reagan announced his tax proposals for "fairness, growth, and simplicity" in a nationally televised speech. The speech appealed to both the spirit of enterprise capitalism and a sense of tax justice—tax justice rooted not in the vertical equity of progressive taxation but in the horizontal equity of a tax that provided uniform treatment to broad categories of taxpayers. His proposal would, he said, "free us from the grip of special interests." He was proposing reduced tax rates "by simplifying the complex system of special provisions that favor some at the expense of others." There would be "one group of losers in our tax plan—those individuals and corporations who are not paying their fair share, or for that matter, any share. These abuses cannot be tolerated. From now on, they shall pay a minimum tax. The free rides are over." The president followed with an open letter to Congress, which struck the same themes. He told Congress that "we face an historic challenge: to change our present tax system into a model of fairness, simplicity, efficiency, and compassion, to remove the obstacles to growth and unlock the door to a future of unparalleled innovation and achievement."[30]

The next day, he hit the same themes in a press conference and a meeting with what the White House described as "200 representatives of blue collar, ethnic, business, agricultural, religious, black, Hispanic and other interest groups." He ridiculed the "tax

---

[30] "The President's Tax Proposals to the Congress for Fairness, Growth, and Simplicity," Summary, May 1985, folder Tax Reform 1985 (3), OA 14862, Frederick McClure Files, RRL; "Address by the President to the Nation," May 28, 1985, folder Tax Reform (5), OA 17746, Beryl Sprinkel Files, OA 17746, RRL. Ronald Reagan to the Congress of the United States, May 29, 1985, folder Tax Reform 1985 (3), OA 14862, Frederick McClure Files, RRL.

breaks for things like windmills and so-called 'educational' cruises on ocean liners and the famous three-martini lunch." They were "tax dodges, which are really no more than windfalls to a privileged few—windfalls that everyone else ends up paying for through higher tax rates." Reagan now identified tax expenditures for what they were, and linked to his earlier fight against government. Some in Congress, he said, "were happier in the bad old days, when they could waste billions of the taxpayers' dollars before breakfast, and there was nobody around to stop them." The tax code, Reagan said, was "an outrage, one riddled through with special privileges and inequities, that violates our most fundamental American values of justice and fair play." He even invoked the myth of the American Revolution as tax revolt:

I don't think Americans can recognize an injustice without trying to change it. That's how this great country got started—our forefathers rebelled against the injustice of oppressive taxation. In place of King George's despotism, they created a government of, by, and for the people, a new democratic Nation in which every individual was treated equally. Today, we are undertaking another great adventure in freedom, a Second American Revolution, a peaceful revolution of hope and opportunity, and one of its first orders of business is to toss our present, moldy tax code overboard and get a new one.[31]

The president then barnstormed around the nation and pounded away at the same points. At times, he became tangled in the specifics of his proposal.[32] But he stayed on the high ground of tax justice

---

[31] Frederick J. Ryan Jr. to Linda Chavez, "Drop by Coalition for Tax Reform, May 29, 1985," The White House, Christena L. Bach Files, RRL; "Presidential Address: Tax Reform Briefing, May 23, 1985," RRL.

[32] E.g., on June 19, when he met with businesspeople in Mooresville, Indiana, Reagan hesitated when someone asked him how his proposal would simplify the tax code. He said, "Wow," and turned to Donald Regan for help in answering. David Hoffman, "President Postpones Tax Blitz," *Washington Post*, July 4, 1985.

and galvanized audiences. The White House was delighted with the polls, and the president relished the applause. Regan recalled that the president's triumphant speaking tour restored his confidence in his own popularity.[33] The proposal seemed to give Reagan's second term a point of focus, just as ERTA had done for the first term. Moreover, both ERTA and Treasury II were quite consistent in the president's mind with his primary goal of tax-rate reduction.

During the months that it took for the tax bill to crawl through the legislative process, the president's radio messages and speeches continued to drum up public support for tax fairness.[34] Whoever wished to attack Treasury II had to invoke principles more compelling than those of the president. The leaders of the congressional tax-writing committees decided that they had to transform themselves and become advocates of horizontal equity and the kind of economic efficiency that results from lowering rates in exchange for a broader base.

Democrat Daniel Rostenkowski (Illinois), chair of the House Ways and Means Committee, became a powerful advocate of the new approach to reform. He did not share Bradley's intellectual enthusiasm for it, but he respected the base-broadening advice he received from the staff of the Joint Committee on Taxation, and he saw ideological merit in joining the movement. He was convinced that the Democrats, as well as the president, had to be visible advocates of reform. He declared, "I'm a Democrat. Reform, fairness— they've all been in the Democratic platform for as long as I've been a Democrat. And I'm not going to let Ronald Reagan get to my left, I'll tell you that much."[35]

---

[33] Regan, *For the Record*, 286.

[34] In the following discussion of congressional deliberations, I draw heavily on Birnbaum and Murray, *Showdown at Gucci Gulch*, 96 ff., and Conlan et al., *Taxing Choices*, 84 ff.

[35] The quotation is from Conlan et al., *Taxing Choices*, 89.

Rostenkowski enthusiastically assumed a highly public role, speaking on television for the party in response to the president's May 1985 call for tax reform. More than 75,000 persons answered his call to write "R-O-S-T-Y, Washington, D.C. . . . and stand up for fairness and lower taxes." Afterward, Rostenkowski bragged that "I really took over the [Democratic] party on that 'Write Rosty' speech."[36]

Rostenkowski also worked for reform behind the scenes, countering the lobbyists representing those who would lose from Treasury II. He even enlisted the help of Bill Bradley, although Bradley was only a marginal player on the Senate Finance Committee. Bradley met with the senior members of the House, with almost every Democratic member of Ways and Means, and with many legislators not on the committee, including the liberal Democratic Study Group. While Bradley courted liberal Democrats, Rostenkowski assured lobbyists that the probusiness Senate would defeat any radical House bill. He told conservative Democrats the same thing, pointing out that this would embarrass Reagan and the Republican Party. Meanwhile, Reagan urged Republicans to support Rostenkowski's reform bill if a Republican version could not win Ways and Means endorsement, and he reassured them that he would veto any bill that imposed a maximum rate higher than in the president's original proposal.[37]

---

[36] The quotation is from Birnbaum and Murray, *Showdown at Gucci Gulch*, 99–100.

[37] On Reagan's lobbying of Republicans early in December, see Ronald Reagan to William Gradison Jr., December 9, 1985, Beryl Sprinkel Files, RRL; "Text of a Letter from the President to the Members of the House of Representatives," December 9, 1985, Office of the Press Secretary, the White House, Frederick McClure Files, RRL; "Radio Address of the President to the Nation," December 14, 1985, Office of the Press Secretary, the White House, Frederick McClure Files, RRL; Ronald Reagan to Robert Michel, December 16, 1985, and Ronald Reagan to Jack Kemp, December 16, 1985, Frederick McClure Files, Ronald Reagan Presidential Archives.

Rostenkowski's tenacity, the effective support of Rostenkowski by the staffs of the Ways and Means Committee and the Joint Committee on Taxation, particularly Chief of Staff David Brockway, and the active lobbying of Republicans by Reagan combined to bring success: enough bipartisan support for the House to pass a reform bill on December 16, 1985. This bill provided for somewhat greater tax benefits for individuals than had Treasury II—deductibility of mortgage interest for second homes, of up to $20,000 of consumer interest, and of 100 percent of state and local taxes. The House bill compensated for the revenue loss from these deductions by increasing corporate tax rates and the top rates on individuals. But many reformers feared the Republican-controlled Senate Finance Committee would sabotage their plans.

The Senate Finance Committee, however, did not bury reform. In fact, it produced an even more radical version of tax reform and approved it unanimously. The chair of the Senate Finance Committee, Robert Packwood (Republican-Oregon), was crucial in keeping reform alive.

Packwood was an even more bizarre candidate for a leader of tax reform than was Rostenkowski. Since becoming chair of the Finance Committee in 1984, Packwood had shown that he was firmly within a tradition of using the position to provide incentives to private industry and social programs. During the eighteen months before the passage of the Tax Reform Act of 1986, Packwood received almost $1 million from political action committees—more than any other member of Congress. But the president's leadership turned Packwood, who was up for reelection in 1986, into a reformer. He did not want to take the blame for the death of reform.

After long weeks in which it looked like tax reform would in fact perish in the Finance Committee, Packwood adopted a bold, alternative plan suggested by the staff of the Joint Committee on Taxation. In April, over a "two-pitcher" lunch at a Washington bar, he and a key political staffer concluded that the only way to win the support of the Finance Committee was to lower the top individual income-tax rate below the rate proposed by the House—to drive it down from 38 to 25 percent, if possible. "No guts, no glory," is the way Packwood later described his attitude.[38]

Packwood, also like Rostenkowski, discovered Bradley as a valuable ally. Packwood praised Bradley's original bill and made him a committee insider. With Bradley's support, Packwood and his staff drafted a plan that lowered the corporate rate from 36 percent in the House bill to 33 percent and retained only two rates for individuals: 15 and 25 percent. The plan proposed abolishing all deductions for mortgage interest, consumer interest, and charitable contributions. Support within the committee grew, and Senate Majority Leader Dole, who had been chair of the Senate Finance Committee until 1984, also signed on. The committee made only a few changes. (The committee increased the highest individual rate to 32 percent and the top corporate rate to 33 percent; it restored certain oil and gas write-offs and protected the ability of banks to deduct for bad-debt reserves; and it added a variety of deductions— those for mortgage interest for first and second homes, charitable contributions by those who itemized returns, and state and local income taxes.)

In May 1986, Packwood's bill won unanimous support from the committee. President Reagan immediately lavished praise on the committee and its chair. On May 10, in his weekly radio address, the president declared: "Thanks to the heroic work of Senator Bob Packwood, members of his Finance Committee and our Administration, the political entrepreneurs have just won a magnificent first

---

[38] The quotation is from Birnbaum and Murray, *Showdown at Gucci Gulch*, 208. For a discussion of the intellectual context for Packwood's conversion to reform see Conlan et al., *Taxing Choices*, 163–65, and for a critical assessment of Packwood see Steuerle, *Taxing Decade*, 115–16. Packwood may have settled the idea of a 25 percent minimum rate as early as July 1985. See White House notes on "Packwood," July 11, 1985, Beryl Sprinkel Files, RRL.

victory over the stagnating forces of the status quo." He went on to urge "Republicans and Democrats to unite to move this legislation through Congress as fast as possible—so that you the people can make America the world's economic superstar through the nineties and the year 2000." On May 14, he told the Tax Reform Action Coalition that Packwood's bill was "the kind of straightforward, hard-hitting proposal that's enough to restore one's faith ... that this truly is a system of the people, by the people, and for the people." Once again, he warned that some people would face higher taxes. But those who would pay more, he said, were "those who have made extensive use of tax shelters and other schemes and have not really been paying proportionately a fair share of the tax burden."[39]

The bipartisan support engineered by Packwood and Bradley moved the bill quickly through the Senate, which adopted it on June 24, 1986. Many lobbyists sought to curry favor with Packwood by supporting the drastic reforms. They hoped to gut the final bill within the conference committee that would reconcile the House and Senate bills.

The two bills contained key elements of agreement. Both bills provided important benefits for lower-income groups through sharp increases in the personal exemption, the standard deduction, and the Earned Income Tax Credit (EITC). The EITC, created as a minor program in 1975, allowed low-income families to count a portion of their income, which declined as their income rose, as a credit against their taxes.

But the bills contained some significant differences, which the conference committee had to iron out. The House bill closed many

[39] "Presidential Radio Talk: Taxes, May 10, 1986, "Remarks by the President to Tax Reform Action Coalition," the White House, Office of the Press Secretary, May 14, 1986, and "Remarks by the President," May 20, 1986, the White House, Office of the Press Secretary, copies in Frederick McClure Files, RRL.

corporate loopholes but was less aggressive in eliminating the tax preferences used by individuals. In contrast, the Senate bill made sweeping reforms on the individual side of the tax code but left more corporate tax breaks unchallenged. And the top rates on both individuals and corporations were lower in the Senate bill— 32 versus 38 percent for individuals and 33 versus 36 percent for corporations.

Rostenkowski and Packwood struck much of the final deal in private, removed from the direct pressure of the contending interests. Rostenkowski, impressed by public enthusiasm for lower rates, agreed to accept rates very close to those proposed by the Senate. In the heyday of the era of easy finance, this might have been the final bargain, with each party claiming credit for significant tax reductions. But at this point, the influence of another factor—a critical factor in differentiating the 1986 tax reforms from earlier ones— came decisively into play.

This new factor was the restrictive fiscal and economic environment. Massive deficits and ERTA meant that Congress could no longer enact its traditional "reform" bills—ones providing significant tax reductions to particular groups—that reduced the overall level of taxation. Nor could Congress any longer rely on inflation- or growth-driven tax increases to finance tax reductions. Congress had to pay for every reduction in tax rates and every increase in tax loopholes by identifying losers—through a reduction in loopholes elsewhere in the tax code.[40]

---

[40] The Gramm-Rudman-Hollings Act, which Congress passed in 1985, also may have contributed to fiscal discipline. The act required automatic reductions in spending whenever the deficit exceeded prescribed levels. But it did not require tax increases, and Congress was often able to work around its requirements. Its effective restraint on expenditures was probably modest. For discussions of the influence of the changed fiscal circumstances, see Steuerle, *Tax Decade*, and "Financing the American State at the Turn of the Century," in *Funding the Modern American State*, ed. Brownlee, 410–45.

In their negotiations, Rostenkowski and Packwood implemented the goal of revenue neutrality. Each of them paid for the rate reductions by sacrificing some of their favorite tax expenditures. Rostenkowski agreed to give up some benefits for individual taxpayers. He agreed to eliminate the deductibility of a variety of items: consumer interest, state and local sales taxes, individual retirement accounts for those with pension plans, and charitable contributions for those who did not itemize their deductions. Packwood agreed to cutting an even wider swath through corporate tax preferences. For example, the final bill repealed for the largest banks the deductions they could take for bad-debt reserves and cut back for the biggest oil producers their write-offs of intangible drilling costs. As a consequence of Packwood's going even further in assaulting "tax socialism," the major losers in 1986 were numerous corporations and industries for whom the loss of benefits from the investment tax credit, the preferential taxation of long-term capital gains, and a variety of tax shelters was greater than their gains from the reduction of the top corporate rate from 48 to 34 percent.

In September, the conference committee approved the deal, and President Reagan again called on the American people for support. In a radio address on September 20, he asked Americans to "support our effort to defeat the special interests and win one for the hardworking taxpayers of this country." At the same time, he wrote to key Republicans in the House, urging their support for the conference bill. He tried to allay their concerns with the pledge that "once this bill is enacted I will not support any legislation that raises its income tax rates."[41] With the support of these House Republicans, Congress approved the conference version. The president signed the

---

[41] "Radio Address by the President to the Nation," September 20, 1986, Office of the Press Secretary, the White House, Frederick McClure File; Ronald Reagan to Jack Kemp, September 23, 1986, Frederick McClure Files, RRL.

legislation into law on October 22. On the White House lawn, he declared: "When I sign this bill into law, America will have . . . the most modern tax code among major industrialized nations. Fair and simpler for most Americans, this is a tax code designed to take us into a future of technological invention and economic achievement, one that will keep America competitive and growing into the 21st century." He concluded, "I feel like we just played the World Series of tax reform. And the American people won."[42]

The reform act (1) reduced individual tax rates across the board; (2) lowered the marginal rate at the highest incomes from 50 to 28 percent;[43] (3) increased personal exemptions and standard deductions, taking 6 million poorer Americans off the tax rolls; (4) expanded the EITC to provide a major increase in the "negative" income tax to millions of poorer Americans; (5) increased capital-gains taxes for those at the highest incomes from 20 to 28 percent; (6) reduced the top corporate rate from 48 to 34 percent; and (7) slashed tax expenditures, particularly those applying to businesses or investment (e.g., it repealed the investment tax credit).

For the first time since World War II, a major piece of tax legislation picked not only winners but also a significant number of losers. The losers in 1986 were the many individuals, corporations, and industries for which the loss of preferences was greater than their gains from the reduction of the top rates. The biggest losers were those that sold tax shelters and some traditional Rust Belt industries. The oil industry emerged with its deductions relatively

[42] Ronald Reagan, "Remarks by the President at the Signing Ceremony for Tax Reform Legislation," October 22, 1986, folder Tax Reform 1985 (4), OA 14862, Frederick McClure Files, RRL.
[43] There was, however, a 33 percent "bubble." This 33 percent rate applied at high (but not the highest) income levels until the individual paid an effective rate of 28 percent on all income. At that point, the 28 percent kicked back in again.

unscathed, largely because of the intervention of Baker and Vice President George H. W. Bush.[44]

In fact, however, those companies benefiting from large deductions actually lost because lower rates made their deductions less valuable. Among businesses, the biggest winners were investment bankers, high-technology industries, service industries, and some multinational firms. The Tax Reform Act of 1986 helped finance cuts in individual income taxes by raising corporate taxes by nearly $120 billion over the next five years, although the net increase in effective rates on capital income was fairly small because of an offsetting drop in personal tax rates.[45]

In his memoirs, Reagan declared: "With the tax cuts of 1981 and the Tax Reform Act of 1986, I'd accomplished a lot of what I'd come to Washington to do."[46]

In sum, in 1986 a bipartisan group of political entrepreneurs, led by President Reagan and Senator Bradley, had successfully championed an approach to tax reform never previously associated with either of the two major parties: focusing reform of the income tax on broadening its income base and creating a more uniform—a more

---

[44] The crucial meeting in which George Bush defended the oil industry was on May 21, 1985; Birnbaum and Murray, *Showdown at Gucci Gulch*, 94. On May 23, the president initialed his approval for the changes favoring the oil industry. James A. Baker III to the President, "Fundamental Tax Reform" [outline of the president's "guidance" on May 21], May 23, 1985, ID 271493SS, FI010-02, WHORM Subject File, RRL.

[45] The increase in corporate taxes can be misleading, however. Many corporations, including IBM and General Motors, favored the reform because they believed that they would profit from being in the competitive, lower-rate environment. Moreover, the effective rate of tax on investment depends on the combination of corporate and individual rates, and this effective rate increased only slightly, mainly through compromises made after Treasury I, on the way to enactment.

[46] Ronald Reagan, *An American Life: The Autobiography* (New York: Simon & Schuster, 1990), 335.

"horizontally" equitable—tax. The resulting legislation—the Tax
Reform Act of 1986—was even more consequential than ERTA.
The 1986 act amounted to the most dramatic transformation of
federal tax policy since World War II.

Both the Reagan administration and many Democratic liberals welcomed the act's emphasis on broadening the income-tax
base. For both, the act was most important because of the way it
moved toward eliminating tax-based privilege. Doing so would promote both fairness—horizontal equity—and economic efficiency.
The Reagan administration and leading Democrats placed different emphases on the other elements of the reform package. Both
Donald Regan and Bill Bradley believed in the importance of bringing down marginal tax rates to promote economic efficiency in the
face of the sluggish growth of national productivity. But overall, this
was of greater interest to Republicans than Democrats. Democratic
liberals, conversely, put more emphasis than did their Republican
colleagues, including many members of the Reagan administration,
on taking poor people off the tax rolls and increasing the negative
income tax.

All participants in the reform process were uncertain as to what
would be the overall distributional effects of the complex reform
package. As it turned out, the combination of loophole closing, on
the one hand, and providing tax benefits to low-income individuals,
on the other hand, was decidedly progressive. In fact, it was so
progressive that it essentially offset the regressive effects of ERTA
and the increases in Social Security taxation. The tax policies of the
"Reagan Revolution" left tax progressivity essentially unchanged.[47]

---

[47] The Congressional Budget Office has regularly published estimates of the
effective federal tax rate on families in various income categories. Its 1990
estimates showed that in 1980 and 1991, the effective tax rates for the five
quintiles of the income distribution from lowest to highest were as follows:
8.4 percent (1980), 8.5 percent (1991); 15.7 percent (1980), 16.7 percent
(1991); 20.0 percent (1980), 20.7 percent (1991); 23.0 percent (1980),

The income tax was in more flux during the 1980s than at any other time since the 1940s. Taxes had turned out to be "up for grabs" to a degree that was surprising to almost all observers. To some tax experts—those who had championed base-broadening reform—the political flux and the substantive content of the 1986 reforms created new opportunities. Joseph Pechman stressed one of them. In 1989 he estimated that, as a consequence of the 1986 elimination of tax shelters, the adoption of a very modest increase in rates—as little as 3 percentage points across the board—could raise as much as $100 billion a year. To Pechman and others, the Tax Reform Act of 1986 seemed to open the way for Congress to reinvigorate the mass-based income tax and thus extend the tax regime created during World War II.[48] Even without further modification, the income-tax system, as reformed by the Reagan administration, had maintained its ability to raise revenue. Although federal tax revenues had weakened in the early 1980s, by 1987 the individual income tax and the corporate profits tax together produced about the same tax revenues, as a percentage of gross domestic product, as they had at the outset of the Carter administration.[49]

22.9 percent (1991); and 27.3 percent (1991), 26.8 percent (1980). This calculation includes Social Security payroll taxes as well as the federal income tax. The average rate for all families barely budged between 1980 and 1991, declining from 23.3 to 23.1 percent. The top 1 percent experienced only a modest drop, from 31.8 to 28.9 percent. For details, see Steuerle, *Tax Decade*, 194–96. See also Richard Kasten, Frank Sammartino, and Eric Toder, "Trends in Federal Tax Progressivity, 1980–1993," in *Tax Progressivity and Income Inequality*, ed. Joel Slemrod (Cambridge: Cambridge University Press, 1994), 9–50.

[48] Joseph Pechman, "More Tax Reform," *Wilson Quarterly* 13 (summer 1989): 141–42.

[49] For all the data on taxes as a share of gross domestic product since 1916, see Bureau of Economic Analysis, Department of the Treasury, National Income and Product Accounts, tables 1.1, 3.2, 3.3, 3.6.

5

Reviving the old regime, 1986–2000

The shifts in national financial policy during the mid-1980s suggested that the United States had the political capacity to embrace a new fiscal regime—especially restructuring its income tax system in a fundamental way and perhaps even breaking what economist Eugene Steuerle has called "the yoke of prior commitments."[1] The tax increases of 1982 and 1984, the Social Security reforms of 1983, and the Tax Reform Act of 1986 (which accepted the principle that tax reductions should be offset by tax increases) all reflected the kind of political leadership and discipline that would be required to usher in a new fiscal regime.

Significant fiscal reform, however, stalled after the passage of the Tax Reform Act of 1986. In particular, fundamental reform of the

---

[1] See C. Eugene Steuerle, "Financing the American State at the Turn of the Century," in *Funding the Modern American State, 1941–1995: The Rise and Fall of the Era of Easy Finance*, ed. W. Elliot Brownlee (Washington, D.C.: Woodrow Wilson Center Press, and Cambridge: Cambridge University Press, 1996), 420–21. By the "yoke," Steuerle means the cost of the many programs, including tax-expenditure programs, which automatically grow more rapidly than does the economy, and which relentlessly narrow the discretion available to legislators.

tax system along the base-broadening lines chartered by the bipartisan architects of the 1986 legislation failed to advance. An essential reason was the continued, growing popular hostility to government. The antigovernment movement that gathered force during the late 1970s and the 1980s grew even stronger in the 1990s, finally capturing both houses of Congress in 1994. This movement, with its popular base in an increasingly alienated middle class, caused politicians to fear recommending the elimination of tax expenditures, such as the home mortgage deduction, that favored large segments of society, and instead to propose tax cuts that favored, or seemed to favor, the middle class. (Politicians who campaigned against government rarely attacked tax expenditures as a means of shrinking government programs.) And the growing enthusiasm for the movement also encouraged the representatives of wealthy and corporate interests to urge tax cuts that would reduce the cost of capital. The most vigorous champions of the movement increasingly harkened back to the tax cut of 1981 during Ronald Reagan's presidency as the epitome of good fiscal policy.

The antigovernment movement, however, did not produce any immediate tax cuts on the scale of the Economic Recovery Tax Act (ERTA). The administrations of both George H. W. Bush and Bill Clinton sponsored or approved significant tax cuts, but they were much smaller than those under ERTA. Three closely linked factors accounted for this blunting of the antigovernment, antitax thrust. First, the Bush and Clinton administrations believed in the economic imperative to reduce deficits. Bush did not favor encouraging deficits as a pretext for cutting entitlements drastically. And Clinton was interested in demonstrating his financial soundness to the constituency of investment bankers. Consequently, Bush and Clinton carried on the effort, begun by the Reagan administration after the passage of ERTA in 1981, to reduce budget deficits.

Second, both the Bush and Clinton administrations, with support from Congress, respected, and deferred to, the power of the

Federal Reserve Board in managing countercyclical policy. This meant—particularly during the economic expansion that stretched throughout the Clinton administration—that the makers of fiscal policy were reluctant to risk tax cuts and deficits that might stimulate harmful inflationary pressures.

Third, public enthusiasm for expensive federal programs, particularly national defense and the entitlements of Social Security and Medicare, remained powerful. The antigovernment movement stimulated far more hostility toward taxation than toward public expenditures. If the public had been enthusiastic about shrinking government, the Bush and Clinton administrations could have more easily delivered major tax cuts or reduced the fiscal burden of entitlements. Only in the twenty-first century, when some of these factors weakened, would the federal government resume the aggressive tax cutting pioneered by the Reagan administration.

During the 1990s, some Republican champions of the antigovernment movement were emboldened to launch the first important assault on the federal income tax since 1932, or at least since the beginning of U.S. involvement in World War II. But they did not win the support of the Clinton administration, which was necessary to advance such reform, let alone the support of the Democratic leadership in Congress. The American public seemed bored or bemused by this brief reform campaign. If anything, Americans retained their attachment to the principle of progressive taxation and were reluctant to sacrifice that principle. Perhaps if the reforms of the Reagan era had not made the income tax economically more efficient and more equitable, at least in a horizontal sense, Americans might have been more ready to consider radical reform. As it was, the fiscal regime inherited from World War II entered the twenty-first century having been invigorated by the Reagan administration, by the two administrations that followed, and by the economic expansion of the 1990s.

PRAGMATIC CONSERVATISM VERSUS
"READ MY LIPS: NO NEW TAXES"

After the Tax Reform Act of 1986, the Reagan administration had abandoned any major effort to reform the income tax. Neither the president nor any of his key advisers wished to press hard for more base-broadening reform of the income tax.[2]

Part of the reason was, no doubt, the fear that additional reform on behalf of horizontal equity would either threaten powerful special interests, such as those of the oil industry (which the Reagan administration had favored during the 1986 reforms), or challenge broad middle-class interests, such as those of homeowners in the deduction of mortgage interest.

In addition, Secretary of the Treasury James Baker may have worried that opening up the tax code for another round of sweeping reform would put the 1986 accomplishments at risk. The consequence might have been some combination of tax cuts that would yield increasing deficits, sacrifice of the base-broadening reforms, and a return to higher marginal rates on the wealthy.[3] Contributing as well to the inertia on tax reform within the Reagan administration was its increasing preoccupation with the Iran-Contra debacle and the related departure of Donald Regan, the White House chief-of staff, and Richard Darman, deputy secretary of the treasury, who had been central players in the Tax Reform Act of 1986.[4]

---

[2] The Omnibus Reconciliation Act of 1987, however, involved some limited base-broadening (and revenue-raising) reform of business taxation. See C. Eugene Steuerle, *The Tax Decade, 1981–1990* (Washington, D.C.: Urban Institute Press, 1992), 166–67.

[3] For this interpretation of Secretary Baker, see Steuerle, *Tax Decade*, 163.

[4] Richard Darman, *Who's in Control? Polar Politics and the Sensible Center* (New York: Simon & Schuster, 1996), 170–72.

In his campaign for president in 1987 and 1988, Vice President George H. W. Bush did nothing to advance tax reform along the bipartisan lines laid out in 1986, and he may actually have impeded any such effort.[5] He said almost nothing, at least directly, about the Reagan administration's record on taxation. And beginning in late 1987, little more than a year after the passage of the Tax Reform Act of 1986, Bush proposed various changes in the tax code, each of which would have rolled back important parts of the package of broad-based reforms.

The first and most important Bush proposal was to slash capital gains taxes from 28 to 15 percent, thus violating the 1986 principle of evenhanded treatment of all income. This proposal advanced the continuing conservative interest in cutting the cost of capital, but the president and his close friend, Nicholas Brady, who would become his secretary of the treasury, may well have been personally enthusiastic about the cuts. They were both members of "old-money" families with capital tied up in highly appreciated assets, and they may well have had a first-hand appreciation of the argument that lowering the taxation of capital gains would encourage the reinvestment of such assets in more productive activities. They believed as well that the cuts would, at least in the short run, increase tax revenues as taxpayers took increased capital gains. Darman, who would become Bush's budget director, also supported lowering the

[5] There is no comprehensive history of fiscal policy during the administration of George H. W. Bush. The best analysis we have is the first-hand account of Richard Darman, and I have drawn heavily on this memoir in my discussion. See Richard Darman, *Who's in Control? Polar Politics and the Sensible Center* (New York: Simon & Schuster, 1996), especially 198–298. However, I place less emphasis than Darman does on the role of the Gramm-Rudman-Hollings Act; see chapter 4 above, note 40. For other excellent accounts, see John Robert Greene, *The Presidency of George Bush* (Lawrence: University Press of Kansas, 2000), 79–88. Herbert S. Parmet, *George Bush: The Life of a Lone Star Yankee* (New York: A Lisa Drew Book / Scribner, 1997), 428–36, 467–70.

rates on capital gains. He argued that the cuts would reduce the taxation of purely inflationary capital gains and increase incentives for long-term investment. He believed as well that the cuts would appeal to "most farmers and middle-class homeowners."[6]

Bush designed two other proposals to appeal to powerful constituencies. One proposal was to further increase the tax breaks provided for the oil and gas industry, thus expanding the special protections that he and James Baker had carved out within the 1986 reforms. The other proposal was for a $1,000 tax credit for every low-income family. Bush made this proposal before an organization of conservative women and intended it to appeal to the interests of the conservative "new right" in strengthening the family.

Bush made one other clear promise—a promise he subsequently regarded as too clear—in the realm of tax policy. In October 1987, in announcing his candidacy, he declared: "I am not going to raise your taxes—period." At the time he made it, he may have been preoccupied with the primary in New Hampshire, which was proud of being a low-tax haven adjoining "Taxachusetts." According to correspondent Elizabeth Drew, some of Bush's campaign aides believed that Bush could change his position after he became president, but others worried about the "period" at the end of his pledge.[7] Despite their worries, after Michael Dukakis won the Democratic nomination for president, Bush turned the "period" into something stronger. In accepting the Republican nomination, he followed the advice of speechwriter Peggy Noonan and intoned her words: "Read my lips, no new taxes."

This blatant imitation of Clint Eastwood's swagger in films became a powerful image in Bush's successful campaign to eliminate the deficit in his polling numbers. The general message was that

---

[6] Darman, *Who's in Control?* 226.
[7] Elizabeth Drew, *Election Journal: Political Events of 1987–88* (New York: William Morrow, 1989), 48–49.

he was a tough guy; he could stand up to powerful, selfish forces like the ones that would seek tax increases to reduce their tax burdens or increase the size of government.[8] The specific message was less clear. Which voters did Bush intend to attract with this anti-tax message? He probably meant to send sympathetic signals to the affluent groups that had borne the brunt of the base broadening under the Deficit Reduction Act of 1984, the Tax Equity and Fiscal Responsibility Act of 1982, and the Tax Reform Act of 1986. And he also probably wanted to tell those who still enjoyed advantages under the tax code that their privileges would stand. He may also have been trying to reassure middle-class families that they would not have to endure further increases in Social Security tax rates or, for that matter, further reductions in their benefits. Millions of middle-class Americans seem to have concluded that he had made such a promise.

His "no new taxes" pledge made it difficult for Bush to explain how he would deal with the continuing problem of the deficit. Part of the problem was that, though the Reagan tax increases had reduced the deficit problem, they had not eliminated it. At the end of the Reagan administration, the deficit was still high, at the embarrassing level of about 3 percent of gross domestic product (GDP). If the economy slowed, the deficit was certain to move back toward the 5 percent level that had raised alarms in the early 1980s. Bush adopted a mild version of supply-side public finance to address the problem. His instrument to reduce the deficit, he said, would be a "flexible freeze." He would freeze the overall increase in public spending at the rate of inflation. Eventually, he argued, following supply-side logic, the economy's expansion would increase tax revenues to a point, which he suggested was only four years away,

---

[8] On at least one earlier occasion, Peggy Noonan had invoked the rhetoric of Clint Eastwood. In an earlier script of hers, Ronald Reagan had challenged Congress to "make my day." See Drew, *Election Journal*, 260.

where the deficit would disappear. Meanwhile, the federal government would be "flexible" in determining the growth rates of the
various federal programs.

Bush's "flexible freeze" finessed, at least for the duration of the
campaign, the difficult economic reality that middle-class entitlement programs such as Medicare and Social Security grew automatically and would push the deficit even higher unless the federal
government either cut back defense spending or increased taxes,
or both. However, Bush could not escape reality once he was in
the White House. And in any case, he may have wanted to address the deficit problem in an effective way, despite the political
fallout from a broken no-tax promise. After all, in the presidential
primaries of 1979, Bush had been a critic of what he called Reagan's "voodoo economics," and during the Reagan administration,
he had supported balancing the budget. Moreover, Secretary of the
Treasury Nicholas Brady, who had been the head of the investment-
banking firm Dillon Read, may have stiffened Bush's resolve to reduce deficits.[9]

Immediately after taking office, Bush faced huge pressures from
outside the administration to address the deficit problem. Former
presidents Gerald Ford and Jimmy Carter rushed in to meet jointly
with Darman on the day Bush nominated him for director of the
Bureau of the Budget. They told Darman that balancing the budget would require a "considerable increase in revenues," including tax increases.[10] Some Republican business leaders, like Paul
O'Neill, chairman of Alcoa, rendered similar advice. And Alan
Greenspan, now chair of the Federal Reserve Board, invited Darman
to lunch and told him that he wanted a program of deficit reduction, which might include tax increases. Without deficit reduction, Greenspan implied, the Federal Reserve would not encourage

---

[9] On Brady's role, see Parmet, *George Bush*, 431.
[10] Darman, *Who's in Control?* 200.

economic expansion for fear that doing so might increase the risk of inflation. Thus, the Bush administration had to worry that unless it undertook deficit reduction, the Federal Reserve, in its efforts to offset inflationary forces, might trigger a recession.

The prospect of working with Congress to reduce the deficit was daunting. The Democrats, who had won control of both the House of Representatives and the Senate, were prepared to support deficit reduction, but they also wanted to protect entitlements and create embarrassment for Bush over his no-tax pledge. Compounding the political problems in Congress was the opposition of Jack Kemp and other supply-side advocates to any tax increases. They were disinclined to give Bush any room to maneuver around his promise. The "dividing lines among Republicans," Darman recalled, "were just as they had been since 1980."[11] He might have added that the tax increases of the mid-1980s had hardened the opposition of supply-side Republicans to any further departure from the orthodoxy of ERTA and the Reagan of 1981.

Bush decided to move forward with a deficit-reduction program, but to do so very slowly and deliberately. To spare himself political embarrassment and to maintain his credibility in other areas, he would stay, temporarily, with the policy of the flexible freeze. During at least his first year in office, he decided, he would propose only modest restraint of expenditures and not propose any tax increases. He would consider a tax increase in the second year but would attempt to appease Republicans in Congress by putting the new tax revenues in a trust fund that would restrict them to deficit reduction, by restraining entitlement growth, and by enacting cuts in the rates of taxation of capital gains. And during the entire process, he would also try to work closely with the Democratic leaders of Congress. In December 1988, Daniel Rostenkowski (Democrat-Illinois), chair of the House Ways and Means Committee, responded positively to

[11] Darman, *Who's in Control?* 202.

Bush's approach at least in the first year. He promised to avoid, in Darman's words, "embarrassing the new President on taxes for one year—but only for one year, in Rostenkowski's version of the conversation."[12]

In April 1989, the Bush administration and the Democratic leadership of Congress rather easily agreed on a revision of the budget that the Reagan administration had proposed earlier for fiscal 1990. But in the process of working out the revision, tension quickly developed between the Bush administration and the Senate majority leader, George Mitchell (Democrat-Maine), over the possibility of cutting capital-gains taxes. The problem over capital-gains taxation began when powerful Republicans in Congress insisted on forcing the issue in the revision of the last Reagan budget rather than waiting, as the Bush administration preferred, until the next budget cycle. These Republicans were generally supply-siders who were eager to resume the process of cutting taxes to reduce the cost of capital.

Early in 1989, partly because of its own enthusiasm for cutting capital-gains taxes, the Bush administration had shifted its position and decided to cooperate with the congressional Republicans in pressing immediately for the cuts. A measure for reduction won some bipartisan support and passed the House. Lloyd Bentsen (Democrat-Texas), chair of the Senate Finance Committee, also supported the measure. But Mitchell, who believed that the Bush administration had violated the agreement to keep taxes off the table, was outraged and persuaded Bentsen to bottle up the cut in committee. Senate Republicans insisted on bringing the cut to the floor, and the Bush administration agreed to help. "Forced to choose between confronting our right flank and confronting Mitchell," Darman recalled, "we chose to confront Mitchell."[13]

Mitchell cooperated in passing the Omnibus Reconciliation Act of 1989, but he blocked a vote on the cut in capital gains taxation

---

[12] Darman, *Who's in Control?* 209.   [13] Darman, *Who's in Control?* 227.

and suspended bipartisan negotiations on the 1991 budget. The last move forced the Bush administration to take the lead in proposing some combination of severe budget cuts and tax increases. Thus, through its accommodation to Republicans who sought to reduce capital costs, the Bush administration made it virtually impossible to deal with the deficit problem and, at the same time, escape political embarrassment over the "no new taxes" pledge.

In proposing the budget for fiscal 1991, however, the Bush administration returned to its original plan and tried to develop a bipartisan compromise in which the president and congressional Democrats would share responsibility for tax increases and some entitlement reform. In January 1990, the administration signaled its willingness to move toward tax increases by proposing some "user fees" as part of a package of modest deficit reduction. This opening encouraged Rostenkowski to take the risk of proposing unpopular measures, including an increase in gasoline taxes of 15 cents per gallon and a freeze on all mandated cost-of-living increases, including those for Social Security benefits. In response, a consensus emerged within the administration to support what Darman described as "revenue measures . . . weighted heavily toward growth-oriented investment, user fees, and revenue measures that directly promote pubic goods (e.g., energy consumption, environmental protection, alcohol abuse reduction)." The latter measures included consumption-based taxes. The president even raised the possibility of a value-added tax, to which Brady was attracted, while Darman and Chief of Staff John Sununu preferred "a broad-based energy tax."[14]

In May, the president launched direct negotiations with the Democratic leaders. Mitchell wanted Bush to make it clear in public that he was willing to consider tax increases, and the president

---

[14] Darman, *Who's in Control?* 246–47.

complied. The White House quickly announced that there would be "no preconditions for negotiation." In late June, after the talks had dragged on with little progress, Bush issued another statement. "It is clear to me," he declared, "that both the size of the deficit problem and the need for a package that can be enacted require all of the following: . . . "—and then listed a wide range of requirements. But the press zeroed in on one of them: "tax revenue increases." Rostenkowski, according to Darman, said that read-my-lips had become "history."[15]

The negotiating process was private, but the bipartisan leaders had great difficulty reaching agreement and took until September to announce the results. A key element in their proposed budget agreement was an increase in tax revenues of $134 billion, largely a result of a series of increases in gasoline taxes and a tax on home heating oil. Nowhere in the package was there a cut in the capital-gains tax. Bush explained that he did not "welcome" the gasoline tax but went on to say that "this way does have the virtue not only of contributing to deficit reduction, but also, over time, of decreasing American's dependence on foreign oil, an objective whose importance has been made increasingly evident in the face of the Iraqi invasion of Kuwait."[16] Thus the president attempted to link the tax increases to the confrontation with Iraq. Two days later, in an address to the nation, he declared that America was standing firm "against Saddam Hussein's oppression" but the

---

[15] George H. W. Bush, "Statement on the Federal Budget Negotiations," June 26, 1990, Public Papers of George W. Bush, Web site of George Bush Presidential Library (http://bushlibrary.tamu.edu/papers/1990/90062600. html; last visited August 29, 2003); Darman, *Who's in Control?* 264.

[16] George H. W. Bush, "Remarks Announcing a Federal Budget Agreement," September 30, 1990, Public Papers of George W. Bush, Web site of George Bush Presidential Library (http://bushlibrary.tamu.edu/papers/1990/ 90093002.html; last visited August 29, 2003).

"cancer" of deficits "was gnawing away at the nation's economic health."[17]

Supply-side Republicans in the Congress pounced on the president for having violated his promise and having abandoned the capital-gains tax. As the president later recalled, they declared it "betrayal—no matter that antitax President Reagan had to raise revenues many times." The leader of the rebels was Newt Gingrich, the Republican (Georgia) whip in the House; he had participated in the process but refused to endorse the outcome. Bush later recalled that the defection of Gingrich "sure hurt me." He explained: "His [Gingrich's] support could have eliminated the flak I took on the tax question and on my credibility."[18] Perhaps most important, Gingrich provided political cover for many Democrats who otherwise would have hesitated to oppose it. These Democrats disliked the regressiveness of the energy taxes, worried as well about the distributional effects of proposed cuts in Medicare and welfare, and saw a golden opportunity to humiliate the president. In October, liberated by Gingrich, they joined with the dissident Republicans to crush the budget agreement on the floor of the House.

Two weeks later, after intense partisanship, Congress passed and the president signed the Omnibus Budget Reconciliation Act of 1990 (OBRA 1990). The defection of Republicans and George Bush's desire to reduce the deficit meant that Democrats were able to recast the elements of the final budget for 1991, including the tax measures, in ways that they preferred. OBRA 1990 dropped

---

[17] George H. W. Bush, "Address to the Nation on the Federal Budget Agreement," October 2, 1990, Public Papers of George W. Bush, Web site of George Bush Presidential Library (http://bushlibrary.tamu.edu/papers/1990/90100206.html; last visited August 29, 2003).

[18] George Bush and Brent Scowcroft, *A World Transformed* (New York: Vintage Books, 1999), 380.

the tax on home heating oil and cut by half the increase in the gas tax. OBRA 1990 also dramatically increased the Earned Income Tax Credit (EITC). Originally, the EITC meant simply to ease the burden of increased Social Security taxes on the working poor; in its dramatic 1990 expansion, the EITC became welfare reform. It encouraged families dependent on welfare to enter the labor market by cushioning the consequent loss of welfare benefits.[19] OBRA 1990 partially made up for the reduction of tax revenues by increasing the highest marginal rates on individual incomes from 28 to 31 percent. In return for the more progressive taxation, the Democrats accepted substantial budget cuts over a five-year period. As a consequence, OBRA 1990 reduced the national budget deficit significantly—by $500 billion over five years, or between 1 and 2 percent of gross national product.

The budget agreement had not been based on coherent principles, but it had strengthened the revenue system, increasing its revenue capacity, and increased the progressivity of the individual income tax.[20] But the president sounded apologetic, rather than proud of his leadership. A reporter asked Bush: "What message will you use now . . . to replace your 'no new taxes' pledge?" Bush responded: "Let me be clear: I'm not in favor of new taxes. I'll repeat that over and over and over again. And this one compromise where we

---

[19] In 1990, for the first time, the EITC provided a rate of credit that was larger than the combined employer and employee Social Security tax rate. For an analysis of the EITC, see three articles in the *National Tax Journal* 47 (September 1994): Anne L. Alstott, "The Earned Income Tax Credit and Some Fundamental Institutional Dilemmas of Tax-Transfer Integration," 609–19; Stacy Dickert et al., "Taxes and the Poor: A Microsimulation Study of Implicit and Explicit Taxes," 621–38; and Janet Holtzblatt et al., "Promoting Work through the EITC," 591–607. See also C. Eugene Steuerle, "The Future of the Earned Income Tax Credit," *Tax Notes* (June 19, June 26, and July 3, 1995).

[20] For analysis of the budget compromise of 1990, especially its lack of coherent principles, see Steuerle, *Tax Decade*, 163–84.

begrudgingly had to accept revenue increases is the exception that proves the rule. That's the way I'll handle it."[21]

Despite the financial soundness of the agreement, it was a political disaster for Bush. He had alienated the Republicans who believed that tax cutting was their party's most popular policy instrument and most efficacious means of stimulating the economy and limiting the growth of government. These Republicans were especially critical of Bush for failing to reduce capital-gains taxation. His effort to do so, however, had antagonized Democratic leaders and limited his ability to reach a bipartisan agreement with them. And, Bush's betrayal of his "No new taxes!" promise, which he later called "rhetorical overkill," handicapped him in both the 1990 and 1992 elections by casting doubt on his public character. And this distrust may have disposed many middle-class Americans, both Republicans and Democrats, to blame Bush for having contributed to the recession that took hold in 1990.[22]

One of the casualties of the 1990 budget agreement was further tax reform along the lines of the Tax Reform Act of 1986. President Bush's championing of cuts in capital-gains taxation represented a return to a more traditional kind of class-oriented tax politics. During the budget process, this opened the door for the congressional leadership to resume the ideologically comfortable position of calling for a return to a higher degree of progressiveness in income taxation. Moreover, the capital-gains tax issue, along with

---

[21] George H. W. Bush, "Remarks on the Federal Budget Agreement and an Exchange with Reporters in Honolulu, Hawaii," October 27, 1990, Public Papers of George W. Bush, Web site of George Bush Presidential Library (http://bushlibrary.tamu.edu/papers/1990/90102700.html, last visited August 29, 2003).

[22] Bush's own assessment was that "the press refused to recognize the [economic] recovery and my political opponents were exceptionally good at reminding people that I had broken my pledge on taxes"; Bush and Scowcroft, *World Transformed*, 380.

President Bush's weakness, cleared the way for presidential candidate Bill Clinton to stress the need for a progressive redistribution of taxation.

CLINTON'S PROGRESSIVISM VERSUS THE "CONTRACT WITH AMERICA"

During his early political career in Arkansas, Bill Clinton developed an interest in vigorously progressive tax reform. In 1974, in his campaign for Congress—his first campaign for higher office—Clinton proposed a minimum tax on corporate income, a reduction of tax credits for companies investing overseas, and excess-profits taxes on "every industry reaping unwarranted profits during inflation."[23] However, as a candidate first for governor and then for president, Clinton modified his tax program. During the 1992 campaign, he proposed a "New Covenant for Economic Change" and "Plan for America's Future," in which he rejected any major tax reforms or introduction of new taxes, such as a national sales tax. With the recent recession in mind, he proposed, instead, a special income-tax cut for the middle class and increases in taxes on the highest incomes. The details of the tax-cut proposal shifted or remained vague, however. Clinton himself probably had serious doubts about making middle-class cuts in the face of budget deficits.[24]

---

[23] Stanley B. Greenberg, *Middle-Class Dreams: The Politics and Power of the New American Majority* (New York: Random House, 1995), 186–88.

[24] In my discussion of the first Clinton administration, I rely on Bob Woodward, *The Agenda: Inside the Clinton White House* (New York: Simon & Schuster, 1994), which focuses on the development of economic policy; Elizabeth Drew, *On the Edge: The Clinton Presidency* (New York: Simon & Schuster, 1994), and *Showdown: The Struggle Between the Gingrich Congress and the Clinton White House* (New York: Simon & Schuster, 1996); and Sidney Blumenthal, *The Clinton Wars* (New York: Farrar, Straus and Giroux, 2003). For Clinton and middle-class tax cuts, see Woodward, *Agenda*, 31, 42, and Drew, *On the Edge*, 59–60.

In the 1992 campaign, Clinton benefited from the impression that George Bush did not comprehend the depth of the economic problems faced by most Americans, and from their sense that government was of little value—and too expensive. Many middle- and low-income people who felt alienated from government and regarded their taxes as excessive had come to agree with the pronouncement of the hotel magnate and convicted tax evader Leona Helmsley: "We don't pay taxes. Only the little people pay taxes."[25] For them, Bush's violation of his pledge not to raise taxes was evidence of his remoteness from the hardship of everyday economic life.

During his first year in office, however, Clinton did little to address popular resentment over tax burdens. He gradually abandoned the middle-class tax cut and focused instead on the need for deficit reduction. The concern of the Clinton administration for deficit reduction was deep. Some within the administration were concerned with responding to pressure from the community of investment bankers. Some others stressed deficit reduction to generate the savings required to fund the eventual retirement of the generation of the post–World War II baby boom. Clinton himself recognized the political importance of following through on Democratic criticism of Presidents Reagan and Bush for deficit spending, and of establishing his credibility as a "New Democrat"—that is, one committed to fiscal soundness as well as social justice.

The impetus for deficit reduction, as well as for energy conservation, led the Clinton administration to advocate major tax increases. The first proposal was for the adoption of a broad-based energy tax that Vice President Al Gore had championed. The energy tax took the form of an all-fuels British thermal unit (Btu) tax, which would have fallen heavily on middle-class consumers. The House narrowly endorsed the Btu tax, although in a drastically modified

---

[25] *New York Times*, July 12, 1989.

form as a consequence of lobbying by corporations, such as aluminum manufacturers and airlines, that consumed huge amounts of energy. But opposition within the Senate Finance Committee—including Republicans and a few Democrats, such as John Breaux of Louisiana and David Boren of Oklahoma—resulted in the demise of the Btu-tax proposal.

The final deficit-reduction actions (in OBRA 1993) replaced the Btu tax with two other major tax increases favored by the Clinton administration. The first was a modest tax on gasoline of 4.3 cents a gallon, and the second was an increase in the marginal tax rates on the highest individual incomes. Also at the suggestion of the Clinton administration, OBRA 1993 provided another substantial increase in the EITC. This increase was not as large an increase as the one George H. W. Bush had approved, but the substantial, cumulative impact of the two increases helped set the stage for the later adoption of the welfare reforms in the Personal Responsibility and Work Opportunity Act of 1996.[26]

Clinton stressed the progressiveness of the OBRA 1993 package by pointing out that the tax increases on families earning more than $200,000 a year would raise 80 percent of the newly imposed tax revenues. Largely as a consequence of the tax increases, OBRA 1993 reduced deficits, according to congressional estimates, by about the same amount—$500 billion over five years—as had OBRA 1990.

---

[26] Eugene Steuerle has argued that "the availability of an increasingly generous EITC," which exceeded in value both the Aid to Families with Dependent Children (AFDC) and the Temporary Assistance for Needy Families (TANF) that replaced AFDC in 1996, "made it easier to push people off the welfare roles and into the work force." See Steuerle, *Contemporary U.S. Tax Policy* (Washington, D.C.: Urban Institute Press, forthcoming 2004), chap. 9. See also Adam Cavasso and C. Eugene Steuerle, "Growth in the Earned Income and Child Tax Credits," *Tax Notes*, January 20, 2003. A full evaluation of Clinton's welfare reform should encompass the expanded, progressive EITC as well as the 1996 legislation.

However, taking into account the fact that 1993 dollars were worth less than 1990 dollars, and that the economy had grown in size, the real value of the reductions of OBRA 1993, in absolute terms and relative to GDP, were less than those of OBRA 1990.[27]

The Clinton administration succeeded in passing OBRA 1993 by only the slimmest of margins. Republicans adopted a tough, partisan stance in opposition to the package. As Hillary Rodham Clinton recalled, "One Republican Congresswoman called me to explain that she agreed with the President's goal to tame the deficit but had been ordered by her leadership to vote no regardless of her convictions."[28] Not a single Republican voted for the reconciliation legislation, and the measure passed by only one vote in each house, with passage in the Senate requiring that Vice President Gore cast a tie-breaking vote. Prospects for passing further revenue legislation along the progressive lines that Bill Clinton preferred were dim.

The Clinton administration, meanwhile, considered further tax increases as part of fulfilling its second priority after deficit reduction—the development of comprehensive health care reform. These increases were likely to fall heavily on middle-class families, either through reduction of the tax revenues lost through the exclusion from taxation of health insurance benefits provided through employers or through the imposition of new taxes.[29] At the outset,

---

[27] For this comparison of OBRA 1990 and OBRA 1993, see Steuerle, *Contemporary U.S. Tax Policy*, chap. 9.

[28] Hillary Rodham Clinton, *Living History* (New York: Simon & Schuster, 2003), 179.

[29] As Eugene Steuerle has pointed out, "the largest tax subsidy in the tax code, as measured by revenues forgone, is the exclusion from taxation of health-insurance benefits provided through employers." According to Steuerle, the Clinton health care proposal "indirectly would have redirected those forgone revenues to finance some of the changes that it sought." The administration's goals in this regard were to reduce both the encouragement of excessive consumption of health services and the subsidizing of health care for the wealthy. See Steuerle, *Contemporary U.S. Tax Policy*, chap. 9. Also

Ira Magaziner, Clinton's health care policy adviser, believed that a substantial tax increase might be necessary, at least in the initial stages of reform. In February 1993, Daniel Rostenkowski, then still the chair of House Ways and Means, told Magaziner, "You guys don't get it; you can't send up another tax." But a few months later, in April, Magaziner's first formal proposal to the president was for the adoption of national sales taxation, in the form of a value-added tax that would raise $60 billion to $80 billion. Donna Shalala, the secretary of health and human services, revealed publicly that the administration was considering the proposal.

There was, in fact, some support for value-added taxation within the administration. Treasury Secretary Lloyd Bentsen had been interested in the Btu tax, in part because it opened the way to adopting a broader-based value-added tax. In February, in an Ohio town meeting, Clinton himself suggested that the value-added tax was "something I think we may well have to look at in the future." But by September, when Hillary Clinton and Magaziner unveiled their health care plan, an awareness of the potential political backlash had sunk in. The tax component of the plan consisted only of a new cigarette tax (75 cents per pack) and a 1 percent tax on the incomes of large businesses that would not join the proposed pools of insurance buyers.[30]

President Clinton evaluated possible increases or decreases in specific taxes without investigating broad-gauged tax reforms that would follow the lines pioneered in the Tax Reform Act of 1986. He displayed a clear preference for the traditional politics of offering

see Leonard E. Burman, "Is the Tax Expenditure Concept Still Relevant?" *National Tax Journal* 56 (September 2003), 613–27.

[30] Woodward, *Agenda*, 147, 168–69, 294. On support within the administration for value-added taxation, see Drew, *On the Edge*, 71, 85, 194. In her memoirs, Hillary Clinton points out that "some Democrats" on the Senate Finance Committee were reluctant to see a health care package with "a tax increase"; Clinton, *Living History*, 152.

tax benefits to specific interests, groups, and classes, rather than a base-broadening strategy. At the same time, no enthusiasm for 1986-style reform emerged from the Department of the Treasury, despite the fact that it was one of the traditional homes of base-broadening expertise within the nation's fiscal policy community. This was to be expected, because Clinton's first secretary of the treasury, former senator Lloyd Bentsen of Texas, had little interest in closing loopholes in the income-tax code, particularly loopholes that favored the oil industry. He had been a reluctant supporter of the 1986 tax reforms, and he had discouraged base-broadening efforts after he became chair of the Senate Finance Committee in 1991. And Clinton's new National Economic Council, which he hoped would lend greater coherence to his economic program, showed no interest in base-broadening strategies.

Clinton, however, failed to offer, let alone deliver, any significant tax cuts for the middle class in 1993 or 1994. This, coupled with his vain effort to enact an ambitious, comprehensive health care program, made him politically vulnerable. Many middle-class voters saw no improvement in the quality of government, failed to see any significant tax relief, and regarded Clinton's deficit reductions as too modest. Some believed that Clinton had betrayed his promise of a middle-class tax cut, and that the president had deliberately misled the public by claiming that an increase in cigarette taxes would be enough to pay for health care reform.

Middle-class rebellion focused on taxation issues may well have contributed significantly to the electoral landslide that swept Republicans into control of both the Senate (for the first time since 1986) and the House (for the first time since 1952). Congressman Newt Gingrich, who became speaker of the House, and his conservative colleagues organized their successful campaign under the banner of a "Contract with America," and key elements of this blueprint for reform concerned taxation. In January 1995, Gingrich and William Archer (Republican-Texas), the new chair of the House Ways and Means Committee, launched their tax program.

The Contract with America had called for a dramatic procedural change in setting fiscal policy: the amendment of the Constitution to require a balanced budget. In January 1995, the House, under Gingrich's leadership, called for an amendment that would oblige the president to submit a balanced budget and would allow Congress to run a deficit only during wartime or when a three-fifths vote of both the House and the Senate approved the deficit. The assumption was that the amendment, if effective, would force the federal government to live within limited tax revenues and make tough choices among competing programs.

Under the rubric of the Contract, Gingrich and Archer also proposed for a significant set of tax cuts. Gingrich called the cuts the "pièce de résistance" of the Contract. Gingrich and Archer aimed almost all the cuts at lowering taxes on capital income, but they designed some of the proposals to remind voters of Clinton's aborted middle-class tax cut. Under what Gingrich and Archer called the "American Dream Restoration Act," tax reform would provide a tax credit of $500 per child to all taxpaying households earning $200,000 or less, provide a new income-tax credit for two-earner married couples, and exempt from taxation contributions to "American Dream Savings Accounts" (similar to individual retirement accounts, or IRAs) that could be used for certain housing, educational, and medical expenses as well as retirement savings. Archer and Gingrich also advanced tax measures that more clearly benefited the wealthy. Under the "Job Creation and Wage Enhancement Act," they proposed cutting in half the rates of taxing capital gains, indexing capital gains for inflation, and allowing the deductibility of losses on the sale of principal residences.[31]

[31] Committee on Ways and Means, U.S. House of Representatives, 104th Congress, 1st Session, "Description of Provisions in the Contract with

In offering both cuts to both the middle class and the wealthy, Gingrich and Archer took a page out of Reagan's 1981 playbook. But the scale of the suggested tax cuts, though substantial, was much smaller than that of the cuts enacted by ERTA. And in contrast to the approach of the Reagan administration after 1981, Archer and Gingrich proposed no base broadening and made no attempt to make the cuts revenue neutral. This approach left some Republicans in the House and many in the Senate worrying that the tax cuts would put at risk deficit-reduction efforts, which had been successful for three years in a row. Also, these Republicans took seriously the advice of economists who told the House Budget Committee that large tax cuts might undermine the successful effort to control inflation. Roger E. Brinner, the chief economist for DRI/McGraw-Hill, described the tax credit of $500 a child as "possibly mediocre politics but definitely bad economics."

In February 1995, the president revived his 1992 campaign idea of middle-class tax cuts. He proposed a $500 credit per child and an expansion of the use of IRAs for family expenses like those identified by the Contract with America, with the addition of long periods of unemployment and the care of an ill parent. And he added a tax deduction of up to $10,000 a year for middle-income families to pay for postsecondary education and training. But Clinton's approach would have phased out benefits to families earning more than $60,000. He claimed that his administration could find enough expenditure cuts in the budget for fiscal 1996 to fund both the tax cut and substantial deficit reduction.[32]

Other Democratic leaders both inside and outside the administration condemned the Contract's program of tax cuts. Congressman

America within the Jurisdiction of the Committee on Ways and Means," January 5, 1995.

[32] "Middle-Class Bill of Rights Tax Relief Act of 1995—Message from the President—PM 17," *Congressional Record* (Senate—February 13, 1995), S2566.

Richard Gephardt (Democrat-Missouri) denounced it as "an af-front to fundamental fairness and decency" because it would take "food from the mouths of children and heat from the homes of se-nior citizens." Vice President Al Gore called tax legislation passed by the House "Robin Hood in reverse," claiming that too many of the bill's benefits would fall to taxpayers earning $350,000 or more. Secretary of the Treasury Robert Rubin and Alice Rivlin, director of the Office of Management and Budget, denounced the proposed tax cuts as "fiscally irresponsible" and urged Clinton to threaten to veto them.[33]

Clinton, however, did not make such a threat. His administration seemed to agree in a general way with the new Republican majority that the federal government should undertake at least some middle-class tax cuts financed by future reductions in the size of federal programs and institutions. One observer described the Democratic Party under President Clinton as a "kinder, gentler version of the Republican Party."[34]

In early March, the Senate majority leader, Robert Dole (Republican-Kansas), failed to win enough Democratic support to assemble the two-thirds majority required to advance the balanced-budget amendment.[35] By May 1995, the amendment, along with a constitutional amendment to impose congressional term limits, was one of the only two provisions of the Contract with America that had been voted down in Congress. Republicans, however, made it

---

[33] Richard Gephardt, "A Victory Party for the Privileged Few," *Congressional Record* (House—March 10, 1995), H2991; Michael Wines, "Gingrich Promises to Tie Tax Relief to Cuts in Deficit," *New York Times*, April 4, 1995.

[34] Felix G. Rohatyn, "What Became of My Democrats?" *New York Times*, March 31, 1995.

[35] Without the defection by Senator Mark Hatfield (Republican-Oregon), Dole would have had the two-thirds majority. On Hatfield's role, see James MacGregor Burns and Georgia J. Sorenson, *Dead Center: Clinton-Gore Leadership and the Perils of Moderation* (New York: Scribner, 1999), 217.

clear that they would make an issue of the defeat of the balanced-budget amendment in the 1996 general elections.

The defeat augmented Republican concerns over future deficits and provided a convenient excuse for moderate Republicans to resist the Contract's tax cuts. Senate Republicans on the Finance Committee took the lead in articulating their doubts. Senator Robert Packwood (Republican-Oregon), chair of the Senate Finance Committee, declared: "Reducing the deficit is the most important thing to do." Senator John Chafee (Republican–Rhode Island), another member of the Finance Committee, said: "Basically, I'm opposed to tax cuts . . . as much as we love to parcel them out." Senator Alfonse D'Amato (Republican–New York), also a Finance Committee member, warned that the federal government had to "cut spending and get the deficit under control, that's number one. . . . Otherwise we're going to end up as Mexico II." Enough Republicans in the House worried about the lack of revenue neutrality to slow down passage of the Archer-Gingrich tax cuts. They held up the tax package in the House until Gingrich and Archer agreed to tie their tax-relief legislation to the achievement of future deficit reductions. Many Republicans in the Senate, however, were not satisfied by this stipulation. In late May 1995, enough Republicans joined Democrats so that the Senate delivered a resounding defeat to the Contract with America's tax legislation.[36]

Meanwhile, both the Senate and the House approved budget resolutions mapping out plans to balance the federal budget. But in their separate resolutions, the two chambers remained far apart on exactly how they would do the balancing. The gap was largest in the area of taxes, where the House proposed $353 billion in tax cuts over the next seven years (following the road map of the Contract with America's tax reforms), whereas the Senate put forward a more

---

[36] Eric Pianin, "Tax Cutters Lose Steam in Senate; House Panel to Unveil GOP Revenue Plan," *Washington Post*, March 14, 1995.

modest $170 billion. The Senate's cuts would take effect only if lower deficits strengthened the economy and created windfalls for the federal government in the form of lower interest payments and larger tax revenues.[37]

The Senate had faced great difficulty in formulating its own tax program for fiscal 1996. The Republican leaders in the Senate realized they had to win significant Democratic support to get any tax measure to a vote of the full body. And Republicans on the Senate Finance Committee continued to have grave doubts about the political and economic risks of excessive cutting of taxes and government. Some preferred to respond to grassroots hostility to taxes with less tax cutting and more tax reform—particularly tax reform that increased horizontal equity and economic efficiency and reduced the costs of government. To bring about a shift of emphasis from middle-class tax cuts to tax reform, several Republican leaders, supported by a few Democrats, began to propose drastic renovation of the federal tax system.

All the radical proposals that emerged had in common the goals of protecting revenues while responding to popular antitax sentiment. The proposals embraced goals of stimulating investment and promoting horizontal equity that had been central to the Tax Reform Act of 1986 but emphasized, as well, the desirability of simplifying the tax system for the taxpayer and reducing the size and power of the enforcement bureaucracy—the Internal Revenue Service (IRS).[38]

Two proposals from within the Senate were similar to ones that had surfaced in earlier periods of fiscal ferment. Senator Sam Nunn

---

[37] Michael Wines, "Fight Now Turns Intraparty, and Battleground Is Taxes," *New York Times*, May 26, 1995.

[38] For a useful introduction to the shape of the radical reform measures, see Peter Passell, "The Tax Code Heads into the Operating Room" and "For Business, the Stakes Are High," *New York Times*, September 3, 1995.

(DemocratGeorgia) and Senator Pete Domenici (Republican–New Mexico), chair of the Senate Budget Committee, put forward the only major bipartisan measure and the only fully articulated piece of legislation. They called their proposal the Unlimited Savings Allowance Tax—the "USA Tax." It was a hybrid of income taxation and consumption taxation.

For individuals, the USA Tax would keep the income tax (including its progressive rates) but eliminate many tax expenditures in return for allowing unlimited deduction for savings, a partial deduction of educational expenses, and a credit for Social Security taxes.

For businesses, the USA Tax would establish an 11 percent value-added tax. By allowing the expensing of an investment (fully writing off the investment during the year it is made), the value-added tax would provide major assistance to capital-intensive industries. The USA Tax also allowed a dollar-for-dollar credit for Social Security payroll taxes. Nunn and Domenici hoped that the latter measure would promote increases in employment.

Overall, the USA Tax proposal was reminiscent of the "spendings" tax suggested by Thomas S. Adams after World War I and favored for a time during World War II by Secretary of the Treasury Henry Morgenthau Jr. Senator Nunn explained that "we are basically going to tax people on what they take out of the economy—above a tax-free level for necessities—rather than what they put into the economy by working and saving."[39]

The more radical idea of replacing all income taxation with a national sales tax—often the favorite conservative alternative to income taxation since World War I—also resurfaced. It was proposed by Senator Richard Lugar (Republican-Ohio) along with William

---

[39] For discussion of S.722 (USA Tax Act of 1995) by Senators Nunn and Domenici, including a description of the development of the bill over a three-year period, see *Congressional Record* (Senate—April 25, 1995), S5664 ff.

Archer. They estimated that a single rate of 16 percent on sales of everything except food and medical services would replace all income-tax revenues. Lugar and Archer hoped to abolish altogether the income tax and the IRS. (The states would collect sales taxes for the federal government.) One House member, Nick Smith of Michigan (Republican), found this aspect of the proposal to be its most attractive feature. He welcomed "repeal of the Sixteenth Amendment and dismantling of the Internal Revenue Department" so that "special interests could [not] again come and complicate the existing Tax Code."[40]

A less familiar proposal came from Dick Armey, the Republican majority leader of the House. In June, he shifted his attention from the provisions of the Contract with America to introduce the "flat tax" in what he called the "Freedom and Fairness Restoration Act (FFRA)."

The flat tax in Title I of the FFRA was a proposal that economists Robert Hall and Alvin Rabushka had advanced in the mid-1980s as a replacement for the existing income-tax system. In Armey's version, the tax would require individuals and corporations to pay a flat rate that would decline from 20 percent in the first year to 17 percent in the third year. Individuals would pay taxes only on wages, salaries, and pensions. They would not have the benefit of any deductions. They would, however, have a general personal exemption that would eliminate taxes for a family of four earning less than, roughly, $37,000. Because of the tax's simplicity, individuals supposedly would have to fill out postcard-size forms with only ten lines. The corporate flat-rate payments would include taxes on all other kinds of income, especially interest and dividends, but would

---

[40] "Just the Job for Jack Kemp," *Economist*, April 8, 1995; Nick Smith, "Alternatives to Our Current Tax System," *Congressional Record* (House—June 8, 1995), H5704; Carolyn Lochhead, "Elimination of Tax Code Gaining Favor," *San Francisco Chronicle*, July 24, 1995.

allow corporations to deduct their investment in capital equipment, structures, and land from their income (in the year those investments were made) before paying taxes. Corporations would no longer withhold the taxes owed by individual taxpayers. Individuals would write monthly checks to the IRS.

In describing the flat tax, Armey emphasized that it would eliminate the double taxation of dividends under both corporate- and personal-income taxation. He claimed it would also promote investment, lose relatively little revenue (about 5 percent a year, according to his estimates), and win popularity because "it combines simplicity and fairness." Jon Fox (Republican-Pennsylvania) added that the tax would "get the IRS and government off the backs of individual and corporate taxpayers, and will allow all of us to redirect our energies to more productive pursuits." Republican presidential candidates Phil Gramm, Lamar Alexander, and Arlen Specter all joined in proposing variations on the tax. Senator Specter's version included deductions for interest on home mortgages up to $100,000 and for charitable contributions (up to $2,500 a year), and it maintained payroll withholding.[41]

In part to help build a Republican consensus behind an approach to tax reform, Gingrich and Dole announced in early April 1995 that they had appointed a commission, chaired by Jack Kemp, to consider a complete overhaul of the federal tax system, including possible repeal of the income tax. (Dole may also have created the commission and appointed Kemp to remove the pressure on Dole to address the issue of tax reform, and to prevent Kemp from endorsing another Republican as the party's presidential candidate in

[41] For descriptions of the flat-tax proposal, see Robert Hall and Alvin Rabushka, *The Flat-Tax*, 2nd ed. (Stanford, Calif.: Hoover Institution Press, 1995), and Dick Armey to the Editor, *New York Times*, April 23, 1995. For supporting comments see, e.g., Jon Fox, "The Flat Tax," *Congressional Record* (House—May 10, 1995), H4790.

1996.)[42] Gingrich and Dole asked the nine-member panel to report its recommendations by October 1995. Kemp had withdrawn from the race for the presidency, but he explained that the appointment "puts me back to the center of the debate for the 1996 campaign." Kemp, however, was far from neutral. He was opposed to punishing consumption and advocated a flat tax, which he believed would turn America into "an enterprise zone from sea to shining sea."[43]

Meanwhile, support for tax reform seemed to be growing across the political spectrum. Conservative organizations mobilized to inundate Iowa and New Hampshire with literature on the flat tax and sales tax, and flat-tax supporters established the "Flat Tax Home Page" on the Internet. On the liberal side, the *New York Times* greeted the Kemp commission by editorializing that "the current tax code is maddeningly complex, costly and unfair." The editor called for a new code that would be "simple, pro-growth, and fair."[44]

In July 1995, House Minority Leader Gephardt proposed the first purely Democratic alternative to the Republican proposals for a shift in tax regimes. Gephardt attacked the flat tax as "the largest redistribution of income in the history of the country" and argued that the income tax should be maintained. But like Armey, he would take more poor families off the income-tax rolls, lower rates dramatically for most people, and pay for both by eliminating deductions. He argued that the simplification would make the IRS "smaller and less expensive." For Americans who no longer had to file a tax return ("the vast majority," according to Gephardt), "the IRS will be reduced to little more than a mailing address." In addition,

---

[42] For this suggestion, see Drew, *Showdown*, 174. For an excellent discussion of the Republican primary campaign waged by Dole, including the significance of the flat tax issue, see Burns and Sorenson, *Dead Center*, 264–68.

[43] *New York Times*, April 4, 1995; "Just the Job for Jack Kemp," *Economist*, April 8, 1995.

[44] "Our Maddening Tax System," *New York Times*, April 16, 1995.

the changes would "dramatically scale back the 300-billion dollar industry of tax advisers and preparers, and the 4.5 billion hours Americans spend each year to prepare their taxes."

Gephardt's treatment of taxpayers differed in some important ways from Armey's. In contrast to Armey, Gephardt suggested a much lower rate (10 percent) for most taxpayers (75 percent of them, according to his estimates), continuing the deduction for home mortgage interest, and retaining the EITC for the working poor. He also would retain capital-gains taxation for individuals and keep the taxation of interest and dividends under the personal-income tax—as part of a plan to maintain or even increase the progressiveness of the federal tax system. In even sharper contrast to Armey, Gephardt suggested a high degree of progression for rates on the highest-income families to pay for these benefits to low- and middle-income taxpayers. On incomes over roughly $32,000, individuals would pay progressive rates rising from 20 to 34 percent. And finally, Gephardt took account of the antigovernment movement by requiring "a national referendum" for Congress to raise tax rates.[45]

President Clinton, however, chose not to become an advocate of fundamental reform. He might have embraced the USA Tax or, following the bipartisan example of Ronald Reagan in 1986, incorporated elements of both the Armey and Gephardt proposals. Perhaps this was a missed opportunity. The Clinton administration might have been able to work with the Senate leadership to devise and sell a compromise based on ideas that a new tax regime must retain or increase progressiveness, enhance horizontal equity, and

---

[45] Richard A. Gephardt, "A Democratic Plan for America's Economy: Toward a Fairer, Simpler Tax Code," Address, Center for National Policy, July 6, 1995; "Gephardt Has His Own Plan on Tax Reform," *San Francisco Chronicle*, July 7, 1995; William M. Welch, "Gephardt Tax Plan Edges Democrats into Debate," *USA Today*, July 7, 1995.

eliminate double taxation and tax loopholes that violate economic efficiency.

On only one occasion, however, had the federal government begun to adopt a new tax regime during the year of a presidential election. That was in 1916, when a major financial crisis, the shadow of war, close cooperation between a Democratic president and a Democratic Congress, and an irresistible insurgency within the Democratic Party launched the modern federal income tax. Nearly eighty years later, Gingrich, Armey, and their insurgent legions in the House called for reform almost as stridently as Claude Kitchin and his supporters had in 1916.

At least two circumstances were very different than in 1916. The economic issues that the federal government would have had to address in making the transition to a new tax regime were far more complex than in 1916. Even more important, partisanship divided the executive from the legislative branches. And Bill Clinton, in contrast to Woodrow Wilson, had no enthusiasm for substantial reform. Without presidential leadership, there could be no dramatic movement toward a new tax regime; the essentials of the tax system introduced during World War II remained in place.

Rather than pursue bipartisan tax reform, Clinton continued to concentrate on short-run budget issues. In his maneuverings, he often followed the advice of Dick Morris, one of his political consultants, and "triangulated," emphasizing the differences between his positions and those of both Republicans and Democrats in Congress. To emphasize his differences from many Democrats, he continued to stress the need to balance budgets. And he abandoned any effort to create large new federal programs. However, to emphasize his differences from leading Republicans, he continued to urge tax cuts that had progressive effects and to suggest and defend entitlement programs.

Clinton and the forces of Gingrich collided over the 1996 budget. In October 1995, the House and Senate reached agreement on budget reconciliation. They compromised on tax cuts by agreeing on a level of $245 billion, which they financed by cuts, including reductions in the EITC and cuts in the growth of Medicare and Medicaid. In addition, they ended the entitlement nature of Medicaid by transforming it into a block-grant program. But on this crucial occasion, Clinton resisted Dick Morris's advice to reach a deal with Congress. Instead, Clinton took the hard line that most congressional Democrats preferred. On December 6, he vetoed the reconciliation bill, using a pen with which Lyndon Johnson had signed Medicare. The resulting stalemate extended to agreement on continuing resolutions to keep "nonessential" departments of government open. Twice they had to shut down for lack of funds.

During the stalemate, Clinton brilliantly navigated the tensions of divided government in a way that seemed to undermine public confidence in Congress. He did so in large part by attempting to seem reasonable, accepting some of Gingrich's critique of government. In fact, in his January 1996 State of the Union address, he used Morris's words and pronounced: "The era of big government is over." However, Clinton immediately qualified the declaration by saying, "But we cannot go back to the time when our citizens were left to fend for themselves," and by asserting that "self-reliance and teamwork are not opposing virtues; we must have both." He went on to propose a wide variety of relatively modest initiatives, including tax credits for college costs and an increase in the EITC.[46]

In April 1996, Clinton and Congress finally agreed on a budget for fiscal 1996 (which was more than half over). Clinton and the Republican leadership of Congress agreed on balancing revenues

---

[46] For firsthand accounts that describe the drafting of the speech and the insertion of the major qualification, see Blumenthal, *Clinton Wars*, 149–152; George Stephanopoulos, *All Too Human: A Political Education* (Boston: Little, Brown, 1999), 411–14; Michael Waldman, *Potus Speaks: Finding the Words that Defined the Clinton Presidency* (New York: Simon & Schuster, 2000), 90–114.

and expenditures within seven years, rather than the nine years that the administration had proposed originally. The budget did cut discretionary spending by $23 billion. But the cut was modest, and the agreement left Medicare and Social Security unscathed, as Clinton and congressional Democrats had wished. Because of the lack of major program cuts, and because of the bipartisan agreement on the importance of balancing the budget, the final agreement included no major tax reductions, which is what congressional Democrats had also wanted.

The debate over the provisions of the Contract with America had failed to produce any consensus among Republicans on how to pursue fundamental tax reform. None of the reform proposals they or Democratic leaders like Gephardt and Nunn floated had caught any waves of public enthusiasm. At the same time, President Clinton had demonstrated that the American public continued to support progressive taxation and would probably fail to support the regressive proposals that the Republicans had offered. Consequently, in the presidential campaigns of 1996, Dole, the Republican candidate, had no difficulty jettisoning the Gingrich agenda. In any event, Dole had never evinced any interest in fundamental tax reform. In his primary contests, he had referred to the flat tax, which candidate Malcolm (Steve) Forbes Jr. championed, as "snake oil."[47] And Dole had co-opted Kemp, the Republicans' most effective advocate of reform, by making him his running mate. Instead of advocating fundamental reform, Dole criticized Clinton for the tax increases of OBRA 1993 and returned to something resembling the Reagan formula: advocacy of a 15 percent across-the-board tax cut. But as journalist Bob Woodward observed, Dole "talked and danced around the issue, betraying his doubts about his own program."[48]

---

[47] For the Dole quotation, see Burns and Sorenson, *Dead Center*, 268.
[48] Bob Woodward, *The Choice: How Clinton Won* (New York: Simon & Schuster, 1996), 438.

In the contest with Dole, Clinton also ignored any possibility for structural reform. He countered Dole's tax-cutting proposal by emphasizing his record of deficit reduction; by arguing that it had been responsible for the prosperity that had taken hold; and by arguing that Dole's tax cut would require major cuts in Medicare, Medicaid, and other programs. Clinton suggested that, in any case, Dole was unlikely to deliver on *his* promise of tax cuts because, as chair of the Senate Finance Committee during the Reagan administration, he bore heavy responsibility for the tax increases of the Tax Equity and Fiscal Responsibility Act of 1982 and the Deficit Reduction Act of 1984.[49]

Clinton was victorious, as were the congressional Republicans, who retained control of the legislative branch. Both Clinton and the Republicans emerged from the 1996 campaign with the intention of making at least a modest round of tax cuts, and they implemented them in the Taxpayer Relief Act of 1997. The biggest cut in terms of revenue lost was the creation of a new child tax credit, designed to reach $500 per child by 1999.[50] It had bipartisan support. Republicans regarded it as a fulfillment of part of the pro-family provisions of the Contract with America, and Democrats like Jay Rockefeller (Democrat–West Virginia), whose National Commission on Children had endorsed it in 1991, regarded it as a progressive measure.[51]

[49] On Clinton's emphasis on the threat of the Dole cuts to entitlement, education, and environmental programs, see Elizabeth Drew, *Whatever It Takes: The Real Struggle for Political Power in America* (New York: Penguin Books, 1997), 150–51.

[50] Steven A. Holmes, "A Generous but Expensive Break," *New York Times*, July 30, 1997.

[51] The economists Eugene Steuerle, who served as principal adviser to the commission, and Jason Juffras proposed the credit to the commission "to more accurately measure ability to pay according to family size and then to tax equally those who have equal ability." See C. Eugene Steuerle, "Why I Favor Child Tax Credits or Allowances: Part One," *Tax Notes*, November 2, 1994; Jason Juffras and C. Eugene Steuerle, *A 1,000 Tax Credit for Every*

The other major progressive cut in the 1997 package was a complicated set of tax subsidies for higher education. Less important in terms of revenue forgone by the federal government was a collection of complicated measures, originating primarily in the Republican ranks, that they intended to promote savings and reduce the cost of capital. These included a gradual increase in the estates that were exempt from estate taxation, a modest reduction of capital-gains taxes, and the creation of Roth IRAs that extended some of the benefits of IRAs to taxpayers who already had employer-provided retirement plans.

The Taxpayer Relief Act of 1997 provided the largest tax cuts since 1981. But the cost of the cuts, in terms of revenue lost, projected down to 2000, was far less, only about 0.3 percent of GDP. Also, Congress and the president paid for these tax cuts with cuts in discretionary spending, particularly in national defense. Meanwhile, the vigorous economic expansion allowed President Clinton to submit, later in January 1998, the first balanced budget in three decades. Pragmatic conservatism, as practiced by Ronald Reagan and George H. W. Bush, and pragmatic liberalism, as pioneered by Bill Clinton, had prevailed.

Divided government and weaknesses in both Democratic and Republican leaderships shaped the final years of the Clinton presidency. Compromises that might have produced substantive policy initiatives were extremely difficult with the legislative and executive branches under the control of different parties, and they became virtually impossible after January 1998, when Clinton began to face public allegations that he had an improper relationship with a White House intern and lied about it under oath. The scandal and ensuing

Child: A Base of Reform for the Nation's Tax, Welfare, and Health Systems (Washington, D.C.: Urban Institute Press, 1991); and National Commission on Children, *Beyond Rhetoric: A New American Agenda for Children and Families—Final Report of the National Commission on Children* (Washington, D.C.: U.S. Government Printing Office, 1991).

impeachment crisis impaired the president's leadership, while Republicans leaders preferred to make the most of the president's situation rather than launch any risky new policy initiatives. On the one hand, Clinton was unable to win congressional support in 1998 for a proposal he made to raise cigarette taxes to finance health care programs. On the other hand, Republicans got nowhere with proposals for additional tax cuts. Neither the president nor Congress could agree on any new programs for spending or taxing. The inability to raise discretionary spending or cut taxes helped restore and increase budget surpluses.[52]

The stalemate between the president and congress over fiscal initiatives did not prevent passage, however, of a measure designed to restructure the IRS. The legislation, the Internal Revenue Service Restructuring and Reform Act of 1998, was the only direct accomplishment of Gingrich's Contract for America and its attacks on the IRS.[53] The legislation added some protections to taxpayers, but the most important changes were probably indirect. The widespread popularity of the measure may have prompted the IRS to make administrative changes, embracing information technology and replacing geographical with functional units. In the short run, the legislation made the IRS more cautious in auditing returns. But in the long run, it will probably make the IRS a more effective enforcer of the law.

At the end of the Clinton administration, and at the end of the twentieth century, the tax regime created during World War II was still in place. Efforts to reform it in a fundamental way had failed,

---

[52] For an interpretation of the presidential-congressional stalemate that places more emphasis on leadership failure than divided government, see Burns and Sorenson, *Dead Center*, 286–87.

[53] In the last phase of the assault on the IRS, a historian who had been employed at the IRS may have contributed to the groundswell of hostility. See Shelley L. Davis, *Unbridled Power: Inside the Secret Culture of the IRS* (New York: HarperCollins, 1987).

and the only systematic reform undertaken since World War II turned out to have been the Tax Reform Act of 1986. Even though the 1986 act did not provide a compelling example for reform during the administrations of George H. W. Bush and Bill Clinton, and even though the two parties drifted back to competition over which could offer more special favors within the tax code, the effects of the 1986 act proved to be quite durable, in three main ways. First, income-tax rates remained significantly lower. Under the Clinton administration, the top marginal rate increased to about 40 percent, but even this rate was still substantially lower than the 70 percent level in place before ERTA. Lower rates may well have increased voluntary compliance with the tax code, and they have certainly reduced the value of the special deductions and exclusions that remained in the tax code after 1986.

Second, the business tax expenditures remained close to the lower levels achieved by the Tax Reform Act of 1986. The act reversed the growth of tax expenditures, which had surged during the 1970s and then continued to grow in the early 1980s, increasing (by one measure) from 6 to 8 percent of GDP in just the five years between 1980 and 1985. Between 1986 and 1990, however, as a consequence of the 1986 measure, tax expenditures declined to less than 6 percent of GDP, and tax expenditures to business declined by two-thirds. Individual—but not business—tax expenditures crept up during the George H. W. Bush and Clinton administrations.[54]

Third, the broadening of the base increased the revenue capacity of the federal income tax. This became especially clear during the dynamic economic expansion of the 1990s, when the broadened base supported rapid growth in tax revenues even without an inflationary stimulus.

[54] Eric Toder, *The Changing Composition of Tax Incentives, 1980–1999*, Research Report (Washington, D.C.: Urban Institute Press, 1999), chart 1.

The Tax Reform Act of 1986 also had important political consequences during the Bush and Clinton administrations. Ironically, the act strengthened the political foundation of the income-tax system that was initially the major target of the "Reagan Revolution." The reductions in the highest rates and the reduction in tax expenditures enhanced support for the federal tax system among those who appreciated that Reagan's tax reforms reduced both the inefficiencies resulting from very high rates and the economic distortions arising from favoritism toward one type of capital over another. In addition, the continuing progressiveness of the federal tax system helped maintain middle- and lower-class support for it. Most Americans still preferred the progressive income tax as the primary means of federal finance. In short, the Reagan tax policies made it more difficult for critics of the income tax to make an appealing case for abandoning it. Consequently, those policies further extended the life span of the tax regime inherited from World War II, at least through the end of the twentieth century.

6

‡‡‡

Threatening the old regime, 2000–present

On January 20, 2001, when George W. Bush took the oath of office as president, the period of divided government and indecisive Republican leadership came to an end. In the November 2000 elections, Republicans had maintained control of both houses of Congress, and the new Republican president, despite the irregularity of his own election, set out to establish control over the legislative agenda. As it turned out, President Bush had a definite top priority for his domestic program: using much of the budgetary surplus that had emerged from the 1990s to fund a large tax cut.

Supply-side economics and tax-cutting populism drove the tax cut that followed in 2001, as they had Ronald Reagan's cut twenty years earlier with the Economic Recovery Tax Act. But there were important differences. On the one hand, Bush's cut in 2001 was smaller than Reagan's in 1981. On the other hand, Bush had in mind a longer-run program of tax cuts. And as his program played out in 2002 and 2003, Bush appeared to have an agenda that was more radical than Reagan's. To be sure, both Reagan and Bush hoped their tax cuts would reduce discretionary spending. But Bush seemed prepared to go further and use tax cutting as a vehicle for containing or reducing the entitlement programs of Social Security and Medicare. Moreover, though Reagan wanted to keep intact the basic structure of the progressive income tax, in 2002 Bush proposed a significant shift of the nation's tax system toward the taxation of consumption. The final tax cut that resulted in 2003 was more modest than Bush had proposed. But for the first time since the Great Depression and World War II, the possibility of a genuine fiscal revolution—one focused on both the income tax and entitlement spending—had become the centerpiece of a presidential agenda.

THE PRESIDENCY OF GEORGE W. BUSH: TOWARD A NEW TAX REGIME

In bidding for the presidency, George W. Bush consistently made tax cutting his highest priority for domestic policy. As governor of Texas, with his presidential campaign in mind, he resisted calls to increase spending on education and turned $2 billion of budget surplus into a tax cut. This record established him as the biggest tax cutter among the Republican candidates for president. In the Republican primaries, Bush invoked his Texas record to outflank Christine Todd Whitman, whose record of tax cutting as governor of New Jersey was not quite as impressive, and Steve Forbes, who continued to advocate replacing the progressive income tax with the confusing "flat tax."[1] During the primaries, Bush advanced a proposal that essentially had three components, which he planned

---

[1] On the development of Bush's tax plan in Texas, see James Moore and Wayne Slater, *Bush's Brain: How Karl Rove Made George W. Bush Presidential* (Hoboken, N.J.: John Wiley & Sons, 2003), 213–17, 228–36, 243–44. In explaining the origins of Bush's tax program, Paul Krugman emphasizes Bush's desire in 1999 to head off a primary challenge from Steve Forbes. See Krugman, *The Great Unraveling: Losing Our Way in the New Century* (New York: W. W. Norton, 2003), 9, 78, 92. Moore and Slater agree that heading off Forbes was important to Bush, but they suggest that he had an

to phase in over a period of several years. Cumulatively, they would save taxpayers about $1.3 trillion, according to Bush campaign estimates. The first component was a set of cuts in tax rates for individuals in most tax brackets. On the extremes, many individuals in the lowest tax bracket would enjoy a cut in their rate from 15 to 10 percent, and individuals in the highest bracket would have a reduction from 39.6 to 33 percent. These cuts included a reduction in the tax rate paid by a married couple with relatively equal taxable incomes. This was a cut in the so-called marriage penalty, which Congress had established as part of the progressive taxation of households.[2] The rate-reduction component would produce, according to the campaign, more than half of the loss in federal revenues that would result from Bush's plan. The second component, accounting for about 10 percent of the cost of the Bush tax cuts, was a doubling of income-tax payers' tax credit per child from $500 to $1,000. The third component was the complete elimination of estate and gift taxation.[3]

In proposing a large tax cut, Bush sought to recapture the magic of Reagan, just as Bush's father and Bob Dole had tried to do during

---

interest in tax cutting as early as 1997 and that he then consulted with Karl Rove and Charls Walker in devising tax policy.

[2] In 1969, Congress created special brackets for married taxpayers. If married couples filed jointly, and their incomes were relatively uneven, they paid less than they would have if they had been single. This was a "marriage bonus," enjoyed by most married taxpayers. But as the incomes of married women increased relative to those of their spouses, the "marriage bonus" increasingly became a "marriage penalty." For the history of the treatment of marriage under the federal tax code, see Dennis J. Ventry, "The Treatment of Marriage under the U.S. Federal Income Tax, 1913–2000" (Ph.D. dissertation, University of California, Santa Barbara, 2001); and Edward J. McCaffery, *Taxing Women* (Chicago: University of Chicago Press, 1997), 29–85.

[3] Richard W. Stevenson, "Bush to Propose Broad Tax Cut in Iowa Speech," *New York Times*, December 1, 1999.

their presidential campaigns. (Like his father and Dole, Bush conveniently ignored the tax-raising dimension of the Reagan legacy.) Both the success of Reagan and the punishment George H. W. Bush had received for breaking his "no-new-taxes" pledge persuaded George W. Bush that, within the realm of domestic policy, a serious tax cut was the most effective campaign promise that Republicans could possibly make. And perhaps the son felt a special impetus to compensate for his father's political error. In any case, Bush and his advisers understood that new budget surpluses lent him a credibility as a tax cutter that his father and Dole—both of whom had been in the position of advocating tax cuts in the face of substantial deficits—had lacked.

In the Republican primaries, Bush developed a new argument for cutting taxes. He did so in order to unite the two often contentious wings of his party: neoconservatives who emphasized tax cuts and deregulation, and those who were more interested in a cultural agenda typified by opposition to abortion. In his unifying appeal, he stressed the reduction of the marriage penalty, the doubling of the child tax credit, and the repeal of estate taxation. These elements of the tax program would, he argued, strengthen the American family. He insisted on describing the estate tax as the "death tax," and he gave the erroneous impression that this tax reached far deeper than the wealthiest 2 percent of American families and thus threatened the ability of large numbers of small businesspeople and farmers to pass on their enterprises to their children.

The Bush campaign carried this theme into the general election but proceeded to put more emphasis on the arguments that Ronald Reagan had pioneered. One argument represented Reagan's brand of tax-cutting populism. Although the bulk of the tax-cut benefits would flow to wealthy Americans, campaign strategists hoped that the rate reduction, which was reminiscent of Reagan's across-the-board proposal, would win broad popular support, just as Reagan's program had done. Following the injunction of Karen Hughes,

Bush's chief media adviser, Bush soothingly described his tax cutting as "relief" rather than cutting.[4]

Bush also followed Reagan's example by promoting tax cuts as an effective way to stimulate the growth of the economy. Within the campaign, Bush's chief economic adviser, Lawrence Lindsey, believed that Reagan's tax cuts had stimulated an increase in work effort and a substantial growth in incomes, thus helping to sustain the economic expansion of the 1980s.[5] After the stock market began to falter in early 2000, and especially after the economic expansion slowed in the latter half of 2000, the supply-side dimension of a tax cut appealed even more to Bush. The cuts would help, he argued, with both the long-term reform of government and the short-run stimulation of economic growth. And perhaps Bush was applying another lesson learned from his father's administration: not to trust Alan Greenspan and the Federal Reserve to move with sufficient vigor in stimulating the economy.

In contrast to Reagan, however, Bush emphasized how tax cuts would force future Congresses to slow the growth of the federal government. David Frum, an economic speechwriter for Bush, re-called that during the campaign he often quoted a grandmother who had told him: "I've learned that if you leave cookies out on a plate, they always get eaten."[6] Bush regarded the tax cuts, phased in over a period of years, as an especially attractive means of pressuring Congress to find ways to slow, or even reverse, the expansion of en-titlements, particularly Social Security and Medicare benefits. At the same time, Bush proposed "privatizing" Social Security by creating

---

[4] David Frum, *The Right Man: The Surprise Presidency of George W. Bush* (New York: Random House, 2003), 38.

[5] For Lindsey's research on this issue, see Lawrence Lindsey, "Individual Tax-payer Response to Tax Cuts 1982–84, with Implications for the Revenue-Maximizing Tax Rate," *Journal of Public Economics* 33 (July 1987): 173–206.

[6] Frum, *Right Man*, 33.

individual accounts for Social Security taxes. By implication, he proposed turning the system into a defined contribution rather than a defined benefit program.

In response to Bush's tax-cutting agenda, the Democratic contender, Vice President Al Gore, sharply criticized Bush for emphasizing tax cuts for the wealthy. And Gore attacked Bush's Social Security ideas, challenging the notion of privatizing the system. He argued that Bush had not demonstrated how, under a privatized system, he would finance the retirement of Americans who had been born during the baby boom that had followed World War II. Even if Bush were able to reform Social Security, the "boomers" would be retiring in huge numbers, beginning in the first decade of the twenty-first century, without having had an opportunity to accumulate adequate savings in private accounts. From its inception, Social Security had financed the benefits of one generation from taxes levied on the next generation. Bush's reform, Gore suggested, would thus break an implicit social contract. Instead, Gore urged putting the part of the surplus required to fund future Social Security benefits into a "lock-box." Gore was willing to consider tax cuts, but only after insuring the solvency of Social Security. Bush accused Gore of "fuzzy math," but public opinion polls suggested that Gore had prevailed in their first debate, which had featured a confrontation over fiscal issues.[7]

Because Gore succeeded in winning the support of a majority of voters in the 2000 contest, Bush could not interpret his election to the presidency as representing a popular mandate for tax cutting or reforming Social Security. Moreover, polls in early 2001 suggested

[7] On the Bush-Gore campaign, see Sidney Blumenthal, *The Clinton Wars* (New York: Farrar, Straus, and Giroux, 2003), 700–72. For Gore's position on Social Security while he was in the Clinton administration, see Michael Waldman, *Potus Speaks: Finding the Words that Defined the Clinton Presidency* (New York: Simon & Schuster, 2000), 192–93.

that the American people had not been energized by the promise of a tax cut. In a Gallup Poll, a majority of Americans ranked debt repayment and continued social spending as higher priorities than tax cutting.[8] But Bush and his administration also noticed that most Americans said they would also like tax cuts. The popularity of cuts, the administration believed, would extend far beyond Republican stalwarts. Following Bush's inauguration, the administration made the tax-cut program its highest priority and structured it along the lines of the campaign proposal. Bush presented his cut to Congress with lines written by Karen Hughes: "Some say my tax plan is too big. Others say it is too small. I respectfully disagree. The plan is just right."[9]

Critics of Bush's tax plan were most vigorous in denouncing the distributional effects of the proposed cuts. Because the very wealthiest Americans paid almost all estate taxes, estimates of the distribution of the benefits of the tax cuts tended to show that most did in fact go to wealthy Americans. William H. Gates Sr., the father of Microsoft founder Bill Gates, denounced the repeal of the estate tax as the elimination of what progressives had rightly regarded "as a practical, democratic restraint on massive concentrated wealth and power." Repeal "today," he charged, "would widen the growing gap in economic and political influence between the wealthy and the rest of America."[10]

This kind of distributional critique of the cuts reinforced another argument made by many Democrats: The cuts would be ineffective in shoring up the sagging economy. These Democrats agreed with

---

[8] "Public Has Mixed Feeling about Tax Cuts," Gallup Poll, January 24, 2001 (www.gallup.com/subscription/?m=f&c_id=9891; last visited September 15, 2003).

[9] Frum, *Right Man*, 50.

[10] William H. Gates Sr., "The Estate Tax: What's at Stake," *Washington Post*, February 16, 2001.

the Bush administration that the economy needed a fiscal stimulus, particularly after a recession began in March 2001. But the Democrats challenged the internal supply-side logic of the cuts. They made a demand-side, Keynesian case that a larger share of the cuts ought to go to poorer Americans, who suffered more during recessions and were more likely to spend their tax savings, thereby providing a more immediate stimulus to the demand for goods and services. In response, Bush took a position that represented an odd amalgam of supply-side and Keynesian ideas. In March 2001, as Frum recalls, Bush told an audience in Billings, Montana: "We want you to have more cash flow so you can expand your business when this economy is slowing down; we want you to have more money in your pocket so you can continue to employ more hardworking people in the great land of America."[11]

Democrats and even some Republicans, including key members of the Senate Finance Committee, focused more on the long-run effects of the cuts than on their potential for short-run stimulation. In so doing, they mobilized arguments of economists such as Paul Krugman, who wrote blistering critiques of the tax plan in his column for the *New York Times*. He challenged the Bush claims that the nation could afford the tax cut, writing that Bush greatly underestimated the likely growth of discretionary spending and obscured how he would have to finance the new programs, particularly a senior citizen drug benefit that he had proposed during the campaign. Moreover, Krugman argued, Bush would have to tap the Medicare surpluses that had been accumulated from Social Security payroll taxes to fund the retirement benefits of the large generation of baby boomers. In short, under the Bush tax plan, the nation would only be able to escape a return to an era of chronic deficits, high interest

[11] Frum, *Right Man*, 58.

rates, and inflationary pressures if it abandoned its commitment to the generation of Americans about to retire.[12]

In the face of the Republican majorities and their desire to support their new president, Democratic criticism of the Bush tax plan gained little political traction. In fact, concerns over the recession led some Democrats to support the tax plan. Consequently, fewer than three months after his inauguration, Bush was able to enact his tax-cut program without having had to revise it significantly. The Economic Growth and Tax Relief Reconciliation Act of 2001, signed by the president in June, enacted provisions that closely resembled the platform on which Bush had campaigned in the primaries and the general election. The act phased in rate reductions—including reductions to 10 percent for the lowest bracket and 35 percent in the highest bracket and a reduction in the marriage penalty—over a five-year period. The act doubled the tax credit for children and added increases in the credits for child care. The act also included, in addition to the features promised in the campaign, expanded incentives for retirement savings and increases in credits and deductions for college education. The most significant departure from the program Bush had proposed resulted from a Senate budget rule that prevented revenue losses after ten years. As a consequence of this rule, the legislation provided that the estate tax would return automatically to the code in 2011. The Bush administration preferred permanent tax cuts but may well have assumed, along with its Democratic critics, that in 2010, or perhaps even sooner, Congress would feel great pressure to make the cuts permanent.[13]

---

[12] For Krugman's critique, see Paul Krugman, *Fuzzy Math: The Essential Guide to the Bush Tax Plan* (New York: W. W. Norton, 2001).

[13] David E. Sanger, "President's Signature Turns Broad Tax Cut, and a Campaign Promise, Into Law," *New York Times*, June 8, 2001.

No one could predict the precise dimensions of the threat of the 2001 tax cuts to the ability of the federal government to fund entitlements in the long run. But set in the context of the history of tax cutting since World War II, the 2001 cuts were not huge. Eugene Steuerle has suggested that the provisions of the 2001 legislation, if "fully implemented," would cost about 1.5 percent of gross domestic product (GDP) each year. In contrast, the Reagan tax cuts, if fully implemented, according to Steuerle's estimates, would have cost about 4 percent of GDP annually. Consequently, even under the 2001 tax cuts, federal tax revenues would be close to 20 percent of GDP in 2010, substantially higher than the 18 percent level of the late 1980s and early 1990s. The repeal of the estate tax further concentrated income and wealth in America, but the rest of the tax cuts, as Steuerle has pointed out, did not alter the distribution of income significantly. The legislation had lowered the top marginal rate, but it was still higher than it had been in 1986. And many low-income families actually improved their economic status as a consequence of the cuts. These were families for whom the creation of the new 10 percent bracket, together with the increase in the child credit, reduced marginal tax rates. One study estimated that the tax cuts, when fully phased in, would save a family of four at or near the poverty line more than $1,700 a year.[14]

The fact that the 2001 cut was smaller in scale than the 1981 cut did not mean, however, that Bush was any less ambitious a conservative than Reagan. In fact, the Bush administration had goals for fiscal and tax reform that were, if anything, more radical than

---

[14] C. Eugene Steuerle, "The 2001 Tax Legislation from a Long-Term Perspective," *National Tax Journal* 44 (September 2001), 427–30. See also Len Burman, Elaine Maag, and Jeff Rohaly, "The Effect of the 2001 Tax Cut on Low- and Middle-Income Families and Children," Urban Institute, April 29, 2002 (www.urban.org./url.cfm?ID=410465; last visited September 12, 2003).

Reagan's. But the Bush administration, perhaps remembering the swift backlash against the huge Reagan tax cut of 1981, adopted a more cautious, incremental political strategy.

After the passage of the 2001 cuts, the Bush administration and congressional Republicans hoped to press forward with additional cuts. These included cuts in capital-gains taxation and the provision of corporate tax breaks. The cuts in 2001 had not included any elements like the investment tax credits that the Reagan administration had made the centerpiece of the Economic Recovery Tax Act in 1981, and business lobbyists looked for favorable treatment in the next round of cuts.[15]

In addition to providing benefits for business and the wealthy, Bush wanted to stoke up the pressure that the 2001 tax cuts placed on discretionary spending and Social Security and Medicare entitlements, as well as on discretionary federal spending. In August 2001, Bush proclaimed that he regarded the disappearance of the surplus as "incredibly positive news." He looked forward to creating "a fiscal straightjacket for Congress," thereby halting the growth of government. At the same time, he suggested the possibility of dipping into Social Security funds to stimulate the weakening economy. "I've said the only reason we should use Social Security funds is in the case of an economic recession or war."[16]

The Bush administration contemplated incorporating tax cuts into a program of fundamental tax reform. Comprehensive reform, if undertaken according to popular ideals, could be a particularly attractive means of making palatable special cuts for businesses and wealthy Americans. By the summer of 2001, the Bush administration was discussing the possibility of tax reform according

---

[15] Robin Toner, "Balance of Power: The Aftermath; Bush Agenda Now Faces Tough Sledding in Congress," *New York Times*, May 25, 2001.

[16] David E. Sanger, "President Asserts Shrunken Surplus May Curb Congress," *New York Times*, August 25, 2001.

to principles, the *New York Times* reported, of "fairer, flatter, simpler." One of the approaches the administration was considering was a comprehensive simplification of the progressive tax system, perhaps following the blueprint of the Tax Reform Act of 1986. In the spirit of simplification, Treasury Secretary Paul O'Neill called the tax code "9,500 pages of gibberish." But he and the rest of the Bush team also discussed adopting a single-rate flat tax on income or moving to consumption taxation. These were, of course, the basic alternatives to the progressive income tax that had been on the table since the champions of the Contract with America had taken up tax reform.

The conservative fiscal reformers, however, remained badly split between proponents of a flat tax and advocates of consumption taxation. In July, Bush adviser Lindsey admitted that there had been no progress in healing that breach. No consensus had emerged in the administration, Congress, the think tanks, academe, or any segment of the media behind any of the basic reform options. "The facts are that one needs a broad consensus before moving on fundamental tax reform," Lindsey acknowledged. This would take time, he said, but "that doesn't mean you shouldn't start the process." The White House believed that it had started the process, but it was noncommittal as to which approach to reform it might favor. "We're going through the merits" of each, said R. Glenn Hubbard, the chair of the Council of Economic Advisers, "and each has a lot of merit."[17] Meanwhile, the Bush administration launched a Social Security Commission, which was studying approaches to "privatizing" the system.[18]

[17] Richard W. Stevenson, "Bush, After Gaining Tax Cut, Is Taking Aim at Tax Code," *New York Times*, July 16, 2001.

[18] Richard W. Stevenson, "President to Name Panel on Social Security Plan," *New York Times*, May 2, 2001.

A series of four surprising, even stunning, events complicated whatever plans the Bush administration was developing for tax cutting, tax reform, and reform of entitlements. First, in April 2001, the defection of Senator James Jeffords of Vermont from the Republican Party forced a reorganization of the Senate, with the Democrats in the majority. Now Bush would have to win the support of the Democratic leadership in the Senate for any major tax cuts.

Second, a recession began in early 2001, and the stock market tumbled lower. The recession, which would last about a year, increased the deficits beyond what the 2001 tax cuts would have produced. The recession weakened tax collections across all tax brackets, and the deterioration of the stock market collapse reduced collections of taxes from the wealthy, particularly in the form of taxes on realized capital gains. In addition, the stock market debacle cast doubt on the wisdom of creating individual retirement accounts within the Social Security system.[19]

Third, the terrorist attacks of September 11, 2001, riveted the attention of the nation and the administration on retaliating with a war on international terrorism. It might now be more difficult, within the administration, to focus on crafting a tax-reform program and, outside the administration, to develop a consensus behind its adoption. Moreover, mobilizing a military response to the attacks would further increase deficits.

---

[19] The commission reported in December 2001, but failed to agree on a plan for creating private investment accounts within the system. The stock market debacle may have contributed to the division within the commission. In any case, as White House spokesman Ari Fleischer explained, reform of Social Security took on a lower priority, "given the fact that we now have a recession and a war." Richard W. Stevenson, "Bush Panel Outlines 3 Plans for Social Security Overhaul," *New York Times*, November 30, 2001; and Richard W. Stevenson, "Social Security Panel Presents Options but No Unified Plan," *New York Times*, December 11, 2001.

Fourth, in December 2001, the Enron Corporation announced that it was filing for bankruptcy. As Bush speechwriter Frum recalled, the news "hit the Bush White House like a death in the family." Not only had "Enron been to Texas what Microsoft was to Washington State," but also "the tone of much of the reporting on Enron insinuated that the Bush team were somehow complicit in the Enron debacle or, at any rate, had benefited from Enron's fraud."[20] Whatever the truth of the matter, as a result of Enron's collapse and other corporate accounting scandals, the Bush team now had to take care in how it presented new tax cuts and tax reforms that provided special favors for businesses and the wealthy.

Despite all of these complications, Bush remained focused on tax cutting and tax reform. The reason was the weakening economy. For one thing, he had before him the example of his father, whose sky-high approval ratings at the time of the Gulf War had disappeared as a recession took hold. He and his economic advisers may well have believed that tax cuts could promote recovery in the short run. For another, Bush may have seen an opportunity in the problem of the recession: the advance of tax cuts for the rich, and of fiscal reform, under cover of a search for fiscal stimulation.

In October, Bush called for tax cuts as the central component of an economic stimulus package. In particular, he sought to accelerate the 2001 cuts in income-tax rates, to increase depreciation rates for business investment, and to eradicate the alternative minimum tax (AMT) for corporations.

Bush began negotiations with Tom Daschle (Democrat–North Dakota), the Senate majority leader, but the two soon clashed. Daschle proposed that Congress roll back the 2001 tax cuts and, in early January 2002, he accused Bush of the "most dramatic fiscal

---

[20] Frum, *Right Man*, 220.

deterioration in our nation's history." Bush dug in; he was so aroused that later that week he departed from a radio script to go far beyond his father's "Read my lips" statement. "Not over my dead body will they raise your taxes," Bush declared to a national audience.[21] He further challenged Daschle by claiming that he had the votes in the Senate to make the 2001 cuts permanent.

Bush, however, decided to compromise, in part to secure the cooperation of Daschle and other Democratic leaders for the war on terrorism and the invasion of Afghanistan. Bush continued to ask for accelerated and permanent cuts, but in March he and the Senate leadership reached agreement on a modest economic stimulus bill that contained a mélange of Keynesian demand-side and neo-conservative supply-side elements. The legislation extended unemployment benefits, provided tax incentives for rebuilding in lower Manhattan, and offered new depreciation benefits for businesses.[22]

Bush's retreat had been only tactical. Little more than a week after he signed the stimulus bill, he called for a third batch of tax cuts. These included two key provisions: first, increasing the amounts of investment that small businesses could deduct in calculating their taxable income and, second, permanently repealing the estate tax. Bush advertised both measures as ones that would come to the aid of small businesses. On April 15, the normal deadline for filing individual tax returns, he raised the stakes by calling once again to make permanent all the 2001 tax cuts. The Republicans in the House of Representatives responded by passing a bill that would

---

[21] Richard W. Stevenson, "A Nation Challenged: The Economy; Bush Wants More Tax Cuts in Effort to Help Economy," *New York Times*, October 6, 2001; and Richard W. Stevenson, "Prospects for Stimulus Plan Hinge on Bush Demand for Tax Cuts," *New York Times*, December 13, 2001. On the tension between Bush and Daschle, see Frum, *Right Man*, 203–4, 219, 274.

[22] Richard W. Stevenson, "Senate Approves Economic Stimulus Bill," *New York Times*, March 9, 2002.

have permanently repealed the estate tax. In the Senate, however, six Democrats who had voted for the 2001 cuts blocked approval of the House measure. Crucial to the defeat in the Senate was the lobbying of some of the wealthiest Americans, including Bill Gates, Warren Buffett, George Soros, and Ted Turner, who had formed a group called "Responsible Wealth" to protect the estate tax.[23]

Meanwhile, the administration, led by the Council of Economic Advisers (CEA) and the Treasury, intensified its review of the options for fundamental reform that advocates for the Contract with America had proposed. In its report for 2002, issued in February, the CEA said that "we must investigate options for tax reform." As the analysis of the CEA and the Treasury proceeded, Treasury Secretary O'Neill repeatedly declared: "Our tax code is an abomination." He told a business group that the tax code "hurts our competitiveness." He went on: "This nation deserves a better tax code, and I believe we can achieve it." He was most critical of the corporate income tax and complained of the "unbelievably complicated" nature of the tax code. However, he remained very vague in public about the likely shape of the Bush administration's reform program. In November 2002, he told the *Financial Times* that the administration had been studying reform "for the better part of a year, cataloguing all the ideas that have been advanced over the last 10 or 20 years about how one might restructure the system," and that the president will "in time ... decide what he wants to do." O'Neill did say that tax simplification was his own priority, and that he thought the most likely reforms were those "minimally

[23] David E. Sanger, "Bush Revives Tax-Cut Plan Providing Aid to Business," *New York Times*, March 19, 2002; Sanger, "Bush Pressing to Make Cut in Tax Rates Permanent," *New York Times*, April 16, 2002; Carl Hulse, "Effort to Repeal Estate Tax Ends in Senate Defeat," *New York Times*, June 13, 2002; and Hulse, "Battle on Estate Tax: How Two Well-Organized Lobbies Sprang into Action," *New York Times*, June 14, 2002.

controversial and not very costly." However, *New York Times* reporters suggested that a more dramatic change might be in the works: a replacement of the progressive income tax with some kind of broad tax on consumption.

As part of its study of tax reform, the Bush administration considered the idea of allowing individuals to exclude dividends from their taxable income. That exclusion appealed to many economists, including Lindsey and Hubbard, because the taxation of dividends by the individual income tax and the taxation of profits (the source of dividends) by the corporate income tax seemed to be double taxation. Lindsey and Hubbard, who had promoted the repeal of the taxation of dividends when he was an adviser in George H. W. Bush's administration, regarded the double tax as unfair, economically inefficient, and an incentive for corporations to borrow excessively. Both the Reagan and George H. W. Bush administrations had taken an interest in the repeal but had been unwilling to pay for the cut by forgoing other cuts. Other conservative economists— including stockbroker Charles Schwab and television commentator Lawrence Kudlow, who had been an economic adviser in the Reagan administration and was reported to be close to Vice President Dick Cheney—had their eyes on Wall Street. They energetically and visibly touted the cut in dividend taxation as a way of stimulating the sagging stock market.[24]

---

[24] *The Economic Report of the President, 2002 together with the Annual Report of the Council of Economic Advisers* (Washington, D.C.: U.S. Government Printing Office, 2002), chap. 1; David E. Sanger, "Bush Pressing to Make Cut in Tax Rates Permanent," *New York Times*, April 16, 2002; Richard W. Stevenson, "Itching to Rebuild the Tax Law," *New York Times*, November 24, 2002; Ed Crooks and Dan Roberts, "O'Neill and Bush Ready to Wrestle with Fiscal Stimulus Proposals," *Financial Times*, November 26, 2002; Elizabeth Bumiller, "Bush and the Economy: Genesis of a Plan; Nurturing the Tax Cut Idea since the Reagan Administration," *New York Times*, January 7, 2003.

As the time neared to present both the president's budget for fiscal 2004 and the CEA's annual report, some conservatives intensified a push toward both additional tax cuts for the wealthiest Americans and consumption taxation. In November, a *Wall Street Journal* editorial titled "The Non-Taxpaying Class" pointed to the fact that the wealthiest Americans accounted for a huge share of income-tax revenues. As the editorial asserted, in 2000 the richest 5 percent of taxpayers accounted for 56 percent of income-tax collections (up from 42 percent in 1986), while the top 50 percent accounted for 96 percent (up from 93 percent in 1986). In contrast, the bottom 50 percent accounted for 4 percent (down from 7 percent in 1986). (The editorial did not point out that incomes had become more concentrated at the top in that same period.) The main thrust of the editorial was against increasing tax benefits for the poor, such as the 16.5 million "lucky duckies" (in the words of the editorial writers) who were "the beneficiaries of tax policies that have expanded the personal exemption and standard deduction and targeted certain voter groups by introducing a welter of tax credits for things like child care and education."

The *Journal* editorial also, by implication, pointed toward reform. It warned that "this complicated system of progressivity and targeted rewards is creating a nation of two different taxpaying classes: those who pay a lot and those who pay very little." The result was that "as fewer and fewer people are responsible for paying more and more of all taxes, the constituency for tax cutting, much less for tax reform, is eroding." Administration figures soon echoed the *Journal*'s distributional analysis. In December, J. T. Young, the deputy assistant secretary of the treasury for legislative affairs, wrote in the *Washington Times* that: "higher earners cannot produce the level of revenues needed to sustain the liberals' increasingly costly spending programs over the long term." This is, he declared, "the end-result of class warfare." Later that month, in a tax forum at the American Enterprise Institute, Hubbard struck the same chord, albeit more gently: "The increasing reliance on taxing higher-income households and targeted social preferences at lower incomes," he said, "stands in the way of moving to a simpler, flatter tax system."[25]

In early January of 2003, the Bush administration proposed a dramatic package of cuts that exceeded in scope what both Democrats and Republicans had expected.[26] Bush reiterated his request that Congress accelerate elements of the 2001 tax-cut package. However, he went well beyond this to urge adoption of a set of dramatic supply-side cuts. These measures would move the nation toward the repeal of all taxes on investment income and accumulated wealth. These proposals included not only making repeal of the estate tax permanent but also allowing individuals to exclude dividends from taxation and to move, each year, $60,000 worth of investments into tax-free savings accounts. The income tax would remain in place, but it would apply largely to wages, salaries, and rents. With some additional adjustments, the individual income tax could become, in effect, a tax on consumption. As the White House advanced these proposals, it indicated that it still favored making private investment accounts an integral part of the Social Security system. The administration had postponed any full-on, comprehensive reform of Social Security; it had decided to pursue the reform

---

[25] "The Non-Taxpaying Classes," *Wall Street Journal*, November 20, 2002, reprinted January 20, 2003; J. T. Young, "Outer Limits of Class Warfare," *Washington Times*, December 3, 2002; Jonathan Weisman, "New Tax Plan May Bring a Shift in Burden," *Washington Post*, December 16, 2002.

[26] On December 6, 2002, both Paul O'Neill and Lawrence Lindsey left the administration, but their departures may have had little to do with the formulation of the tax cut package. See Richard W. Stevenson, "Upheaval in the Treasury: The Context; Paying a Price for a Shaky Economy," *New York Times*, December 7, 2002; "Fifty Ways to Say Goodbye," *Financial Times*, December 7, 2000.

of Social Security in an incremental fashion, and to use tax reform as a cover to do so.[27]

The Bush administration estimated that the new tax cuts would cost the federal government about $726 billion over the next ten years. Some conservatives quickly declared that they welcomed the deficits that this cost would produce. In the *Wall Street Journal*, economist Milton Friedman wrote: "There is one and only one way" of cutting "government down to size." This was, said Friedman, harkening back to Reagan, "the way parents control spendthrift children, cutting their allowance." Friedman said he did not know whether or not cutting allowances would stimulate the economy in the short run, but he was confident that "a major tax cut will be a step toward the smaller government that I believe most citizens of the U.S. want."[28]

In early February, Hubbard adopted Friedman's argument and said that the deficits were designed to reduce the size of government. In its annual *Economic Report of the President*, which appeared in February, Hubbard's CEA made clear the president's context for tax reform. Before assessing the various options for major reform of the income tax, the CEA declared: "An important goal of fiscal policy is to promote growth by limiting the share of output commanded by the federal government." Nowhere in the report, however, did the CEA compare the level of taxation in the United States with that elsewhere in the world. Such a comparison would have revealed

[27] Richard W. Stevenson, "Politics and the Economy: The Overview; Bush Unveils Plan to Cut Tax Rates and Spur Economy," *New York Times*, January 8, 2003. Probably the most significant, and politically difficult, adjustment required to shift the basis of taxation to consumption would be the elimination of the deductibility of interest payments (or the addition of borrowings to the tax base).

[28] Milton Friedman, "What Every American Wants," *Wall Street Journal*, January 19, 2003. It is possible that the metaphor of the spendthrift child was originally Friedman's, and that Reagan had borrowed it.

that in 2000, among the thirty nations that belonged to the Organization for Economic Cooperation and Development (OECD), total tax revenue as a share of GDP was lower in the United States that anywhere except for Japan, South Korea, and Mexico. Federal, state, and local taxes claimed 29.6 percent of GDP in the United States. Japan and Korea had slightly lower levels (respectively 27.1 and 26.1 percent), and only Mexico had a significantly lower level (18.5 percent). The average (unweighted) for all OECD members was 37.4 percent, and it was 39.5 percent for European OECD members.[29]

The Republican Study Committee, consisting of about seventy of the most fiscally conservative members of the House of Representatives, quickly voiced their agreement with Friedman and Hubbard. The group's chair, Sue Myrick (North Carolina), said: "Anything that will help us stop spending money, I'm in favor of." Patrick J. Toomey (Pennsylvania), the chair of the group's budget task force, dismissed the possibility that the larger deficit might push up interest rates and asserted: "There's a much better case to be made that the deficit will force spending down."[30]

By this logic, conservatives should have been pleased in March, when Douglas J. Holtz-Eakin, the director of the Congressional Budget Office (CBO) and, until February, the chief economist for the CEA, estimated that the cost of the new tax cuts was more likely to be on the order of $2.7 trillion. In addition, he suggested that the

---

[29] *The Economic Report of the President Together with the Annual Report of the Council of Economic Advisers 2003* (Washington, D.C.: U.S. Government Printing Office, 2003), introduction and chapter 5 ("Tax Policy for a Growing Economy"); and OECD, "OECD Report Shows Tax Burden Falling in Many Countries," table A, October 10, 2002 (www.oecd.org/documentprint/0,2774,en_2649_37427_1062312_1_1_1_37427,00.html; last visited September 16, 2003).

[30] David Firestone, "Washington Talk: Conservatives Now See Deficits as a Tool to Fight Spending," *New York Times*, February 11, 2003.

federal government might have to double its debt to finance the tax cuts over the ten-year period. In contrast to the House conservatives, he suggested that this new debt might crowd out new corporate investment. A bipartisan group, which included Paul Volcker, former chair of the Federal Reserve Board, and Robert Rubin, former secretary of the treasury, pointed out that the level of federal debt would grow even larger if the federal government not only cut taxes but also provided a Medicare prescription drug benefit and adjusted the AMT. They warned that this would happen "before the fiscal going gets tough" as a consequence of the "unfounded benefit promises" of Social Security and Medicare. They also rejected supply-side analysis and called for "no new tax cuts beyond those that are likely to provide immediate fiscal stimulus."[31]

The bipartisan critique did not slow the Bush package in the House, but it did so in the Senate. Democrats in that body were generally willing to accept some tax cuts, but they wanted ones that put cash into the hands of middle-class Americans to stimulate, Keynesian style, economic recovery. The Democrats had lost control of the Senate, but they found allies among a few Republicans who had difficulty living with estimates like those of the CBO, and with the certainty that war and reconstruction in Iraq, which began in March, would push deficits even higher. They did not entirely agree with John W. Snow, who had replaced Paul O'Neill as secretary of treasury, when Snow told the House Ways and Means Committee that "we can afford the war, and we'll put it behind us." For the first time since the Mexican War, an administration rallied the nation for war without calling for any financial sacrifice.[32] In

---

[31] Daniel Altman, "The End of Taxes as We Know Them," *New York Times*, March 30, 2003; Bob Kerrey, Sam Nunn, Peter G. Peterson, Robert E. Rubin, Warren B. Rudman, and Paul Volcker, "No New Tax Cuts," *New York Times*, April 9, 2003.

[32] The only other possible exception was the Persian Gulf War in 1991. It is true that the federal government did not raise taxes that year. But it did so

the closely divided Senate, two dissident Republicans, Olympia J. Snowe (Maine), who served on the Senate Finance Committee, and George V. Voinovich (Ohio), prevented the Senate from adopting the full range of Bush's reform proposals and from adopting any package of cuts that would cost more than $350 billion.[33]

Bush never made a coherent, principled appeal to the public on behalf of the broad shift toward consumption taxation that he had proposed. If he was aware of Reagan's vigorous, effective campaign on behalf of reform in 1985 and 1986, he did not follow that example of political entrepreneurship. He seemed to prefer the tactics of reform by stealth. He worked largely inside the government, mobilizing Republican partisanship and congressional support for cuts that would, according to CBO estimates, cost the Treasury about $320 billion. This was even lower than the Senate ceiling, but the Republican architects of the legislation had adopted many of the cuts that the president and the House had wanted. They achieved the relatively low $320 billion figure by attaching sunset clauses to the cuts. Most observers doubted that future Congresses would allow the tax cuts to expire. And the Republicans made sure to include many of the cuts that the president cared most strongly about— substantial cuts (down to a rate of 15 percent) in the taxation of dividends and capital-gains taxation. The final legislation, the Jobs and Growth Tax Relief Reconciliation Act of 2003, cut the taxation of dividends and capital gains down to 15 percent. Calculation of the reduced dividend taxes would, however, be a highly complicated matter. The act also included accelerations in implementing the rate

in 1990, and President George H. W. Bush linked the increase in gasoline taxes to the confrontation in Iraq. The 1990 tax increases first generated revenues in 1991. See pp. 189–90.

[33] David E. Rosenbaum, "Tax Cuts and War Have Seldom Mixed, *New York Times*, March 9, 2003; David E. Rosenbaum, "Negotiators Reach Rare Deal on Tax Cut," *New York Times*, April 10, 2003.

reductions and child credit authorized in 2001, and it provided for significant increases in depreciation allowances for corporations.[34]

Estimating the ultimate cost of all the Bush tax cuts would require a great deal of guesswork, but the cuts certainly augmented the current deficits, which had become formidable by 2003. Toward the end of the summer of 2003, the CBO forecast that the deficit for fiscal 2003 (ending on September 30) would reach a record $401 billion. This would be twice as large in absolute terms as the deficit for fiscal 2002 and a great departure from the $127 billion surplus for fiscal 2001. The CBO believed that the 2003 package of tax cuts would account for about $53 billion of the $401 billion deficit, and for more than $117 billion of the projected deficit for fiscal 2004 of about $480 billion.

In comparison with the size of the economy, the 2003 deficit was still smaller than the deficits of the Reagan era, which had reached roughly 5 to 6 percent of GDP. By 2004, however, the CBO estimated that the deficit would reach about 4.2 percent of GDP. The CBO, however, had not reckoned on possible increases in spending. In September, President Bush asked Congress for an additional $87 billion to fund the reconstruction of Iraq. With such a large increase, the deficit seemed likely to rise above the biggest of the Reagan era. The three tax cuts, the wars and reconstructions in Afghanistan and Iraq, and the weak economy all had worked together to turn the budgetary surpluses of the late 1990s into deficits that would begin to rival those that drove the pragmatic Reagan administration to seek major tax increases.[35]

---

[34] David E. Rosenbaum and David Firestone, "$318 Billion Deal is Set in Congress for Cutting Taxes," *New York Times*, May 22, 2003; Rosenbaum, "A Tax Cut without End," *New York Times*, May 23, 2003; Richard W. Stevenson, "Bush Signs Tax Cut Bill, Dismissing All Criticism," *New York Times*, May 29, 2003.

[35] Rosenbaum, "Tax Cut without End"; Edmund L. Andrews, "New Deficit Estimate: 401 Billion," *New York Times*, August 9, 2003; Andrews,

As the Bush administration neared the end of 2003 and approached an electoral test in 2004, it could claim to have made some progress in advancing a fiscal revolution. With the tax cuts, the president had shifted the federal tax code toward the taxation of consumption. But Bush's progress overall had been limited. Significant taxation of investment remained, and the repeal of the estate tax was not yet permanent. The corporate income tax remained. Further, despite the Bush administration's complaints about complexity and promises of tax simplicity, the tax code was more complicated than it had been before the three cuts in taxes. In any case, news of a shift toward a consumption regime had probably not reached most Americans. The president had yet to dramatize and win popular support for such a shift. He had not demonstrated that he knew how to use experts, the media, and bipartisan cooperation on behalf of reform. Despite the desire of the Bush administration to make taxes more predictable, the future of the tax code had become more uncertain than at any time since World War II. Finally, Bush had not yet developed a coherent program to reform entitlements, and there was no indication that such a program would win popular support.

Perhaps it will turn out that the 2003 tax cuts marked the end of the Bush administration's effort to shift tax regimes and dramatically scale back entitlements. The administration never displayed an interest in an open campaign for such reforms, and perhaps the administration will lose interest in, or the ability to pursue, the tactics of stealth. Also, Bush might come to regard the growing deficit as a

"Leap in Deficit Instead of Fall Is Seen for U.S.," *New York Times*, August 27, 2003; Congressional Budget Office, "The Budget and Economic Outlook: An Update," August 2003 (www.cbo.gov/showdoc.cfm?index=4493&sequence=0&; last visited September 21, 2003); David Firestone, "Dizzying Drive to Red Ink Poses Stark Choices for Washington," *New York Times*, September 14, 2003; Firestone, "Afghanistan and Iraq Tab of $87 Billion Is Submitted," *New York Times*, September 18, 2003.

serious problem and pragmatically turn to "revenue enhancement," just as Reagan did after the 1981 tax cuts. And the presidential election of 2004 might return the White House to the Democratic Party. By the fall of 2003, all the candidates for the Democratic nomination for the presidency had denounced the Bush tax cuts, and all had advocated rolling back the tax cuts that had favored the wealthy.[36]

If the Bush administration survives the 2004 election and continues on its course of tax reform, its best prospects for success may rest with a future financial crisis. An expanded reconstruction effort in Iraq, other international problems, and domestic problems, such as a collapse of real estate markets might trigger, would all increase deficits and the likelihood of a financial debacle.

At the same time, as Paul Krugman and others have argued, the costs of new federal programs—such as reducing the AMT and creating a Medicare drug benefit, and the implicit social contract that requires funding the Social Security benefits of the baby-boom generation—could also expand deficits and contribute to the seriousness of a financial crisis. Such a crisis, rife with high interest rates and inflationary pressure, would require either a dramatic reduction of entitlements or large tax increases.[37] The Bush

---

[36] David E. Rosenbaum, "Tax Cuts Split the Democratic Presidential Field," *New York Times*, September 12, 2003.

[37] See, e.g., Krugman, *Fuzzy Math*; Krugman, "Stating the Obvious," *New York Times*, May 27, 2003; and Krugman, "The Tax-Cut Con," *New York Times Magazine*, September 14, 2003. Pressures to reduce or repeal the AMT are likely to become powerful. The AMT entered the tax code in 1986 as a measure designed to cap certain deductions taken by high-income taxpayers. But Congress has never indexed the minimum for inflation. Consequently, in 2003, almost 2.5 million taxpayers are likely to have to pay the AMT, and estimates suggest that as many as 33 million taxpayers will pay it by 2010, including almost all couples with two children and incomes between $75,000 and $100,000. Economist Leonard Burman describes this as "a problem people don't know they have." See Shailagh Murray, "Firestorm

administration might wager on the former, but the lessons of history tend to point to the latter as the more likely outcome.

THE NEXT FISCAL CRISIS: GUIDELINES FROM HISTORY

If Americans are unwilling to scale back their demands for the services of the federal government, and especially for social entitlements and national defense, the next major fiscal crisis may be severe enough to require the federal government to go beyond tinkering with existing taxes and carry out fundamental tax reform. Put somewhat differently, solving the crisis might require new tax revenues on a scale possible only if the federal government simultaneously undertook systematic tax reform.

In crafting a new regime, reformers could find some substantive guidance in the history of federal tax regimes. The most fundamental fact for reformers to bear in mind is that the introduction of a new tax regime has never stood alone. Every new regime has always been an integral part of a larger transformation of government that became a necessary part of the resolution of a national emergency. As such, each new regime had a reciprocal relationship with the larger transformation of government: The tax regime enhanced trust in the larger transformation of government. The best example of this was the adoption of highly progressive corporate and individual taxation during World War I. Creating this tax system built public trust in the intervention in World War I and the mobilization that accompanied it. The tax system of World War II was less progressive, but it also helped Americans accept wartime sacrifice. Yet

Looms on Minimum Tax," *The Wall Street Journal*, July 1, 2003, and Leonard E. Burman et al., *The Individual AMT: Problems and Potential Solutions*, Tax Policy Center Discussion Paper 5 (Washington, D.C.: Urban Institute Press, 2002).

the new tax regimes also received support and legitimacy as a consequence of the larger institutional transformation. For example, public confidence in the democratic purposes of American participation in World War I increased support for a new tax regime. More dramatically, the popularity of the massive mobilization for World War II helped win acceptance for the mass-based income tax. In short, all earlier, transforming episodes of fiscal reform have taken place in the context of public trust in the federal government and augmented that trust.

If the federal government did attempt to fabricate a new fiscal regime, it would succeed only if it recaptured public trust. Americans must believe that the federal government is working effectively to solve the nation's structural problems—perhaps in part through tax reform—before they would be willing to support significant tax increases, embrace new taxes, or accept reductions in the tax benefits they receive from the federal government. Until that trust returns and tax policy contributes to building that trust, special-interest politics will continue to dominate the shaping of taxation. Both the affluent and middle- and low-income families who are alienated from politics and government will tend to fear that any reform measures—especially the introduction of new taxes that promise to reduce tax burdens—are nothing more than covert devices to increase their taxes or remove their tax benefits.[38]

[38] There are numerous elements that might enter into fundamental tax reform that would be rather different from the flat tax or broad-based consumption taxation, such as the architects of the Contract with America proposed, and the administration of George W. Bush favors. Reformers could carry out a full-scale implementation of the principles that guided the Tax Reform Act of 1986. A new consumption tax system could include substantial exemptions of spending for low-income taxpayers, or even be progressive in their rate structure. Energy taxes, designed for the purposes of conservation or internalizing the external costs of pollution, might play a greater role in a reformed tax system. Replacement of Social Security payroll taxes with income taxes or value-added taxes would represent a very substantial change

Historically, the introduction of new tax regimes that enhance confidence in American government has required several key institutional elements. In particular, the successful creation of new tax regimes in the United States has included some combination of three elements: (1) enhanced progressiveness in rate structure, (2) allocation of revenues raised by regressive taxes to programs whose benefits are distributed progressively, and (3) regulation of behavior in ways that were widely regarded as improving the national well-being.

The Civil War tax regime, which was based on high tariffs, incorporated the second and third elements. The second element was financing Civil War pensions, and the third was encouragement of a national market in which wages and profits were high. The World War I regime swept in not only on an ethos of national sacrifice but also on the conviction that government should tax away or deter the accumulation of ill-gotten or socially dangerous assets (e.g., excess profits and incomes, large estates, undistributed profits) and punish "sinful" behavior. The New Deal tax regime encompassed all three elements, and the regime introduced during World War II justified mass-based income taxation in terms of not only sacrifice for national survival but also progressive social justice.

The Tax Reform Act of 1986 did not signal a new tax regime, but it constituted the most important change in tax policy since World War II. To a significant extent, it represented an effort to promote

in the current tax regime. For suggestions of how a new tax regime might be a central element in a program of "liberal nationalism," see Michael Lind, *The Next American Nation* (New York: Free Press, 1995), 101, 182, 188 ff., 216, 310, 319, 322 ff. Robert Shiller has also proposed strengthening the progressive income tax by turning it into a kind of "inequality insurance." Under this system, the government would automatically adjust progressive tax rates to prevent a worsening of the distribution of income. See Robert J. Shiller, *The New Financial Order: Risk in the 21st Century* (Princeton, N.J.: Princeton University Press, 2003), 149–164.

horizontal equity and enhance economic productivity while protecting the overall progressivity of the income-tax system. The success
of this act may well have signaled that definitions of fairness that
stress horizontal equity had grown in their political appeal during
the 1970s and 1980s. Popular support for the principle of horizontal fairness may also have helped George W. Bush's campaign
for relief of the double taxation of dividends. But in contrast to
Reagan's campaign in 1986, Bush's larger campaign for consumption taxation has not yet acquired the aura of an idealistic crusade
for greater tax equity. Part of the reason may well be that basing
federal finance on regressive consumption taxation still remains at
odds with American ideals of progressive equity. An important indi-
cator of that strength has been the Bush administration's agreement
to, and even support for, significant tax reductions for Americans
in the lowest income groups.

In addition to offering guidance on the substance of tax policy,
the history of the great transformations of American taxation could
provide the architects of future tax reform with several lessons on
the process of reform. On the one hand, the history of taxation in
America has been turbulent, ridden with conflict involving the interests of both the state and the modern corporation, and heavily
constrained by constitutional rules, institutional habits, and technology. It has always been uncertain in its outcome, and today the
future of taxation in America may still be very much "up for grabs."
On the other hand, the history of national fiscal crises suggests that
the federal government, in league with other powerful interests, has
the capacity to produce dramatic, strategic changes in tax policy.

The history of national crises suggests that the cause of tax reform must have effective presidential leadership. As party loyalties
and party discipline have waned in significance during recent years,
presidential leadership has become more important. Whatever the
national objectives might be—promotion of domestic savings (public and private), increase in economic productivity, advance of

distributional equity, or growth in jobs—they must be stated with coherence, with a clear sense of internal priorities, and with drama. If taxes are to be increased or decreased significantly, the specific purposes of the increases or decreases must be identified with clarity and cogent justification, linked to the general purposes of government, and developed through a process of consensus building with outreach to contending groups in civil society. Such consensus building will offer the greatest potential for success by embedding any changes in tax rates within a reform program that is comprehensive in scope—one that involves a systematic integration of all the modes of federal taxation and expenditure.

Presidents must not only articulate and dramatize goals but also lend coherence to the process of legislation. The exigencies of major wars and depressions forced—or enabled—presidents to approach tax reform with a sense of mission and a degree of procedural coherence rarely possible under the U.S. constitutional order. But the experience during the Reagan presidency suggests that a national emergency is not a necessary condition for coherent reform. Despite the absence of an emergency, the Reagan administration approached tax reform in 1986 with an appreciation of this kind of coherence. The administration of George W. Bush has launched an even more ambitious reform program, but it may not have done so in the coherent way that is necessary for sustained success.

The history of tax policy during periods of national crisis also suggests that reformers must be alert to the play of historical contingency. They must watch, in particular, for the moments in which key players may be willing to change their minds. Tax reformers would do well to listen to the advice of Thomas S. Adams, the most important economist in the Treasury between 1917 and 1933. Although he viewed taxation as heavily shaped by class politics, he found that on some tax issues, "a majority of legislators and voters are unaffected and disinterested; they may cast their votes as a more or less disinterested jury." And "in the adoption of tax legislation

there come zero hours, when the zeal of the narrowly selfish flags."
The challenge that Adams saw was for experts, and for politicians,
to take advantage of such openings. "There are thus many important tax problems," he declared, "which may be settled on the broad
basis of equity and sound public policy, if one is wise and ingenious
enough to find the right solution."[39]

The most dramatic changes in American tax regimes have occurred when administrations have been able to take advantage of
the opportunities, identified by Adams, for what political scientists
have called "social learning." For dramatic change, administrations
must approach tax reform in a comprehensive fashion, articulate
the goals of reform in ways that rise above the interests of particular
groups, and organize the process of reform to insulate experts from
political pressure. In the politics of tax reform, conflict has always
been severe and the outcome uncertain. But in this turbulence, the
successful architects and managers of the most significant transformations of tax policy have been able, despite their immersion in a
grinding political process, to define and articulate a transcendent
public interest.

[39] Thomas Sewell Adams, "Ideals and Idealism in Taxation," presidential address delivered at the Fortieth Annual Meeting of the American Economic
Association, December 27, 1927, *American Economic Review* 18 (1928):
1–7.

Historiography and bibliography

Toward the end of World War I, the Austrian sociologist Rudolf Goldscheid proposed a "fiscal sociology" as a new way to study the public budget. He wanted to analyze the budget as "the skeleton of the state stripped of all misleading ideologies."[1] Goldscheid explained that "nowhere [is] the entirety of any given order of society and economy... reflected as clearly [as] in the public household, that the State cannot be very different from its financial system, [and] that every single private household is intimately connected with the State household."[2] Another Austrian scholar, the

---

[1] Rudolf Goldscheid, *Staatssozialismus oder Staatskapitalismus* (Vienna, 1917), quoted by Joseph A. Schumpeter, *Die Krise des Steuerstaats, Zeitfragen aus dem Gebiete der Soziologie* (Graz and Leipzig, 1918), translated as Schumpeter, "The Crisis of the Tax State," in *International Economic Papers: Translations Prepared for the International Economic Association*, no. 4, ed. Alan T. Peacock et al. (London: Macmillan, 1954), 5–38.

[2] Rudolf Goldscheid, "Staat, offentlicher Haushalt und Gesellschaft, Wesen und Aufgaben der Finanzwissenschaften vom Standpunkte der Soziologie," in *Handbuch der Finanzwissenschaft*, vol. 1, ed. W. Gerloff and F. Meisel (Tübingen, 1925), translated as "A Sociological Approach to Problems of Public Finance," in *Classics in the Theory of Public Finance*, ed. Richard A. Musgrave and Alan T. Peacock (London: Macmillan, 1962), 202–13.

economist Joseph Schumpeter, seconded Goldscheid's proposal and stressed that the fiscal sociology should have a historical basis. In 1918, Schumpeter declared:

The spirit of a people, its cultural level, its social structure, the deeds its policy may prepare—all this and more is written in its fiscal history, stripped of all phrases. He who knows how to listen to its message here discerns the thunder of world history more clearly than anywhere else.[3]

The severe wartime fiscal crisis and attendant debates over the meaning of the modern state within the ruins of the Austro-Hungarian Empire stimulated Goldscheid and Schumpeter to develop their interest in fiscal sociology, fiscal history, and the history of taxation.

In a similar fashion, the fiscal anguish of the U.S. federal government during the 1980s and 1990s and the related political discourse over the proper role and scope of the national government have prompted some American scholars to reconsider the history of public finance and especially of taxation. From a variety of political perspectives, they have begun to revive tax history in order to understand contemporary policy options and to enrich our knowledge of American society and government.

Professional historians, however, have rarely shared Schumpeter's enthusiasm for the potential for understanding a society through the history of its taxation. They have contributed relatively little to broad-gauged scholarship on the history of American taxation, even during the recent revival of interest in tax history within other disciplines. To be sure, historians have provided some monographic research on specific aspects and periods of tax development, and they have occasionally commented on tax policy

---

[3] Schumpeter, "Crisis of the Tax State," 7.

while writing on broader or related topics. But historians have left the overarching interpretations and the comprehensive surveys to policy scientists, primarily political scientists and economists. No historian has ever authored an extended history of taxation, or of taxation at the federal level, in America.

Many of the comprehensive book-length histories of American taxation have been written by members of other disciplines: Roy G. Blakey and Gladys C. Blakey (economists), Randolph E. Paul (an attorney), Edwin R. A. Seligman (an economist), Frank W. Taussig (an economist), and John Witte (a political scientist). Their books, in part because of the paucity of historical scholarship, remain valuable to the contemporary student. The only comprehensive history of United States taxation written by a historian is Sidney Ratner's *American Taxation: Its History as a Social Force in Democracy* (1942). It is still the best single volume on the history of federal taxation through the adoption of mass-based income taxation during World War II. He somewhat updated the book twenty-five years later, in *Taxation and Democracy in America* (1967).[4]

The other general histories provide useful supplements to Ratner's survey. The many editions of Taussig's *The Tariff History of the United States* placed Taussig in a class by himself as a historian of the tariff system, where he remains today, two generations later. His general conclusion that American tariffs, however distasteful in theory, had only limited effects on the domestic economy remains

---

[4] See Ratner, *American Taxation: Its History as a Social Force in Democracy* (New York: W. W. Norton, 1942) and *Taxation and Democracy in America* (New York: W. W. Norton, 1967). Ratner had considerable economic as well as historical expertise. After earning his Ph.D. at Columbia University in 1942, he served as an economist for the Board of Economic Warfare, the Foreign Economic Administration, and the planning division of the State Department. He joined the history department at Rutgers University in 1946. See Reed Ableson, "Obituary: Sidney Ratner, 87; Specialized in Economic History," *New York Times*, January 17, 1996.

the conventional scholarly wisdom.[5] Edwin Seligman made a variety of contributions to the history of taxation, but most notable was his *The Income Tax: A Study of the History, Theory and Practice of Income Taxation at Home and Abroad* (1914), which is the best history of American income taxation, including its European background, prior to World War I.[6] The Blakeys, in *The Federal Income Tax* (1940), amplify Ratner's scholarship, particularly with regard to the development of the federal income tax during World War I and the 1920s.[7] The most informative overview of the articulation of mass-based income taxation during the 1940s and 1950s is Randolph Paul's *Taxation in the United States* (1954), even though Paul, who was a central participant in crafting the World War II tax legislation, did not document his history with footnotes.[8] John Witte's *The Politics and Development of the Federal Income Tax* (1985) provides the most detailed survey of federal tax policy from the 1960s through the early 1980s.[9]

With the exception of John Witte, all of these scholars wrote within a "progressive" intellectual framework. Sidney Ratner articulated the approach most clearly. He argued that the main theme of public finance and tax history during the twentieth century was the struggle between "the thrust for social justice and the counter-thrust for private gain." In 1942, when Ratner's book appeared, the

---

[5] The last edition was Taussig, *The Tariff History of the United States: The Eighth Revised Edition* (New York: G. P. Putnam's Sons, 1931).

[6] See Seligman, *The Income Tax: A Study of the History, Theory and Practice of Income Taxation at Home and Abroad* (New York: Macmillan, 1914). For his contributions to the history of other aspects of taxation, including property and corporate taxation, see Seligman, *Essays in Taxation*, 9th ed. (New York: Macmillan, 1921).

[7] Blakey and Blakey, *The Federal Income Tax* (London: Longmans, Green, 1940).

[8] See Paul, *Taxation in the United States* (Boston: Little, Brown, 1954).

[9] See Witte, *The Politics and Development of the Federal Income Tax* (Madison: University of Wisconsin Press, 1985).

New Deal seemed to have established a clear victory for social justice by having secured progressive income taxation, which Ratner
described "as preeminently fit for achieving and preserving the economic objectives of a democracy." Moreover, the adoption and expansion of income taxation appeared to have created the basis for
a well-funded welfare state and for a federal government that could
defend the cause of democracy around the world. Ratner's interpretation of tax history was an expression of a larger progressive view
of the history of government and reform during the twentieth century. That view regarded the reform movements that culminated in
the New Deal as an expression of social democracy and as a stream
of victories for working people—farmers and factory laborers.[10]

THE POSTPROGRESSIVE ANALYSIS
OF SOCIAL INTERESTS

The political scientists and economists who have recently explored
the history of the federal tax system have dramatically challenged
the "progressive history" of income taxation. They have done so
by focusing on the question of "who or whose interest it is that sets
the machine of the state in motion and speaks through it," to use
Schumpeter's words yet again. In the process, they have produced
a rich menu of descriptions of the configuration of the "interests"
shaping tax policy.[11]

Scholars who have challenged a progressive interpretation of social interests include, among others, neoconservative economists
searching for historical foundations for the Reagan "revolution"
and its attack on government. They have presented the history of
taxation in the twentieth century not as a victory for principled

---

[10] Ratner, *American Taxation* and *Taxation and Democracy*, 14 and 16, in
both editions.
[11] Schumpeter, "Crisis of the Tax State," 19, n. 19.

forces of democracy but as the capture of "the state" by narrowly self-interested groups of "tax-eaters." Central to this neoconservative story is the adoption and expansion of the federal income tax. Ben Baack and Edward J. Ray, in an important article, argue that "the current issue of the impact of special-interest politics on our national well-being has its roots in the bias of discretionary federal spending at the turn of the century" and in the enactment of the federal income tax. They claim that the passage of the Sixteenth Amendment, which authorized income taxation, was intended to raise significant new revenues and was a result of special-interest groups that sought greatly expanded funding for military and social-welfare programs.[12] The most comprehensive statement of a neo-conservative interpretation of the expansion of the public sector is the book by economist and economic historian Robert Higgs, *Crisis and Leviathan: Critical Episodes in the Growth of American Government* (1987). Higgs sees the passage of the Sixteenth Amendment as the thin edge of the wedge for interest groups who wanted to use government to redistribute income in their direction, largely by funding their favorite programs.[13]

The progressive and the neoconservative interpretations, despite their differences in identifying and characterizing socially powerful interests, agree that the federal income tax significantly enhanced the power of the state. But most recent scholars of tax history, when tracking group and class influence, have started from quite a different point. Rather than seeking to explain the rise of Leviathan,

[12] Ben Baack and Edward J. Ray, "The Political Economy of the Origin and Development of the Federal Income Tax," in *Emergence of the Modern Political Economy: Research in Economic History* (Supplement 4), ed. Robert Higgs (Greenwich, Conn.: JAI Press, 1985), 121–38.

[13] See Higgs, *Crisis and Leviathan: Critical Episodes in the Growth of American Government* (New York: Oxford University Press, 1987).

they have emphasized and tried to understand the weaknesses of the modern federal government.

In so doing, the analysts of weakness have begun by noting three seemingly interrelated fiscal characteristics. The first is the relatively small size of American tax revenues as a percentage of national income, when compared with tax revenues in Western Europe over much of the post-1941 tax regime. The second is the Swiss-cheese quality of the progressive income tax, a characteristic created by preferential rates of taxation and by tax expenditures. The third is the federal government's huge budget deficit, which has grown in absolute size in most years since 1980. Many scholars regard the deficit as a reflection of both a weak tax-state and a national civic decline.

In the process of identifying these characteristics, a few analysts of weakness have written innovative histories of the international development of twentieth-century institutions of public finance, including those in the United States. Two examples are Sven Steinmo, *Taxation and Democracy: Swedish, British and American Approaches to Financing the Modern State* (1993), and Carolyn Webber and Aaron Wildavsky, *A History of Taxation and Expenditure in the Western World* (1986).[14]

---

[14] Steinmo, *Taxation and Democracy: Swedish, British and American Approaches to Financing the Modern State* (New Haven, Conn.: Yale University Press, 1993), and Webber and Wildavsky, *A History of Taxation and Expenditure in the Western World* (New York: Simon & Schuster, 1986). Two excellent international comparative histories do not encompass the United States but focus rather on Europe from the early modern era through the industrial revolution. See Gabriel Ardant, "Financial Policy and Economic Infrastructure of Modern States and Nations," in *The Formation of National States in Western Europe*, ed. Charles Tilly (Princeton, N.J.: Princeton University Press, 1975), 164–242; and D. E. Schremmer, "Taxation and Public Finance: Britain, France, and Germany," in *The Cambridge Economic History of Europe, Volume 8, The Industrial Economies:*

The scholars who explore the weakness of the American tax-state have developed two very different analytical approaches, but both of the approaches are based on the analysis of what Schumpeter called "social power relations."

The first group of scholars who focus on governmental weakness works within a tradition of fiscal analysis that extends back to Rudolf Goldscheid. His central conclusion was that class politics had impoverished the state. Capitalism, he argued, had emasculated feudal states, which he believed had often possessed great fiscal power because of the assets they owned. "The rising bourgeois classes," Goldscheid argued, "wanted a poor State, a State depending for its revenue on their good graces, because these classes knew their own power to depend upon what the State did or did not have money for." So the capitalists "conquered the State by stripping it of its wealth" and created a "tax State," which was dependent on taxing or begging from the very capitalists who controlled the state. The capitalists used its fiscal instruments only when necessary "to enhance their profits and extend their power."[15]

Modern "capitalist-state" theorists follow the general thrust of Goldscheid's interpretation as they attempt to understand what they regard as the failures of the American state to adopt significant programs of social investment or progressive wealth redistribution. These scholars, primarily political scientists, accent the influence of the leadership of the corporate sector and argue that in the nineteenth century, large corporations and the wealthiest Americans captured federal fiscal policy in order to protect the investment system—and their own power. As a consequence, these scholars argue, the federal government abstained from redistributing wealth

The Development of Economic and Social Policies, ed. Peter Mathias and Sidney Pollard (Cambridge: Cambridge University Press, 1989), 315–494.

[15] Goldscheid, "Sociological Approach," 203, 205, 209, 211.

in a progressive fashion and, instead, reinforced the process of capital accumulation. In so doing, the capitalist-state theorists argue, American government had to wrestle with an inherent dilemma created by democratic political institutions: How could it respond to democratic pressures for redistributional equity while maximizing capital accumulation?

Prominent among the capitalist-state theorists who focus on fiscal history is the historian and political scientist Robert Stanley, who describes the early history of the federal income tax, from the Civil War through 1913, in *Dimensions of Law in the Service of Order: Origins of the Federal Income Tax, 1861–1913* (1993). He sees the passage of the Civil War law, the enactment of the Sixteenth Amendment, and the reenactment of a federal income tax in 1913 as an expression of capitalist desire "to preserve imbalances in the structure of wealth and opportunity, rather than to ameliorate or abolish them, by strengthening the status quo against the more radical attacks on that structure by the political left and right."[16] Consistent with Stanley's history of the income tax is a history of New Deal tax reform, *The Limits of Symbolic Reform: The New Deal and Taxation* (1984), written by historian Mark Leff, who argues that Franklin D. Roosevelt looked only for symbolic victories in tax reform and was never willing to confront capitalist power by undertaking a serious program of income and wealth redistribution or by significantly expanding taxation of the incomes of upper-middle-class Americans. Thus Stanley and Leff regard income-tax initiatives before World War II as hollow, primarily symbolic efforts to appease the forces of democracy.[17]

---

[16] See Stanley, *Dimensions of Law in the Service of Order: Origins of the Federal Income Tax, 1861–1913* (New York: Oxford University Press, 1993), viii–ix.

[17] See Leff, *The Limits of Symbolic Reform: The New Deal and Taxation* (Cambridge: Cambridge University Press, 1984).

The political scientist Ronald King has also advanced an elaborate expression of the capitalist-state approach to fiscal history, in
*Money, Time and Politics: Investment Tax Subsidies and American
Democracy* (1993). King carries the story told by Stanley and Leff
into the post–World War II era, in which income-tax revenues came
mainly from wages and salaries rather than profits, dividends, and
rents, as had been the case earlier. He puts less emphasis on the symbolic use of the language of progressive redistribution to appease
democratic forces. Instead, he stresses the role of a "hegemonic tax
logic," based on the needs of American capitalism, which first appeared during the 1920s but prevailed only after World War II. This
logic, King argues, called for the federal government to adopt tax
policies that promoted capital accumulation but at the same time
to trumpet them as measures that increased productivity, average
wages, and jobs. He argues that all of the presidents after World
War II invoked this logic in devising their tax programs. But he finds
the administration of John F. Kennedy to have been the most creative in mobilizing investment tax subsidies to accommodate the
potentially conflicting interests of business and labor. Kennedy's
was, therefore, according to King, "the quintessential presidency
of the postwar American regime." Thus, in King's formulation, the
loopholes in the federal tax code become more than "random loopholes drilled primarily to satisfy the demands of selfish factions."
King argues that the loopholes "reflect a more conscious intention
consistent with systematic policy purpose."[18]

The second approach used to explain the fiscal weakness of the
modern American state is that of scholars who have described

---

[18] See King, *Money, Time and Politics: Investment Tax Subsidies and American
Democracy* (New Haven, Conn.: Yale University Press, 1993), 37, 316; and
his essay "From Redistributive to Hegemonic Logic: The Transformation of
American Tax Politics, 1894–1963," *Politics and Society* 12, no. 1 (1983):
1–52.

themselves, in various ways, as "pluralists" because they emphasize the multiplicity of contending groups shaping tax policy, and
because they detail the ways in which the American political system
encourages fragmentation of the polity into local and special interests. Whereas the capitalist-state theorists tend to consider tax policy as rationally advancing the interests of capitalists, the pluralists
who have written at length about fiscal history stress the economically dysfunctional character of federal tax policy, especially the
complex webs of special tax rates and tax expenditures. In this pluralist view, the federal tax code often distorts economic decisions
and weakens the federal government by undermining the income-
tax base. The political scientist John Witte has written the most
comprehensive pluralist history of the income tax, *The Politics and
Development of the Federal Income Tax*. In it, he describes the tax
system as one of "enormous complexity, which may have reached
the limits of legitimacy, the capacity to meet revenue demands, and
the capability of reform." The economist Charles Gilbert, in his
American Financing of World War I (1970), rendered a similar verdict on American tax policy during World War I.[19]

For the sake of clarity, it should be emphasized that this description of pluralist scholarship as rendering negative judgments of the
political process applies only to those pluralist scholars who have
written extensive fiscal histories. Other scholars have described politics as pluralist but have rendered much more favorable judgments.
But virtually none of the pluralists with more favorable normative
evaluations have made substantial contributions to fiscal history.[20]

[19] John Witte, *The Politics and Development of the Federal Income Tax*
(Madison: University of Wisconsin Press, 1985), 23; Charles Gilbert,
American Financing of World War I (Westport, Conn.: Greenwood Press,
1970).
[20] Robert A. Dahl and Samuel P. Hays are two of the most obvious examples
of more optimistic pluralists. See Dahl, *Democracy and Its Critics* (New

The pluralist analysis of "social power relations" also contrasts sharply with that of the capitalist-state theorists. Pluralists emphasize the extent to which a broad range of middle-class groups has prevailed in the political process. Thus the political scientists Carolyn Webber and Aaron Wildavsky, in *A History of Taxation and Expenditure in the Western World* (1986), wrote: "As Pogo might have put it, we—the broad middle and lower classes—have met the special interests, and 'they is us.'" The outcome, in the words of John Witte, is a system that "essentially exempts the poor, taxes the broad middle class at a very stable rate, and taxes the rich at varying rates depending on political and ideological shifts." Influential political scientists who have analyzed the history of America's Social Security system, including its financing, have reached similar conclusions about the distribution of power. The leading examples of this scholarship include Martha Derthick, *Policymaking for Social Security* (1979), and Carolyn L. Weaver, *The Crisis in Social Security: Economic and Political Origins* (1982).[21]

The pluralist interpretation of the tax-state as historically weakened by the grinding of middle-class interest groups has, in turn, influenced public discourse through "declinists." These are scholars such as historian Paul Kennedy, in *The Rise and Fall of the Great Powers: Economic and Military Conflict from 1500 to 2000* (1988), and the political scientist David Calleo, in *Beyond American Hegemony: The Future of the Western Alliance* (1987) and *The Bankrupting of America: How the Federal Budget Is Impoverishing*

Haven, Conn.: Yale University Press, 1969); and Hays, *The Response to Industrialism, 1885–1914* (Chicago: University of Chicago Press, 1957).

[21] Webber and Wildavsky, *A History of Taxation and Expenditure*, 531; Witte, *The Politics and Development of the Federal Income Tax*, 21; Martha Derthick, *Policymaking for Social Security* (Washington, D.C.: Brookings Institution Press, 1979); and Carolyn L. Weaver, *The Crisis in Social Security: Economic and Political Origins* (Durham, N.C.: Duke University Press, 1982).

the Nation (1992), who bemoan the decline in civic culture in America and regard the great size of federal budget deficits as a symptom of that decline. They have blamed the massive deficits on the failure to raise sufficient tax revenues and, in turn, on middle-class preferences for lower taxes, especially taxes that subsidize middle-class consumption patterns over public social investment. Calleo diagnosed America's economic troubles as in large part the price paid for democratic tax politics. He implied that significant reform of the public sector can come only if the process of tax politics is first reformed—by insulating the tax system from democratic politics.[22]

Thus political scientists and economists have dramatically reinterpreted the forces of democracy lauded by Sidney Ratner. Within the new tax history, democracy has been subverted by narrowly selfish tax-eaters (the neoconservative interpretation) or captured by capitalists or their agents (the capitalist-state view) or transmogrified by the excessive grind of competitive interest groups (the pluralist analysis).

POSTPROGRESSIVE VIEWS OF THE ROLE
OF THE STATE

Each of the major postprogressive interpretations of American tax history is "society centered" rather than "state centered." That is to say, in explaining the development of the federal government and its fiscal policies, each attaches greater importance to the influence

---

[22] See Kennedy, *The Rise and Fall of the Great Powers: Economic and Military Conflict from 1500 to 2000* (New York: Random House, 1988), especially 434, 527, and 534–35; and Calleo, *Beyond American Hegemony: The Future of the Western Alliance* (New York: Basic Books, 1987), especially 109–13 and 126, and *The Bankrupting of America: How the Federal Budget Is Impoverishing the Nation* (New York: Morrow, 1992).

of interests outside the government than to the role of interests within it.

At the same time, however, the neoconservative, capitalist-state, and pluralist interpretations all pay close attention methodologically to the role of the state; each has a more clearly articulated vision of the role of the state than did the progressive histories. Even the pluralist interpretation, which dwells on the weakness of the state, theoretically defines the role of the state. And both the neoconservative and the capitalist-state arguments accord a degree of autonomy to institutions and actors within the government.

The neoconservative fiscal story offers little detailed analysis of the institutions of the federal government, but in the story, the federal government acquired considerable autonomy during the course of the twentieth century. In particular, neoconservative scholars highlight the success of the federal government in manipulating politics to undermine traditional American resistance to taxpaying, particularly during the New Deal and World War I. Neoconservative scholars feature agents of the state who gain control of the instruments of national communication, manipulate federal power to discourage or suppress grassroots challenges to the state, and cultivate a class of experts capable of designing taxes whose effects are difficult to detect. The historian David Beito, for example, in *Tax Payers in Revolt: Tax Resistance during the Great Depression* (1989), emphasizes the power of a tax-resistant culture that, he claims, dates back to John C. Calhoun. Beito argues that this culture was vital at the state and local levels as late as the 1930s and claims that the New Deal played a crucial role in breaking its back.

The result, the neoconservatives argue, is government growth that impairs productivity—growth fueled both by interest-group politics and self-interested, relatively autonomous agents of the state. In a sense, they echo one of Schumpeter's warnings about the growth of social programs: "If the finances have created and partly formed the modern state, so now the state on its part forms

them and enlarges them—deep into the flesh of the private economy." Neoconservative scholars emphasize the need to limit state
autonomy in order to restore the health of the republic, and they
offer historical evidence to support political movements designed
to impose new constitutional restraints, such as balanced-budget
amendments and Proposition 13–style limits on tax rates.[23]

For their part, capitalist-state theorists of fiscal policy have
moved beyond simplistic models of state capture to express an appreciation for the complexity of the relationship between political leaders and capitalists and for the extent to which the former
can acquire autonomy and exercise initiative in establishing policy.
Robert Stanley, for example, argues that "political officials" were
far more than tools of the capitalists. They acted "as relatively autonomous trustees . . . through the use of multiple dimensions of the
law." Thus, Stanley sets the history of early income taxation in what
he calls an "omnipresent legal environment" and explores "the full
network of lawmaking agencies in their symbiosis with other dimensions of the social structure." Legislatures and courts were aware
of the "crucial rhetorical consequences" and the distributional implications of tax law and used their autonomy, through the law,
Stanley proposes, to shape popular values and beliefs. He attributes
overwhelming responsibility for the enactment of income taxes during the Civil War, in 1894, and again in 1913 to the initiative of
the capitalists' "trustees," who he believes acted to preempt the
adoption of more radical measures. And he views the fight over the
constitutionality of income taxation not as a confrontation between
classes but as an argument within the state for control over "cen-
trist" mechanisms of allocation. Thus, Stanley interprets *Pollock v.
Farmers' Loan and Trust Co.* (1895), which invalidated the 1894

---

[23] See Beito, *Tax Payers in Revolt: Tax Resistance during the Great Depression*
(Chapel Hill: University of North Carolina Press, 1989); and Schumpeter,
"Crisis of the Tax State," 19.

income tax, as a Jacksonian attack by the Supreme Court on the dominant role of Congress in "statist capitalism" rather than as an assault on income taxation.[24]

Ronald King also finds considerable state autonomy, based on the responsibility of political leaders to reconcile the interests of contending groups and classes. It was by working effectively under this responsibility, King argues, that the architects of the post–World War II tax regime took into account the interests of labor—as well as their own fundamental devotion to capital accumulation—and replaced the "zero-sum redistribution game" with "the politics of non-zero-sum productivity" and a tax policy of economic "growthmanship." By manipulating both tax policy and tax symbolism, state managers induced labor to reduce its pressure for short-run economic and fiscal gains in favor of long-run gains "within overall capitalist hegemony."[25]

In contrast, the federal government portrayed in the pluralist histories of public finance is one of pathetic weakness. Pluralists complement their stress on the power of middle-class interests with a view of the American state as so fragmented that it cannot stand up to the grinding of interest-group competition. The weak political structures cited by the pluralist scholars of tax history include fragmented political parties, a decline of partisanship after World War II, a system of federalism that reinforces local interests, a bureaucracy paralyzed by multiple decision points, and a federal government constitutionally fractured along the legislative-executive fault line. The pluralists argue that these structural weaknesses, combined with a high degree of democratic access to government and with a tax system that encompasses virtually all households and businesses, will necessarily produce an inefficient tax policy that

---

[24] Stanley, *Dimensions of Law*, especially vi–x, 3–14, 136–75.
[25] See King, *Money, Time and Politics*, 47–85, for the core of his theoretical argument.

is an incoherent jumble of complexity and that fails to raise adequate revenue. And because of these structural weaknesses, those who would reform public finance are condemned to a frustrating process of slow and incremental change.[26]

The most important recent expression of the pluralist understanding of the role of the state in tax policy comes from a political scientist, Sven Steinmo, in *Taxation and Democracy: Swedish, British and American Approaches to Financing the Modern State* (1993). Steinmo concluded that a "fragmentation of political authority"—checks and balances and the localism encouraged by American federalism—strengthens special-interest groups at the expense of political parties and frustrates tax reformers who would broaden the income-tax base or adopt national consumption taxes in order to expand social programs. The fragmentation encourages groups to be exceptionally hostile to any increase in their tax burdens. Steinmo's invocation of comparative analysis and the framework of political science's "new institutionalism" has sharpened the pluralist analysis of the development of American taxation.[27]

THE DEMOCRATIC-INSTITUTIONALIST APPROACH

This book and its companion volume, *Funding the Modern American State, 1941–1995: The Rise and Fall of the Era of Easy Finance* (1995), represent efforts to organize an approach that

---

[26] For a brief pluralist history of the relationship between American public finance and the structure of the American state, see the chapter "Paying for Modern Government" in Ballard C. Campbell, *The Growth of American Government: Governance from the Cleveland Era to the Present* (Bloomington: Indiana University Press, 1995), 175–200.

[27] See Steinmo, *Taxation and Democracy.* For a description of the "new institutionalism," which attempts to embrace the full range of institutional factors in comprehensive models of public-sector development, see James G. March and Johan P. Olsen, *Rediscovering Institutions: The Organizational Basis of Politics* (New York: Free Press, 1989).

differs significantly from the pluralist, capitalist-state, and neoconservative approaches to the history of taxation. This new interpretation might be described as "democratic institutionalist."[28]

In its "democratic" dimension, this approach recognizes the
power of democratic forces outside the federal government. These
were forces that contributed, for example, to the progressively redistributional cast of the twentieth-century tax regimes. At the same
time, the interpretation stresses the potency of ideas as independent
creative forces. Thus concepts of progressive equity, often expressed
as the criterion of the "ability to pay" taxes, shaped and gave intention to democratic pressures. In recognizing the power of democratic forces and ideas of equity, this approach has much in common
with older progressive histories.

Democratic institutionalism breaks with progressive history in
three important ways. First, the "institutionalist" dimension of this
interpretation accents the influence of governmental institutions—
particularly the presidency and congressional leadership, professional experts within government, political partisanship, and constitutional structures—in shaping policy. Within these governmental institutions, ideas figure centrally in a process of social learning.
Presidents and other policy entrepreneurs, including professional
experts, use ideas to understand social change. Moreover, they invoke those ideas to form alliances beyond the formal boundaries of
government. Building those alliances, in turn, often encourages the
development of supportive policy communities.

The second break with progressive history by scholars of taxation
who adopt a democratic institutionalist model is an emphasis on historical contingency, rather than a relentless advance of democracy.

---

[28] See W. Elliot Brownlee, ed., *Funding the Modern American State, 1941–
1995: The Rise and Fall of the Era of Easy Finance* (Washington, D.C.:
Woodrow Wilson Center Press, and Cambridge: Cambridge University
Press, 1996).

Most important, the approach suggests that national emergencies have heavily influenced the specific ways in which ideas, democratic forces, and policy networks have interacted to shape important changes in fiscal institutions. In each of the great modern wars, for example, presidents employed tax reforms and invoked democratic ideals of taxation to mobilize the economy, to win support for their administrations, and to unify the nation behind the war effort. The approach also stresses the idea that the transitions between regimes have been heavily "path dependent." In other words, the tax regime imposed in each emergency changed economic, political, and intellectual conditions in ways that made it difficult or even impossible for the federal government to return to the tax regime in force before the emergency. Consequently, today's tax system has a stratified quality. Each layer of tax institutions, almost like a layer of the earth's crust, represents the legacy of an earlier epoch, or fiscal regime.[29]

The third break is an emphasis on how economic development shaped the organizational options available to the architects of tax

---

[29] While the democratic-institutionalist interpretation of both state and society differs substantially from the neoconservative, one important neoconservative scholar also stresses the importance of national crises and path dependency to institutional development. See Higgs, *Crisis and Leviathan*, especially 3–74. The first, and most influential, work of historical scholarship to focus attention on the upward-ratchet effect of wars on public expenditures in industrial democracies was Alan T. Peacock and Jack Wiseman, *The Growth of Public Expenditure in the United Kingdom* (Princeton, N.J.: Princeton University Press, 1961). The leading theorist of the influence of path dependency on historical change is economic historian Paul David; see, e.g., David, "Clio and the Economics of QWERTY," *American Economic Association Papers and Proceedings* 75 (May 1985): 332–37; and David, "Path-Dependence and Predictability in Stochastic Systems with Network Externalities: A Paradigm for Historical Economics," in *Technology and the Wealth of Nations*, ed. Dominique Foray and Christoper Freeman (New York: St. Martin's Press, 1993).

policy. The democratic-institutional approach attempts to assess how, over time, the changing condition of economic structure and organization has defined the institutional possibilities for the expression of democratic ideals. For example, the interpretation recognizes that the federal government could not embody the ideal of "ability to pay" in its modern form until economic development created the administrative underpinnings for an effective income tax. More generally, economic development, defined to include the emergence and refinement of modern technology and organizational structures as well as economic growth, shapes the public finance options available to policymakers.[30]

A significant collection of monographic scholarship on the history of taxation could be described as democratic institutionalist, although the scholars do not use that term. Some of this scholarship addresses the origins of the federal tax system during the early republic. Most important, Robert A. Becker, in *Revolution, Reform, and the Politics of American Taxation, 1763–1783* (1980), Roger H. Brown, in *Redeeming the Republic: Federalists, Taxation, and*

---

[30] Public finance economist Richard Musgrave has led his profession in thinking about the relationship between structural economic change and the development of fiscal regimes. He has proposed an even stronger view of the relationship than the one suggested here. He argues that structural change in highly developed economies has, in fact, driven dramatic changes in tax structure, which he claims would have occurred even without major wars. See Musgrave, *Fiscal Systems* (New Haven, Conn.: Yale University Press, 1969), 125–206. Musgrave does not take up, however, the reciprocal relationship: the effects of taxation on economic development. More generally, neither economists nor historians have undertaken sustained analyses of such effects. However, for suggestions on the effects of the pre–Civil War tax system on economic development, see Richard Sylla, "Experimental Federalism: The Economics of American Government, 1789–1914," *The Cambridge Economic History of the United States, Volume II: The Long Nineteenth Century* (Cambridge: Cambridge University Press, 2000), 483–541.

the Origins of the Constitution (1993), E. James Ferguson, in *The Power of the Purse: A History of American Public Finance, 1776–1790* (1961), and Thomas P. Slaughter, in *The Whiskey Rebellion: Frontier Epilogue to the American Revolution* (1986), all emphasize the role of democratic forces, concepts of equity, and historical contingency in the development of the federal government's first tax regime.[31]

Other specialized scholarship reinforces a democratic-institutionalist interpretation of tax reform by pointing to the importance of democratic forces during the post–Civil War industrial era. Some monographs have suggested the strength of the appeal of the single-tax movement to Americans and its great influence on the mainstream of tax reform, although most scholars of tax history, including those writing from a progressive point of view, have discounted its role. Notable are Charles Barker's biography *Henry George* (1955) and two histories of the movement: the historian Arthur Dudden's *Joseph Fels and the Single-Tax Movement* (1971) and the economist Arthur Young's *The Single Tax Movement in the United States* (1916).[32] In an influential article written more than fifty years ago, Elmer Ellis provided

---

[31] Robert A. Becker, *Revolution, Reform, and the Politics of American Taxation, 1763–1783* (Baton Rouge: Louisiana State University Press, 1980); Roger H. Brown, *Redeeming the Republic: Federalists, Taxation, and the Origins of the Constitution* (Baltimore: Johns Hopkins University Press, 1993); E. James Ferguson, *The Power of the Purse: A History of American Public Finance, 1776–1790* (Chapel Hill: University of North Carolina Press, 1961); and Thomas P. Slaughter, *The Whiskey Rebellion: Frontier Epilogue to the American Revolution* (New York: Oxford University Press, 1986). For an approach that places more emphasis on top-down, conservative forces in shaping the early tax system, see Sylla, "Experimental Federalism."

[32] Charles A. Barker, *Henry George* (New York: Oxford University Press, 1955); Arthur P. Dudden, *Joseph Fels and the Single-Tax Movement* (Philadelphia: Temple University Press, 1971), 199–245; and Arthur N.

evidence that buttressed Sidney Ratner's emphasis on the role of farmers in shaping the inception of the federal income tax.[33] The development of federal taxation must be understood in the context of the history of taxation at all levels of government, and the histories of taxation at the state and local levels—albeit few and far between—tend to support a democratic-institutionalist interpretation. A number of studies have illustrated how small-property owners—both farmers and middle-class people in towns and cities—pushed for the adoption of new, more progressive taxes at the state and local levels and then supported the adoption of income taxation at the federal level. W. Elliot Brownlee, in *Progressivism and Economic Growth: The Wisconsin Income Tax, 1911–1929* (1974), found the impetus for the adoption of income taxation in Wisconsin to be primarily agrarian. Recently, Phil Roberts, in *A Penny for the Governor, A Dollar for Uncle Sam: Income Taxation in Washington*, reached a similar finding for the passage of the short-lived income taxation in Washington State. David P. Thelen, in *The New Citizenship: Origins of Progressivism in Wisconsin, 1885–1900* (1972), presented persuasive evidence that in the late 1890s urban tax issues transformed Wisconsin mugwumps, many of whom were "conservative businessmen," into "crusaders against corporate arrogance." The most comprehensive account of state and local tax reform between the Civil War and World War I is Clifton K. Yearley's *The Money Machines: The Breakdown and Reform of Governmental and Party Finance in the North, 1860–1920* (1970). Like Thelen, Yearley emphasized the support for tax reform among urban property owners. By contrast, John D. Buenker, in *Urban Liberalism and Progressive Reform*

Young, *The Single Tax Movement in the United States* (Princeton, N.J.: Princeton University Press, 1916).

[33] Elmer Ellis, "Public Opinion and the Income Tax, 1860–1900," *Mississippi Valley Historical Review* 27 (September 1940): 225–42.

(1973), found strong support for tax reform among Democratic "representatives of the urban new stock working class." Buenker is not clear as to the possible overlap between "working class" and the "urban middle class," but like Brownlee, Thelen, and Yearley, he emphasizes the play of democratic forces. Morton Keller, in *Regulating a New Economy: Public Policy and Economic Change in America, 1900–1933* (1990), reinforces this general view by finding that "a welter of conflicting goals and interests determined tax policy and practice" in cities and states during this period.[34]

Recent scholarship focused on federal income taxation—from congressional proposal of the Sixteenth Amendment in 1909 through World War I—also supports democratic institutionalism. John D. Buenker's *The Income Tax and the Progressive Era* (1985), which is the standard source on the movement to ratify the Sixteenth Amendment, discovers broad-based, democratic support for

---

[34] W. Elliot Brownlee, *Progressivism and Economic Growth: The Wisconsin Income Tax, 1911–1929* (Port Washington, N.Y.: Kennikat Press, 1974); Phil Roberts, *A Penny for the Governor, A Dollar for Uncle Sam: Income Taxation in Washington* (Seattle: University of Washington Press, 2002); David P. Thelen, *The New Citizenship: Origins of Progressivism in Wisconsin, 1885–1900* (Columbia: University of Missouri Press, 1972), 202–22; Clifton K. Yearley, *The Money Machines: The Breakdown and Reform of Governmental and Party Finance in the North, 1860–1920* (Albany: State University of New York Press, 1970), 193–250; John D. Buenker, *Urban Liberalism and Progressive Reform* (New York: W. W. Norton, 1973), especially 103–17; and Morton Keller, *Regulating a New Economy: Public Policy and Economic Change in America, 1900–1933* (Cambridge, Mass.: Harvard University Press, 1990), 208–15. A recent study, however, warns that tax reform varied widely across the states. It was less threatening to business in what the author calls "corporate states" such as New York than in states "guided more by political ideas that were more in line with those of Thomas Jefferson. See R. Rudy Higgens-Evenson, *The Price of Progress: Public Services, Taxation, and the American Corporate State, 1877 to 1929* (Baltimore: Johns Hopkins University Press, 2003), 9–10.

income taxation within the nation's cities. W. Elliot Brownlee's essays emphasize all of the elements of democratic institutionalism in World War I taxation. Another study that appreciates the role of political contingencies, and the radical thrusts of Congress between 1916 and 1921, is Jerold L. Waltman's *Political Origins of the U.S. Income Tax* (1985). Steven Weisman's recent history of the development of the income taxation through World War I also emphasizes the role of democratic forces, although he finds them divided over "two basic conflicting principles," which he defines as "justice" and "virtue."[35]

A few scholars have stressed the importance of democratic idealism to the development of federal taxation after World War I. Benjamin Rader, in an article that deserves greater visibility, pointed to the expression of progressive ideals even in the tax initiatives of the 1920s. R. Alton Lee describes how progressives, into the 1920s, invoked federal taxing power, rather than the commerce clause of the Constitution, to regulate industrial society. Walter

[35] John D. Buenker, *The Income Tax and the Progressive Era* (New York: Garland, 1985); W. Elliot Brownlee, "Wilson and Financing the Modern State: The Revenue Act of 1916," *Proceedings of the American Philosophical Society* 129 (1985): 173–210; Brownlee, "Economists and the Formation of the Modern Tax System in the United States: The World War I Crisis," in *The State and Economic Knowledge: The American and British Experiences*, ed. Mary O. Furner and Barry E. Supple (Washington, D.C.: Woodrow Wilson Center Press, and Cambridge: Cambridge University Press, 1990); Brownlee, "Social Investigation and Political Learning in the Financing of World War I," in *The State and Social Investigation in Britain and the United States*, ed. Michael J. Lacey and Mary O. Furner (Washington, D.C.: Woodrow Wilson Center Press, and Cambridge: Cambridge University Press, 1993), 323–64; Jerold L. Waltman, *Political Origins of the U.S. Income Tax* (Jackson: University Press of Mississippi, 1985); and Steven R. Weisman, *The Great Tax Wars: Lincoln to Wilson—The Fierce Battles over Money and Power That Transformed the Nation* (New York: Simon & Schuster, 2002).

Lambert, in an unpublished 1970 dissertation that is the best survey of New Deal tax policy, found that the administration of President Franklin Roosevelt had a deep ethical commitment to the principle of "ability to pay." But the way is open for a substantial democratic-institutionalist history of tax policy between World Wars I and II.[36]

The volume *Funding the Modern American State, 1941–1995: The Rise and Fall of the Era of Easy Finance*, which accompanies the present volume, applies a democratic-institutionalist perspective to the history of taxation since 1941.

In *Funding the American State*, three scholars explore the relationship between the development of post-1941 taxation and the most important objectives of the federal government's tax policies—financing war, financing Social Security, and promoting economic stability. Carolyn C. Jones, a legal scholar, discusses the financing of World War II, the introduction of mass-based income taxation, and the creation of the taxpaying culture that served as the foundation for the mass-based tax. The historian Edward D. Berkowitz examines the development of the financing of Social Security from its origins in 1935 through its dramatic expansion in 1950–2 and up to the contemporary fiscal crisis. And Herbert Stein, an economist, brings up to date his classic survey of the history of fiscal policy, *The Fiscal Revolution in America*.[37]

---

[36] Benjamin G. Rader, "Federal Taxation in the 1920s: A Reexamination," *The Historian*, May 1971; R. Alton Lee, *A History of Regulatory Taxation* (Lexington: University Press of Kentucky, 1973); and Walter K. Lambert, "New Deal Revenue Acts: The Politics of Taxation" (Ph.D. dissertation, University of Texas, Austin, 1970).

[37] Carolyn C. Jones, "Mass-Based Income Taxation: Creating a Taxpaying Culture, 1940–1952"; Edward D. Berkowitz, "Social Security and the Financing of the American State"; and Herbert Stein, "The Fiscal Revolution in America, Part II: 1964 to 1994"—all in *Funding the Modern American State*, ed. Brownlee. See also Herbert Stein, *The Fiscal Revolution in America* (Chicago: University of Chicago Press, 1969).

In *Funding the Modern American State*, two other scholars focus on the politics of post-1941 tax reform. Julian Zelizer, a historian, takes up congressional politics. He studies the career of Wilbur Mills, a longtime chair of the House Ways and Means Committee (1958–75), and considers Mills's relationship to the development of a fiscal community that shaped tax policy in the late 1950s and early 1960s. The political scientist Cathie Jo Martin focuses on the presidency. She explores the dynamic relationships among business interests, the ideas of the business community, and presidential leadership since World War II.[38]

The concluding essay in *Funding the Modern American State* is an effort by C. Eugene Steuerle, an economist, to apply history to the forecasting of what is likely to be the next tax regime. He does this in the context of looking closely at the way in which economic change can both constrain and create opportunities for new tax regimes. He concludes that the nation must now do more than adopt new taxes or shift to a new tax regime in order to fund programs to meet new social needs. Economic as well as political conditions dictate, he argues, that the United States adopt a new fiscal regime—one that pays for changing priorities, at least in part, by a reallocation of resources from existing governmental programs.[39]

One important episode in post-1941 tax history—the Tax Reform Act of 1986—has received substantial scholarly attention. The scholarship reinforces a democratic-institutionalist framework. Eugene Steuerle's *The Tax Decade, 1981–1990* (1992) stresses

---

[38] Julian Zelizer, "Learning the Ways and Means: Wilbur Mills and a Fiscal Community, 1954–1964," and Cathie Jo Martin, "American Business and the Taxing State: Alliances for Growth in the Postwar Period"—both in *Funding the Modern American State*, ed. Brownlee. See also Julian Zelizer, *Taxing America: Wilbur D. Mills, Congress, and the State, 1945–1975* (Cambridge: Cambridge University Press, 1998).

[39] C. Eugene Steuerle, "Financing the American State at the Turn of the Century," in *Funding the Modern American State*, ed. Brownlee.

two factors that figure centrally in the democratic-institutionalist framework. First, he emphasizes the role of experts, especially the Treasury lawyers and economists (of which he was one), in influencing base-broadening reform in 1986. He argues that they had a coherent vision of reform, derived from the intellectual legacy left by their predecessors within the Treasury. Second, Steuerle emphasizes the way in which economic change—patterns of economic growth and inflation—structured the post-1941 tax regime. Strong support for Steuerle's analysis is found in the book by political scientists Timothy J. Conlan, Margaret T. Wrightson, and David R. Beam, *Taxing Choices: The Politics of Tax Reform* (1990). In addition to the role of the president, the Treasury experts, and their ideas in 1986, Conlan and his colleagues identify the role of congressional entrepreneurs such as Senator Bill Bradley, who acted as brokers between professional experts and the larger political arena, and the media, which enabled the "policy entrepreneurs" to build public support for reform. These political scientists go so far as to claim that the Tax Reform Act of 1986 illustrates that "politics of reform" has now replaced interest-group pluralism. Finally, a first-rate piece of journalism by Jeffrey H. Birnbaum and Alan S. Murray, *Showdown at Gucci Gulch: Lawmakers, Lobbyists, and the Unlikely Triumph of Tax Reform* (1987), documents the contribution of experts, concepts of tax equity, presidential leadership, and historical contingency to the passage of the 1986 act.[40]

---

[40] C. Eugene Steuerle, *The Tax Decade, 1981–1990* (Washington, D.C.: Urban Institute Press, 1992); Timothy J. Conlan, Margaret T. Wrightson, and David R. Beam, *Taxing Choices: The Politics of Tax Reform* (Washington, D.C.: Congressional Quarterly Press, 1990); and Jeffrey H. Birnbaum and Alan S. Murray, *Showdown at Gucci Gulch: Lawmakers, Lobbyists, and the Unlikely Triumph of Tax Reform* (New York: Random House, 1987). The leading proponent of a "politics of reform" analysis is James Q. Wilson; see his *The Politics of Regulation* (New York: Basic Books, 1980). Steuerle

Despite the recent scholarship, much remains to be done before we have an adequate understanding of the nation's fiscal history. We lack modern histories of tariffs and excise taxes, which remained dynamic sources of revenue well into the twentieth century. A comprehensive history of property taxation would tell us not only about the nation's fiscal systems but also about its political culture.[41] There is no modern history of the single-tax movement. We lack any substantial histories of taxation during the Civil War or World War II, and much remains to be explored with regard to taxation during World War I and the New Deal. We have no histories of the administration of income taxation, and only a preliminary understanding of its relationship with the cultural dimensions of taxpaying. We have no analytical histories of central institutions in the formation and administration of federal tax policy such as the Department of the Treasury, the Bureau of Internal Revenue, the House Ways and Means Committee, and the Senate Finance Committee.[42] And,

has updated and expanded *The Tax Decade*; see his *Contemporary U.S. Tax Policy* (Washington, D.C.: Urban Institute Press, forthcoming in 2004).

[41] The most useful modern history of American property taxation draws largely on data from Kansas. See Glenn W. Fisher, *The Worst Tax? A History of the Property Tax in America* (Lawrence: University Press of Kansas, 1996).

[42] There are, however, excellent reference works written within two of these institutions. On a Treasury bureau, see Jeffrey A. Cantor and Donald R. Sabile, *A History of the Bureau of the Public Debt: 1940–1990 with Historical Highlights from 1789–1939* (Washington, D.C.: U.S. Government Printing Office, 1990). A useful older survey of Treasury borrowing is Robert A. Love, *Federal Financing: A Study of the Methods Employed by the Treasury in Its Borrowing Operations* (New York: Columbia University Press, 1931). On another arm of the Treasury, see Shelley L. Davis, *IRS Historical Fact Book: A Chronology, 1646–1992* (Washington, D.C.: U.S. Government Printing Office, 1992). On the House Ways and Means Committee, see Donald R. Kennon and Rebecca M. Rogers, *The Committee on Ways and Means: A Bicentennial History, 1789–1989* (Washington, D.C.: U.S. Government Printing Office, 1989).

we lack broad-gauged assessments of the effects of American taxation on the history of economic growth, economic stability, the distribution of income and wealth, and economic development.[43]

Modern scholarship on the history of taxation might well contribute to public discourse on the fiscal condition of the nation. A firmer understanding of the nation's fiscal history could help policymakers to identify the possibilities and constraints that must be taken into account in evaluating, and reforming, the ways in which the nation pays for government. The nation is almost certainly coming to the end of the post-1941 regime, and we need, in particular, a comprehensive history of the "era of easy finance" to help guide the development of a new tax regime.

---

[43] For a discussion of the state of historical knowledge about the economic effects of one aspect of taxation—taxation of the rich—see W. Elliot Brownlee, "Economic History and the Analysis of 'Soaking the Rich' in 20th-Century America," in *Tax Justice: The Ongoing Debate*, ed. Joseph J. Thorndike and Dennis J. Ventry Jr. (Washington, D.C.: Urban Institute Press, 2002), 71–93.

Index

279

Other books in the series *(continued from page iii)*

James M. Morris, editor, *On Mozart*

Blair A. Ruble, *Money Sings: The Changing Politics of Urban Space in Post-Soviet Yaroslavl*

Theodore Taranovski, editor, *Reform in Modern Russian History: Progress or Cycle?*

Deborah S. Davis, Richard Kraus, Barry Naughton, and Elizabeth J. Perry, editors, *Urban Spaces in Contemporary China: The Potential for Autonomy and Community in Post-Mao China*

William M. Shea and Peter A. Huff, editors, *Knowledge and Belief in America: Enlightenment Traditions and Modern Religious Thought*

W. Elliot Brownlee, editor, *Funding the Modern American State, 1941–1995: The Rise and Fall of the Era of Easy Finance*

W. Elliot Brownlee, *Federal Taxation in America: A Short History*

R. H. Taylor, editor, *The Politics of Elections in Southeast Asia*

Sumit Ganguly, *The Crisis in Kashmir: Portents of War, Hopes of Peace*

James W. Muller, editor, *Churchill as Peacemaker*

Donald R. Kelley and David Harris Sacks, editors, *The Historical Imagination in Early Modern Britain: History, Rhetoric, and Fiction, 1500–1800*

Richard Wightman Fox and Robert B. Westbrook, editors, *In Face of the Facts: Moral Inquiry in American Scholarship*

Morton Keller and R. Shep Melnick, editors, *Taking Stock: American Government in the Twentieth Century*

Richard Grassby, *Kinship and Capitalism: Marriage, Family, and Business in the English-Speaking World, 1580–1720*

Charles E. Butterworth and I. William Zartman, editors, *Between the State and Islam*

Blair A. Ruble, *Second Metropolis: Pragmatic Pluralism in Gilded Age Chicago, Silver Age Moscow, and Meiji Osaka*

Anthony Pagden, editor, *The Idea of Europe: From Antiquity to the European Union*

David Schimmelpenninck van der Oye and Bruce W. Menning, editors, *Reforming the Tsar's Army: Military Innovation in Imperial Russia from Peter the Great to the Revolution*

Made in the USA
Lexington, KY
02 November 2010